Annotations on the Revelation of St. John the Theologian

by Johann Gerhard

Annotations on the Revelation of St. John the Theologian

by Johann Gerhard

Doctor of Theology and at one time a public Professor of the same at the illustrious Salana

Submitted by Johann Ernst Gerhard

1643

Printed in Jena
at the expense of Johann Ludwig Neuenhahn
by Johann Jacob Bauhoffer

1665

Translated by Paul A. Rydecki

Repristination Press
Malone, Texas

A translation of *Johannis Gerhardi Adnotationes in Apocalypsin D. Johannis Theologi* (Jena, 1643), by Johann Gerhard. Copyright 2015 by Paul A. Rydecki. Published by permission of the translator. No part of this publication may be reproduced, stored in a retrieval system, or transmitted in any form or by any means, electronic, mechanical, photocopying or otherwise without the prior written permission of Repristination Press.

Published in 2016

REPRISTINATION PRESS
P.O. BOX 173
BYNUM, TEXAS 76631

www.repristinationpress.com

ISBN 1-891469-69-X

Table of Contents

Foreword	7
Prolegomena	9
Chapter 1	11
Chapter 2	23
Chapter 3	33
Chapter 4	45
Chapter 5	53
Chapter 6	63
Chapter 7	71
Chapter 8	79
Chapter 9	87
Chapter 10	99
Chapter 11	105
Chapter 12	115
Chapter 13	127
Chapter 14	139
Chapter 15	151
Chapter 16	155
Chapter 17	163
Chapter 18	173
Chapter 19	181
Chapter 20	187
Chapter 21	199
Chapter 22	209

6

Foreword

It is a pleasure to publish Pastor Rydecki's translation of Johann Gerhard's *Annotations on the Revelation of St. John the Theologian* (1643). Just as was the case with the *Annotations on the First Six Chapters of St. Paul's Epistle to the Romans* (1645), Gerhard's *Annotations on the Revelation* was first published through the efforts of Gerhard's son, Johann Ernst Gerhard (1621–1668), who, though a young man who earned his Master's degree in 1643, demonstrated a profound commitment to the preservation of his father's writings. Though Gerhard's son is often overshadowed by the praise heaped on his father, one might well wonder how much of Johann Gerhard's legacy would have been lost to the ages if not for the labors of Johann Ernst Gerhard.

Today, a revival of the study of the theology of the Age of Lutheran Orthodoxy (1580–1713) is underway, and it is a joy to see Repristination Press continue to take a leading role in the publication of English translations from writings of the chief theologians of that age. The recent publication of Gerhard's *On the Legitimate Interpretation of Sacred Scripture* (1610), the *Annotations on the First Six Chapters of St. Paul's Epistle the Romans* (1645), and the current volume help readers come to a better understanding of the historic Lutheran approach to the interpretation of God's Word. Pastor Rydecki's ongoing translation work from the writings of Aegidius Hunnius, Johann Gerhard, and other theologians of the Age of Lutheran Orthodoxy is a tremendous service to the Church in our age.

+James D. Heiser,
Bishop, The Evangelical Lutheran Diocese of North America
Publisher, Repristination Press

8

JOHANN GERHARD'S ANNOTATIONS ON THE REVELATION OF ST. JOHN, APOSTLE AND EVANGELIST

Prolegomena

1. *The principal efficient cause* of the Revelation is the Holy Spirit, who was poured out upon John, as upon the other Apostles, on the Day of Pentecost (Acts 2:3), and drove him not only to preach the Gospel with the living voice, but also to summarize the evangelical doctrine in writing as he does in the Revelation. (Cf. 2 Pet. 1:21, 2 Tim. 3:16.)

2. *The ministerial cause* or *secondary author* of the Revelation is John, the evangelist and apostle of Jesus Christ. This is clear from the inscription which is attributed to John the theologian, for it says: Ἀποκάλυψις Ιωάννου τοῦ θεολόγου, that is, the *Apocalypse* or the *Revelation of John the Theologian*. That this "theologian" is the Apostle John is especially clear: (1) From the conformity of the introduction to this book with that of John's Gospel History, as well as his First Epistle. The author of this book writes in Rev. 1:1–2, "Jesus Christ gave this revelation to His servant John, who bore witness to the Word of God and the testimony of Jesus Christ, and of whichever things He saw." John speaks about himself in practically the same way in the Gospel History, John 21:24: "This is that disciple who presents the word concerning these things, and He has written them, and we know that his testimony is true." He also introduced his First Epistle in a similar way: "That which was from the beginning, which we have heard, which we have seen with our eyes, which we have looked upon, that we announce to you." (2) From the style. It is peculiar to John, more than to the other writers of the New Testament books, to call the Son of God Λόγον, the Word (John 1:1, 1 John 1:1). And now the same name is applied to the Son of God in this book (Rev. 19:3). See many examples of this in *Exeg.*, locus I *de Script. S.*, par. 306 ff.

3. *The canonical authority of this book* is proven with many arguments in the above-referenced work (par. 307).

4. *The subject matter.* This book contains not only prophetic visions, but also dogmatic ones. It deals with the state of the Christian Church in the New Testament from the time at which John lived until the end of the world.

5. *The structure.* The book is divided into seven visions. The first deals with the time of John, chapters 1–3. The second deals with the time following that, chapters 4–7. The third vision has to do with the time of heresies, chapters 8:1–11. The fourth portrays the general state of the Church from the time of John until the end of the world, chapters 12–14. The fifth treats the seven last plagues, chapters 15–16. The sixth deals with the destruction of the Antichrist, chapters 17–19. The seventh is a repetition of the earlier ones, chapters 20–22. (Cf. Augustine, Book XX, *De Civitate Dei*, ch. 17.) Thus he repeats the same things in many ways, so that he seems to say some things and then other things, when, in reality, he is actually saying the same things in different ways.

6. *The purpose.* The general purpose of the book is the fourfold purpose expressed in 2 Tim. 3:16. The specific purpose is the consolation of the Church.

7. *Special features* of this book include (1) *obscurity.* Jerome writes, *ad Paulin.:* "The Revelation of John contains as many mysteries (*sacramenta*) as words." Augustine, *ad Paulin.:* "Many things are said obscurely in this book so as to exercise the mind of the reader, and there are few things in it that, even when clarified, help to explain the rest." The only remedy to this obscurity is the fulfillment of those prophecies.

Another special feature is (2) its *similarity with the Book of Daniel.* First, with regard to the authors; both were dear to Christ and joined to Him by a bond of blood. Second, with regard to the subject matter; in both places, the history of the special circumstances of the Church and the mystery of the Antichrist are set forth. Third, with regard to the structure; both bear the mark of a sublime sermon, that is, succinct and symbolic, given by means of visions. Fourth, with regard to authority; the Book of Daniel was not received without some hesitation, being counted among the *Ketuphim*.

Chapter 1

There are four parts to this chapter:
  I. The address and salutation, vv. 1–9;
  II. The occasion of the first vision, vv. 9–12;
  III. The first apparition or vision, vv. 12–17;
  IV. Three consequences: consolation, explanation, exhortation, vv. 17 to the end of the chapter.

v. 1 Ἀποκάλυψις Χριστοῦ, *a revelation of Christ,* made to Christ, as one concludes from the following verses. Lyranus thinks the phrase means "that it had been made to an angel who was impersonating Christ." But John clearly distinguishes between Christ and the angel.

Αὐτῷ, *to Him,* because Christ (1) is Mediator between God and men. (2) He is the supreme Prophet of the Church, through whom God speaks to us (John 1:18; Heb. 1:2). Viegas suggests this means "that all things were revealed to Christ at the first moment of His conception."

Τοῖς δούλοις, *to the servants.* (1) To all Christians in general. (2) To the ministers of the Church in particular.

ἐν τάχει, *immediately.* "The time is near" (v. 3). But certain things have taken a long time to happen, haven't they?

We reply: 1. It is sufficient that certain things happened immediately, by synecdoche. 2. If the brevity of this life is compared with eternity (1 Cor. 10:11; 1 Pet. 4:7; 1 John 2:18; James 5:8; Rev. 22:10), then they still happened "quickly." 3. Aretas: It seems like a long time "because of the desire of the godly, who are prepared to suffer many things for Christ."

But we reply more appropriately that this is said, either with reference to the beginning of these things, or from God's perspective.

ἐσήμανεν, *he confirmed.* Rupert thinks that the word in this passage means the same thing as "to sign, to seal." But the word is not used that way in the Scriptures. In the previous sentence, it is explained with τὸ δεῖξαι, "to show."

v. 2 ἐμαρτύρησε, *he testified,* namely, in the Gospel History. In it, he noted the things he saw Christ do and heard Christ say (John 10:35; 21:24). The apostles were to be eyewitnesses (Acts 1:8; 10:39). Some understand it to refer to this prophecies of this book.

ὃς ἐμαρτύρησε, *who testified,* pertains to all three parts that follow.

v. 3 ὁ ἀναγινώσκων καὶ οἱ ἀκούοντες, *blessed* (the μακάριοι is understood) *is the one who reads and blessed are those who hear.* Anselm says that the reading refers to the clerics, whereas the hearing refers to the laymen. But it is better to apply it to all men, whatever their order may be. The three concepts are joined together: reading, hearing, keeping.

τηρεῖν, *to keep,* refers to the "keeping" of the memory and the "obedience" of the life (Luke 8:15).

With τοὺς λόγους τῆς προφητείας, *the words of this prophecy,* he means the prophecies written in this book. But in general, he means everything contained in it.

v. 4 Ταῖς ἑπτὰ ἐκκλησίαις, *to the seven churches.* The title "seven churches" has in view the whole Church, (1) because the number seven in Holy Scripture signifies perfection and universality (Pro. 24:16; Psa. 119:164; Augustine in Book XI, *De Civitate Dei*, ch. 31); (2) because the whole Church is breathed upon with the grace of the sevenfold Spirit (Petrus Damianus, *De Excell. Joh.*).

Augustine in Book XVII, *De Civitate Dei*, ch. 4: "Perfection is ascribed to the whole Church in 1 Sam. 2 with the number seven, on account of which John also writes to the seven churches, thus showing that he is writing to the fullness of one. The same thing is symbolized beforehand in the Proverbs of Solomon, where Wisdom built for herself a house and propped it up on seven columns."

Those churches in Asia Minor are listed individually in v. 11.

Χάρις, *grace,* the free favor of God; εἰρήνη, *peace,* the result of grace. That is, it denotes the peace of the conscience.

ἀπὸ Θεοῦ ὁ ὢν, καὶ ὁ ἦν καὶ ὁ ἐρχόμενος, *from God who is, and who was, and who is to come.* Aretas: "'Who is' refers to the Father; 'who was' refers to the Son; 'who is to come' refers to the Holy Spirit." But it is better to say that all these things refer to the Father, since it mentions the Holy Spirit and the Son later. Aretas admits that "this is possible, since the Father contains in Himself all things that are, the source, and the means, and the end."

Primasius and Thomas apply these words to the Son: "Who is, on account of immutability; who was, on account of eternality; who is to come, on account of equity. Who is, namely, alive; who was, before He was born of the Virgin; who is to come, to judge."

This is another way of referring to the eternal and immutable essence of God. This immutability is also indicated with this unusual manner of speech in which those three names are used. Although they should be governed by the preposition, they are not inflected according to the rules of the Greek language; they remain unchanged. It seems to be taken from Exo. 3:14: "I am who I am." Galatinus (Book 2, ch. 14) translates: "Who was, and am, and will be."

The same is true of the personal essence of the Father. He is, on account of immutability. He was, on account of eternity. He is to come, because (1) He remains the same for all eternity, and (2) He will judge through the Son.

Καὶ ἀπὸ τῶν ἑπτὰ πνευμάτων, ἃ ἐνώπιον τοῦ θρόνου αὐτοῦ, *and from the seven spirits that are before His throne.*

1. Some take this to refer to the angels. Blasius de Viegas on Rev. 4: "These words refer to the seven chief angels who preside over human affairs." Others take it to refer to the entire company of angels, but Viegas refutes them. "The seven spirits in Holy Scripture are said to stand before God, Tob. 12:15; Rev. 8:2, 15:16."

2. Others take it to refer to the saints. Petrus Cudsemius in *De Desperata Calvini Causa*, p. 132: "If the saints come before God in order to participate in the distribution of celestial gifts, why not also for prayer and supplications? For if you receive something good from someone, surely you can also rightly and piously seek it from him."

3. Socinus, Epist. 3, *Ad Volkelium*, p. 483, writes: "Those spirits are nothing other than the manifold power and authority of Christ which were

granted to Him by God Himself." Later he says that it is an explanation of the preceding phrase. He proves this from chapter 5, "where the seven eyes that the Lamb has are said to be seven spirits that are sent out into the whole earth."

4. Still others take it to refer to the gifts of the Holy Spirit. But "grace and peace" cannot be sought from themselves.

5. The best interpretation is that the seven spirits refer to the very person of the Holy Spirit, who is described by way of metonymy, not with regard to His essence or person, but with regard to His gracious gifts. For in communicating His gracious gifts to those seven churches, He worked so perfectly that it is as if they were all spirits working perfectly in each of His churches. Justin, *Cohortatio ad Graecos*: "The holy prophets said that one and the same Spirit was divided into seven spirits." *Glossa Ordinaria*: "One in nature, manifold in diversity of gifts."

Therefore, the Holy Spirit is understood to be the author of the seven—that is, of all—the spiritual gifts in the Church (Isa. 11:1; 1 Pet. 4:10). Grace and peace can only come from God alone, and the apostles only pray to God alone for it. The seven spirits are said to be before the throne of God, because the Holy Spirit is of one essence and glory with the Father and governs all things together with Him. "To stand before the throne" indicates ministry, but here another phrase is used.

v. 5 ὁ μάρτυς ὁ πιστός, *the faithful witness*. This is a reference to the prophetic office of Christ, which He faithfully carried out by revealing to us God's counsel concerning our salvation, even sealing His testimony with blood (John 8:14, 8:37). He is "the Apostle of our profession" (Heb. 3:1).

Christ is placed after the Holy Spirit, (1) lest anyone should imagine that the order implies inequality; (2) because Christ is the Mediator between God and men; (3) because John goes on to describe the office of Christ more fully.

Christ (1) is the Word of the Father, and therefore, by virtue of such a relationship, He can testify and enunciate the Father's counsel. (2) He sealed with His death and blood everything that He enunciated as the Word of the Father. (3) He sought the glory of the Father alone.

ὁ πρωτότοκος ἐκ τῶν νεκρῶν, *the firstborn from among the dead*. This is a reference to the kingly office of Christ. He is called the "firstborn from among the dead," not with regard to time, but (1) because He arose by His own power, and we, too, will arise to eternal life by His power and merit (1 Cor. 15:14; Heb. 2:14). (2) We are subject to Him, to our Lord, just as the firstborn was the ruler of his brothers (Gen. 49:3; 2 Chr. 21:3). (3) He receives the nations and the ends of the earth as an inheritance (Psa. 2:8, Heb. 1:6), just as the firstborn was the genuine heir of the paternal property. (4) He was the first, not to return to this natural, earthly life, but to enter into glory. (Cf. 1 Cor. 15:20, Col. 1:18.)

ὁ ἄρχων τῶν βασιλέων τῆς γῆς, *the ruler of the kings of the earth*. This again refers to the kingly office of Christ, for He is the *King of kings* (Rev. 19:16), who, according to His human nature, has been placed at the right hand of God over angels and all creatures (Eph. 1:20).

He joins this to the previous statements because Christ obtained this kingship by His death.

Τῷ ἀγαπήσαντι ἡμᾶς, *to Him who loved us*. Erasmus applies this to the Father, but (1) other things are inserted that undoubtedly refer to Christ. (2) The phrase "in His blood" is added, which cannot refer to the Father.

Therefore, some think that it should be read, "of Him who loved"; others, "He who loved." But Aretas relates it with, "to Him be glory," Rom. 5:8; and Gal. 2:10, "He loved me."

λύσαντι ἡμᾶς, *who washed us*. This is a reference to the priestly office of Christ. The word "washed" demonstrates the power of the blood of Christ, which was sufficient, not only to sprinkle all men, but also to wash them.

Love is ascribed to the one who washes. Rupert: "He would not have washed, if He had not loved. For He did not first wash and then love, but first He loved, and then He washed."

v. 6 Καὶ ἐποίησεν ἡμᾶς βασιλεῖς καὶ ἱερεῖς, *and He made us kings and priests*.

1. Spiritual kings, because they rule over the devil and his ministers. Ambrose, Book II, *De Abraham*, ch. 10: "They, too, are kings who are not slaves to sin and are not conquered by evil."

2. Priests, because they offer spiritual sacrifices (Rom. 12:1, 1 Pet. 2:5). Irenaeus, Book IV, ch. 20, p. 245: "All the righteous possess the priestly order."

ἡ δόξα καὶ κράτος, *glory and strength.* Understand either ἔστι or ἔστω, *it is* or *let it be.* "Glory and strength," that is, the glory of strength and power—an example of hendiadys.

v. 7 Ἔρχεται, *He,* namely, Christ, *is coming,* inasmuch as He has been established by God as Judge. The present tense is used for that which is coming shortly in the future.

ὄψεται αὐτὸν πᾶς ὀφθαλμὸς, *every eye will see Him.* For He will come in His visible human nature. And especially "those who pierced Him" (Zec. 12:10). Not only those who pierced Him on the cross, but also those who pierced Him with their blasphemous tongues.

κόψονται ἐπ᾽ αὐτὸν πᾶσαι αἱ φυλαὶ τῆς γῆς, *all the tribes of the earth will strike over Him.* This refers to all men (Gen. 28:14; Psa. 72:37; Mat. 24), that is, the ungodly from among Jews and Gentiles.

They will strike. They will tear their bodies asunder due to their inability to endure the pain "over Him," that is, on account of Him, because they rejected His Word and persecuted the members of His body.

v. 8 Ἐγώ εἰμι τὸ Α καὶ τὸ Ω, *I am the Alpha and the Omega.* The explanation is given immediately, "I am the beginning and the end." The metaphor is drawn from the order of the letters of the Greek alphabet. 'I am He before whom nothing is, through whom was made everything that was made; I am He who remains, while all things perish. Eternity, creation, our glorification.'

These are the words of Christ by which eternity is ascribed to Him, as well as the *homoousia,* the same essence with the Father. Only God speaks thus about Himself (Isa. 41:4, 44:6, 48:12). It further indicates that Christ is "the author and perfecter of our faith" (Heb. 12:2). "He is the First because of His divinity, and the Last of men because of His humanity," Andreas Caesariensis, ch. 66, f. 99.

But the previous explanation is simpler.

Clement of Alexandria, Book IV, *Stromata,* f. 230: "For this reason the Word is called the Alpha and the Omega, because of Him alone does the end become the beginning, and it again ends in that which is the beginning from above, having neither distance nor dimension."

The heretics Marcus and Colorbasus played a sort of anagram game with the order of the letters of the alphabet and extracted many inept and dangerous doctrines from it, impudently misusing this example of Christ in defense of their own vanity, as Tertullian testifies, *De Praescriptione*, ch. 50.

Ὁ ὤν, *who is*, who, with the Father and the Holy Spirit, is immutable in essence (Heb. 13:8).

ὁ ἦν, *who was*, not only in the Old Testament, but also before the world was formed (Psa. 90:1). ὁ ἐρχόμενος, *who is coming*, who will be forever and will come to judge visibly, according to His human nature.

Ὁ Παντοκράτωρ, *the Almighty*, who is powerfully able to carry out the things that are promised in this book.

v. 9 συγκοινωνός, *companion*. There is a threefold communion of the godly: (1) in the cross, (2) in spiritual gifts, among which is patience, and (3) in glory.

Θλίψει, *tribulation*, on account of the confession of the Gospel.

βασιλείᾳ, *the kingdom*, the kingdom of grace and of glory. The kingdom is combined with tribulation, because nothing is more regal than to suffer for Christ's sake.

ὑπομονῇ τοῦ Χριστοῦ, *the patience of Christ*. (1) Christ gives it. (2) Christ is the shining example of patience. (3) The godly endure persecution on account of Christ and for the sake of Christ, by whose power and protection they patiently bear their afflictions.

Ὑπομονὴ signifies, not only the patience with which we endure evil things, but also, by virtue of the Word, the patient expectation with which we persevere in bearing these evil things, with the hope of reward.

Πάτμῳ, *Patmos*, is one of the islands in the Aegean Sea called the Sporades islands, where John had been exiled by Domitian (Eusebius, Book 3, *Hist.*, ch. 16). It is commonly called the island of palms, known for its trade in precious metals, but it is most famous for the exile of John.

Since John was being punished by the emperor with an earthly exile on account of the faith, he was then refreshed by the heavenly Prince with greater delights and favors.

v. 10 ἐν πνεύματι, *in spirit*.

1. From a sense of external things I was turned inward so that my spirit, that is to say, my soul, might be entirely occupied in contemplating the images or visions that were being divinely set before me.

2. Ambrose on this passage: "So many mysteries could not be seen with carnal, but with spiritual eyes."

3. An ecstasy fell upon me. (Cf. Acts 10:10, 22:17; 2 Cor. 12:2.) Haymo on this passage: "It is clearly demonstrated that Blessed John saw this vision, not bodily, but in spirit, yet not in a dream. He was caught up in a state of ecstasy."

ἐν τῇ κυριακῇ ἡμέρᾳ, *on the Lord's Day*, because it had been hallowed by Christ's resurrection. (Cf. Athanasius, *Sermo de Semente*, p. 721. Augustine, Book XXII, *De Civitate Dei*, ch. 30.)

Ignatius, Epist. 3: "He calls that regal day the most preeminent of all days—the day on which our life arose and our victory over death was won in Christ." Chrysostom (Homily 5, *De Resurr.*) says that this day was "of bread and of light, for on it we perceived the bread of heavenly resurrection in which the darkness of our mind fled away."

From this passage, one concludes that the first day of the week was set aside by the apostles as the Sabbath, in memory of the resurrection of Christ. (Cf. Acts 20:7, 1 Cor. 16:2.)

v. 11 Γράψον, *write*. Therefore the apostles received the command to write.

Ephesus is a famous city in Asia Minor, in the province of Ionia. Smyrna, likewise, was a city of Ionia, in which the peoples of Asia Minor used to celebrate their assemblies (Pliny, Book V, ch. 29). Pergamum is a city of Asia Minor in the province of Troas, the homeland of Galen. Thyatira, not far from Ephesus, lies in the province of Lydia. Sardis, likewise, is a city of Lydia, the royal seat of Croesus. Philadelphia is a city of Mysia. Laodicea is situated in Caria.

v. 12 Βλέπειν τὴν φωνὴν, *to see the voice*. (1) Flacius: "To see the author of the voice who was speaking to me." (2) R. Maimonides (*More Nebuchim*, part. 1, ch. 46) teaches that, in sacred language, often that which is apprehended by one sense is explained as being apprehended by the other, and since sight is nobler than the other senses, therefore it is often used in place of the others. Jer. 2:31, "See the word of the Lord!" Gen. 27:27, "See the smell of my son." Exo. 20:18, "All the people saw the thunderings." Rom. 7:23, "I see another law." 1 Cor. 1:26, "See your calling." In Hebrew, "to see a vision" refers to a vision of the eyes, but it is also transferred to the apprehension of the intellect.

The seven churches (listed above) are symbolized by the seven golden lampstands.

v. 13 ὅμοιον υἱῷ ἀνθρώπου, *similar to a son of man*. Viegas concludes from this (p. 62) that an angel had appeared to John in the person and likeness of Christ. But John speaks this way because, in a state of ecstasy and in spirit, he saw Christ. Christ walks in the midst of the lampstands. Therefore, He is present for His Church according to both natures (Mat. 18:20, 28:20).

Irenaeus says the following about the form of this apparition, Book IV, ch. 37, p. 270: "In these images is signified something about the glory He received from His Father with the appearance of His head. Something priestly is signified with His robe, and, for this very reason, Moses vested the High Priest, as a type. Something of the end is signified, like *bronze refined in the furnace*, which is the firmness of faith and the enduring quality of prayers, on account of the refining fire when He comes at the end of time."

ἐνδεδυμένον ποδήρη, *dressed in a long robe*. Lyranus suggests this word is a combination from the Greek and the Latin: from *pos*, which is "foot," and *haereo*, which "adheres" to the ankles.

A type of clothing is meant. It refers to a robe that hung down to the feet.

This robe that reached to the ankle is a symbol of the priesthood, for the Old Testament priests wore this kind of clothing.

Περιεζωσμένον, *girded around*. The belt is a symbol of alacrity and swiftness in administering the priesthood, in defending the godly. Some think that it signifies the priest's self-mortification and abnegation. For we gird ourselves, they say, near our kidneys, which are the seat of evil emotions in man. But such a belt is not needed for Christ, who is immune to all depraved emotions. In Isa. 11:5, righteousness is said to be the belt of His loins, and fidelity the belt of His kidneys.

But the belt in this passage appears around his breasts as a testimony to His love for the Church, for He wants us to suck the milk of love—even blood, and the grace of the Holy Spirit—from His girded and compressed breasts.

Ζώνην χρυσᾶν, *a golden belt*, which signifies (1) Christ's royal dignity; (2) His glorious triumph over His enemies; (3) that this priest far surpasses the priests of the Law, for they would use a belt interwoven with golden threads.

v. 14 ἡ δὲ κεφαλὴ αὐτοῦ καὶ αἱ τρίχες λευκαὶ ὡσεὶ ἔριον λευκὸν, ὡς χιών, *and His head and hair were white like white wool, like snow*. This denotes: (1) the eternal deity of Christ (Dan. 7:9); (2) His divine wisdom (Job 32:7, Pro. 20:29); (3) the purity and holiness of His judgments.

Οἱ ὀφθαλμοὶ αὐτοῦ ὡς φλὸξ πυρὸς, *His eyes like a flame of fire*. They are a symbol: (1) of the omniscience with which Christ also looks into hidden things as He dispels the darkness with His fiery eyes; (2) of wrath and vengeance against the ungodly.

v. 15 Οἱ πόδες αὐτοῦ ὅμοιοι χαλκολιβάνῳ, *His feet like brass*. Chalcolibanon is a species of electrum, more precious than gold. Suidas, the ancient translator, interpreted it as orichalcum, which was, to the ancients, the most precious kind of metal that could be dug out of the ground. Pliny says that it was long admired on account of its unique beauty, but by his time it had long since been exhausted from the earth. It seems that orichalcum refers to something that is born in the mountains, or that is dug out of a Lebanese mountain.

If the etymology indicates the meaning of the word, then it is something composed of metal and frankincense. For *chalcos* is metal, and *libanon* means frankincense. Thus some think it is a kind of frankincense that refers to a kind of metal. But the following description hardly seems to permit this.

For His feet are said to be *burning or fiery like chalcolibano*.

It signifies: (1) the wrath by which Christ crushes His adversaries—He consumes them like fire; (2) the purity of the life of Christ during His entire time on earth; (3) the last judgment to be administered by Christ at the end of the world.

ἡ φωνὴ αὐτοῦ ὡς φωνὴ ὑδάτων πολλῶν, *His voice like the voice of many waters*. The voice of many waters is noisy and loud. It refers to: (1) the majesty of Christ; (2) the multitude of people who are to be converted to Christ (Rev. 17:15); (3) the judgment of Christ which will suddenly come upon the ungodly like a torrent (Eze. 1:24); (4) the very rapid passage of the Gospel throughout the whole world.

v. 16 ἔχων ἐν τῇ δεξιᾷ αὐτοῦ χειρὶ ἀστέρας ἑπτὰ, *having seven stars in His right hand*. Those seven stars refer to the seven teachers of the churches in Asia Minor (v. 20). He has them in His right hand, that is, He defends and preserves them, lest anyone snatch them out of His hand (John 10:28). He is the author and defender of the ministry.

ἐκ τοῦ στόματος αὐτοῦ ῥομφαία δίστομος ὀξεῖα ἐκπορευομένη, *a sharp two-edged sword proceeding out of His mouth*, a sword with two mouths, that is, two edges. It refers to: (1) the Word of Christ that converts the godly and kills the ungodly (Isa. 11:4; 2 The. 2:8; Heb. 4:12; Rev. 2:16, 19:15, 21); (2) vengeance against His foes.

Christ bears a sword in three ways: (1) girded upon His thigh (Psa. 45:3); (2) in His mouth; (3) in His hand (Psa. 7:12). This represents God's progression as He inflicts punishment. First, He has a sword girded as He shows His power in order to frighten. Then He places the sword in His mouth as He threatens in order to terrify. Finally, when neither of these is sufficient, He brandishes His sword in order to strike.

ἡ ὄψις αὐτοῦ ὡς ὁ ἥλιος φαίνει ἐν τῇ δυνάμει αὐτοῦ, *His face like the sun shining in its strength*, that is, at about midday. The sense is that His face was very bright, like the blazing sun into which no one can hold his gaze and look.

It represents: (1) the divine majesty and glory of Christ (Mat. 13:43, 17:2); (2) the glorification of His body; (3) omniscience.

v. 17 ἔπεσα πρὸς τοὺς πόδας, *I fell at His feet*, like a dead man, from fear and terror. But He placed His right hand on me to raise me up and comfort me (Dan. 10:18).

v. 18 ὁ ζῶν, *the living One*. Not only do I (1) live forever, but (2) I am also able to give life to others, (3) because I am life itself (John 11:26, 14:6).

After the resurrection, I now live forever, because death shall have no dominion over Me (compare Acts 13:34 with Rom. 6:9).

ἔχω τὰς κλεῖς τοῦ θανάτου, *I have the keys of death*. I am Lord of death and hell. To Me belongs the supreme dominion over death and hell, so that I can free from both and damn to both.

v. 19 *The things that are and the things that will be*, that is, this vision of the seven lampstands which represents the present state of the churches, and also the visions that follow, namely, the seven seals, the seven trumpets, and the seven bowls, which represent the future state of the Church and the world.

v. 20 The ministers of the Church are called (1) angels (2) and stars.

Angels, (1) because God has entrusted to them the task of announcing His commandments (Justin, *Dialogus cum Tryphone*, p. 214); and (2) they should stand in the same state of righteousness and have their conduct in heaven.

Stars, (1) because they announce the heavenly doctrine, which is light; (2) and because of their example of a holy life (2 Cor. 5:20, Phi. 2:15-16, 1 Tim. 4:12). Jude calls the heretics "planets," wandering stars.

They should be burning with the fervor of love, set on high with sublime contemplation, gleaming with the conduct of an excellent life, established and fixed as they persevere in doing good works, facing toward the earth with compassion on its inhabitants, and quick to obey God.

They are conferred upon the lampstands of the Church as those who keep the lamps burning, for God kindles the light of His Word in the Church.

The lampstands are golden: (1) because they are precious before God, and (2) because they should pursue purity (Mat. 5:15-16, Phi. 2:15).

Chapter 2

The second chapter contains four letters to four of the churches in Asia Minor:
    I. To the angel or bishop of the church in Ephesus, vv. 1–7;
    II. To the bishop of Smyrna, vv. 8–11;
    III. To the bishop of Pergamum, vv. 12–17;
    IV. To the bishop of Thyatira, v. 18 to the end of the chapter.

v. 1 These letters are addressed to the bishops of the churches, (1) because it is their office to announce the will of God to the hearers who are committed to their trust; (2) because they are more in need of consolation and correction than the rest.

But it must always be understood that He says, "Write these things to the angel," so that he may then make it known to his church.

v. 2 Οἶδα, *I know*. In this passage, the word "knowledge" implies affection. I am pleased with your patience.

Τὰ ἔργα, *the works*, refers to works of kindness toward the poor, especially those who are exiles because of their confession of God's Word.

Τὸν κόπον, *the labor*, refers to diligence in the works of the ecclesiastical office. But the word κόπος signifies labor combined with a sense of toil.

ὑπομονήν, *patience*, in enduring the afflictions that are brought upon you because of your confession of the Gospel.

He also commends the bishop's zeal in that he cannot tolerate the wicked, that is, those who spew false doctrine and those who live in manifest sins. One concludes from the antithesis that he has excommunicated them and thrown them out of the Church.

Καὶ ἐπείρασω, *and you have tested*, you have investigated them (1 John 4:1) and exposed their deceit.

Τοὺς φάσκοντας εἶναι ἀποστόλους, *those who say they are apostles.* They boast that they are teachers who have been divinely sent. Ebion and Cerinthus were notable examples of such teachers, who taught that Christ is only a man and that works of the Law are necessary for justification.

v. 3 Καὶ ἐβάστασας, *and you have borne*, namely, the yoke of the cross that has been imposed on you, the calumnies and the disgrace brought upon you by those false teachers for My name's sake.

Κεκοπίακας, *you have labored*, you continue to labor in the works of your office for the glory of My name.

Οὐ κέκμηκας, *you have not fainted*, in spite of those calumnies and persecutions, you have not left anything out of that diligence, nor have you failed to confess the doctrine.

v. 4 ἔχω κατὰ σοῦ, *I have a complaint against you.*

ὅτι τὴν ἀγάπην σου τὴν πρώτην ἀφῆκες, *that you have left your first love.* You do not burn with as much zeal in faith and love toward Me, and you have abandoned much of the kindness and works of mercy that you used to show to the poor.

Primasius, Ambrose, and Bede take this statement to be about "the loss of love through mortal guilt, not in the bishop himself, whom Christ has praised up to this point, but in many of his subjects."

But the context shows that this pertains to the bishop himself, which is also made clear from the threat that is added. Therefore it is understood that he has abandoned some of the fervor of love, that he has fallen from the height of virtue to a lower level.

v. 5 Πόθεν ἐκπέπτωκας, *from which level you have fallen.*

Τὰ πρῶτα ἔργα ποίησον, *do the first works*, put on your earlier zeal in faith and love.

ἔρχομαί σοι, *I will come to you*, that is, against you.

Κινήσω τὴν λυχνίαν σου, *I will remove your lampstand.* I will remove the bishop from his office. I will take away the treasure of the Word from the church, so that it will no longer have a place among the lampstands.

v. 6 Epiphanius writes about the Nicolaitans, Book I, Vol. 2, *Haeres.*, 25: "The devil entered into Nicolaus, one of the seven deacons, and deceived his heart with that same error as those previously named, so that he was wounded even more than they." He is talking about the Basilidians and the other heretics who were hostile to marriage. "For although he had a beautiful wife and had kept himself from her in imitation of those whom he saw as devoted to God, he endured for a time, but he was finally unable to control his intemperance. So, then, he fell from his purpose and, not at all surprisingly, had intercourse with his own wife. But afterwards, feeling ashamed that he had been overcome and fearing that it would be discovered, he dared to say that, unless someone engages in sexual activity every day, he cannot participate in eternal life. For he fled from one extreme to the other." Cf. Irenaeus (Book I, ch. 27) and Eusebius (Book III, *Hist.*, ch. 26).

They taught that (1) wives should be held in common; (2) it is permissible to eat the sacrifices of the Gentiles; (3) fornication is permissible.

A follower of Nicolaus—a soft and effeminate man—had been assigned to the people of Asia Minor. But the Apostle John, who taught in Asia Minor at that time, zealously opposed that impostor.

v. 7 ἀκουσάτω, *let him hear*. The outcome is understood from what came before. Let him properly attend to what the Spirit of God says in general to all the churches.

Τῷ νικῶντι, *to the one who overcomes* (1) the devil's temptations; (2) the lust of the flesh; (3) the hatred and persecutions of the world; (4) the seductions of depravity. First, it is not spoken to the one who fights, but "to the one who overcomes." Second, it is not spoken in the past tense, to the one who was victorious, but in the present, because it is not enough to have overcome once or more often if one does not always overcome. Third, it is spoken in absolute terms to the one who overcomes. No definite enemy is mentioned, so that we should understand that all things are to be overcome.

"I will give to eat from the tree of life," that is, I will give him the heavenly Paradise (Luke 23:43, Rev. 22:2,14), of which the earthly Paradise was a type, for in the middle of it was the tree of life (Gen. 2:9), the fruits of which would have preserved man in perpetual youth and health.

The tree of life is said to be "in the midst of Paradise," because (1) it shows everyone the path to Christ. No one has been excluded from its benefits by an absolute decree. (2) Christ is the Church's Mediator, walking in the midst of the golden lampstands (Rev. 1:13). (3) The means of salvation are near to us in the Church (Rom. 10:6).

v. 9 Τὴν θλῖψιν, *the tribulation*, the persecutions that you are suffering for My name's sake.

Τὴν πτωχείαν, *the poverty*, that your resources have been snatched away from you by your persecutors on account of your confession of the Word (Heb. 10:34).

Πλούσιος εἶ, *you are rich*, namely, in God (Luke 12:21), in the saving knowledge of God, in faith, in spiritual goods.

Τὴν βλασφημίαν, *the blasphemy*, with which the false Jews slander you. Indeed, you are even in danger as you labor to refute their blasphemy. The words immediately following indicate what kind of blasphemy this was, that they were cloaking their wickedness with the holy name of God.

They say that they are Jews, God's elect people, but they are not the true seed of Abraham nor are they the people of God (John 8:39, Rom. 2:28, 9:6, Gal. 6:16). According to the flesh they are descended from Abraham, but they do not follow in his footsteps (Rom. 4:12), nor do they do his works (John 8:39).

v. 10 Μέλλει βάλλειν ὁ διάβολος εἰς φυλακὴν, *the devil is about to throw into prison*. The devil, through his instruments, namely, the persecutors, will throw some of you into prison, ἵνα πειρασθῆτε, *that you may be tested*, that your faith, patience and perseverance may be tried and made evident (1 Pet. 1:7).

ἡμερῶν δέκα, *for ten days*. (1) Some interpret this as ten years (Dan. 9:24). "From the tenth year of the reign of Trajan until he would be succeeded by Hadrian." (2) But it is better to say that the number of ten days is used to indicate a short period of time (Amos 5:3).

ἄχρι θανάτου, *until death*, that you may even be prepared to suffer death for the confession of the Christian faith.

Στέφανον, *crown*, corresponds to τὸν νικῶντα, *the one who overcomes*, in verse 7. (Cf. James 1:12.)

v. 11 The second death is eternal death (Rev. 20:14, 21:8).

v. 13 ὅπου ὁ θρόνος τοῦ σατανᾶ, *where the throne of Satan*. Luther: *des Satans Stuhl*. In the midst of the enemies and persecutors of the Word, and also in the midst of the heretics.

Κρατεῖς τὸ ὄνομά μου, *you hold onto My name*, the confession of My name. You remain steadfast in the truth of the doctrine.

Οὐκ ἠρνήσω τὴν πίστιν μου, *you have not denied My faith*, My doctrine which is centered around faith, concerning My person, office, and benefits. You are fighting for the faith once delivered (Jude 3).

Καὶ ἐν ταῖς ἡμέραις, *and in the days*, in which Antipas was killed. Luther: *Und in meinen Tagen ist Antipas getodet*. Antipas was a faithful teacher of the church in Pergamum and a steadfast confessor of Christ.

ὅπου κατοικεῖ ὁ σατανᾶς, *where Satan dwells*, who incites tyrants to persecute the godly.

v. 14 ἔχεις, *you have*, you tolerate, you grant a place.

Τὴν διδαχὴν Βαλαάμ, *the doctrine of Balaam*. He calls the doctrine of the Nicolaitans "the doctrine of Balaam" by way of analogy, for Balaam gave Balak, king of the Moabites, the counsel that he should invite the Israelites to his sacrifices and seduce them to commit fornication (Num. 25:1, 31:16). Likewise, the Nicolaitans would eat of the sacrifices of idols and commit fornication, contrary to the decree of the apostles (Acts 15:29).

v. 16 Πολεμήσω μετ' αὐτῶν ἐν τῇ ρομφαίᾳ τοῦ στόματός μου, *I will fight with them with the sword of My mouth*. I will fight against them with the sword of the Word (Rev. 1:16), by means of a new teacher with whom I will replace you. And if they are not converted, then I will exercise My judgment against them, and I will destroy them in My wrath (Job 4:9, Isa. 11:4). He has in mind the story of Balaam, whom the angel restrained with his drawn sword (Num. 22:23), and who was also killed by the sword (Num. 31:8).

v. 17 Ἀπὸ τοῦ μάννα, *from the manna*. The manna with which God fed the Israelites for forty years in the desert was a type (1) of the Gospel, which is hidden from the wise men of the world (Mat. 11:25), for through it souls are fed in the desert of this world; (2) of Christ Himself (John 6:32); (3) of joy and refreshment, for by it the elect will be satisfied in eternal life. "I will make him a partaker of the heavenly goods that are reserved for the saints in heaven, just as an omer of manna was reserved in the tabernacle" (Exo. 16:32; Heb. 9:4).

Some think that "manna is a symbol of the divine grace obtained through Christ," which agrees with the second explanation above.

The sense is that he who overcomes by the inward consolation of the word and the Spirit in this life will also be satisfied by the beatific vision of God in the life to come.

Δώσω αὐτῷ ψῆφον λευκήν, *I will give him a white stone*. When judges would absolve the accused, they would cast a white stone into the voting jar as a testimony of innocence. Ovid, Book XV, *Metamorphoseon*: "The custom was to use old stones, both black and white. The defendants were condemned with the former, while they were absolved from guilt with the latter."

The sense is that he who overcomes will be absolved from sin, from the curse of the Law, and from eternal damnation. Christ will also confess him on the Day of Judgment (Mat. 10:32). Luther: *Ich wil ihm geben ein gut Zeugnüß*.

ὄνομα καινὸν, *a new name*. When a person was to be elected to the magistrate, his name was written on a white stone and cast into the voting jar, where it was hidden until it was revealed in the election. The sense is that he who overcomes will be called and will be a child and heir of God, a brother and coheir of Christ (Rom. 8:16), a citizen of the heavenly Jerusalem. But all of that is still hidden in this life (1 John 3:2). This glory of the godly will be revealed on the Day of Judgment.

No one knows the name of God's children except the one who receives it, because the faith by which that name is applied to a person cannot be seen by others (1 Cor. 2:11). The speech is elevated: "Not only will they be absolved from damnation, but they will also be heirs of eternal life."

v. 19 Τὴν διακονίαν, *the service*, the labor which you endure in your office, the care with which you look after the saints (Rom. 12:13).

Τὰ ἔσχατα πλείονα τῶν πρώτων, *the last works are more than first*, that you daily abound in faith and in zeal for good works; that you are performing more works of mercy on a daily basis and are more fruitful in good works (Col. 1:10).

Τὴν γυναῖκα Ἰεζάβελ, *that woman Jezebel*, some ungodly woman similar to Jezebel in idolatry and in ungodliness (1 Kings 16:31).

ἐμοὺς δούλους, *My servants*. Christ calls them "His servants," not after they were seduced, but when Jezebel approached them in order to seduce them (Mat. 21:31).

Πορνεῦσαι καὶ εἰδωλόθυτα φαγεῖν, *to fornicate and to eat of the sacrifices of idols*, namely, in those public banquets which the Gentiles would hold from the meat of their sacrifices in honor of their idols and to which they would invite the Christians (1 Cor. 10:20). This could not be done without causing the weak to stumble. The Nicolaitans are again in view, for they boasted that they had the spirit of prophecy and taught that it was permissible for Christians, as a matter of Christian freedom, to eat the idol sacrifices and to fornicate. Apart from those banquets and when there was no danger of offense, it was permissible to eat idol sacrifices (1 Cor. 10:25, 27).

v. 21 *I gave her*, namely, the prophetess, time to repent, that she may stop her spiritual and physical fornication.

v. 22 Βάλλω αὐτὴν εἰς κλίνην, *I will cast her onto a bed*. I will inflict her with an illness.

Τοὺς μοιχεύοντας μετ' αὐτῆς, *those who commit adultery with her*, those who assented to idolatry and committed fornication with her.

v. 23 Τὰ τέκνα αὐτῆς, *her children*, her disciples who assent to her heresy. ἀποκτενῶ ἐν θανάτῳ, *I will kill in death*. They will perish by the sword, just as Jezebel and the prophets of Baal were killed (1 Kings 18:40; 2 Kings 9:33, 10:25).

ὁ ἐραυνῶν νεφροὺς καὶ καρδίας, *the One who searches minds and hearts*. All things are known to Me, even the things that are hidden in the innermost recesses of the heart (Psa. 7:10; Jer. 11:20, 17:10).

Κατὰ τὰ ἔργα, *according to your works*, which are the external witnesses of the faith hidden in the heart.

v. 24 Τὰ βάθη τοῦ Σατανᾶ, *the deep things of Satan*. Those heretics referred to their doctrine as "profound mysteries," but John calls it "the deep things of Satan." They boasted that they had learned these mysteries from a revelation of the Holy Spirit, but John—or rather, Christ—says that they had come from Satan (1 Tim. 4:1).

Οὐ βάλλω ἐφ᾽ ὑμᾶς ἄλλο βάρος, *I will not cast another weight upon you*. I will not impose on you the kind of afflictions with which I threatened the Nicolaitans.

Others suggest, 'I will not require anything further of you than what follows in verse 25.'

v. 25 Πλὴν ὃ ἔχετε, κρατήσατε ἄχρις οὗ ἂν ἥξω, *but hold onto what you have until I come*. Hold onto the deposit of pure doctrine, true faith that is accompanied by love and the remaining virtues, until I take you to Myself through death. Take care that the sound doctrine is also propagated to those who come after you and preserved until the end of the world.

v. 26 Τὰ ἔργα μου, *my works*, that is, the works that I have commanded (John 6:29, 1 John 3:23).

Δώσω αὐτῷ ἐξουσίαν ἐπὶ τῶν ἐθνῶν, *I will give him authority over the nations*. Because such a one who overcomes is a true and living member of My mystical body, I will give him a share in the victory that I obtained against My foes. And since this member of My body belongs to Me as the Head, My victory is, in a real sense, also attributed to him (Eph. 2:6). For when he fights in true faith against the devil, the world, and the ungodly persecutors, when he remains in the confession of the true doctrine and prays to God to preserve the Church and to vanquish the enemy, he is ruling the nations with a rod of iron and is dashing them to pieces like vessels of clay, so that they may either be converted in this life and brought to the obedience of faith, or judged by him on the day of judgment (Mat. 19:28, 1 Cor. 6:2).

Lyranus: "I will give him authority over the nations in the final judgment, in which the perfect will be judged with Christ, and thus they have authority to pass judgment on the nations. And he will rule them with a rod of iron, with inflexible justice. And he will break them to pieces like vessels of clay, because at that time sinners will be cast into hell."

Bellarmine contends that the phrase, "to rule with a rod of iron," must necessarily be understood "about the time prior to the resurrection." But the context demonstrates that the message is about the Last Day, for it also says that he will dash them to pieces like vessels of clay. This will not happen until the Last Day.

v. 28 *Morning star* signifies: (1) the perfect knowledge of God in eternal life; (2) heavenly glory and brightness, for such a one who overcomes will "shine like the stars" (Dan. 12:1, 1 Cor. 15:41), or even "like the sun" (Mat. 13:43); (3) Christ, who calls Himself the "Morning Star" (Rev. 22:16), will give Himself to the one who overcomes as his very own.

Chapter 3

This chapter contains the three letters to the remaining three churches of Asia Minor:
    I. To the bishop of Sardis, vv. 1–6;
    II. To the bishop of Philadelphia, vv. 7–13;
    III. To the bishop of Laodicea, v. 14 to the end of the chapter.

v. 1 ὁ ἔχων τὰ ἑπτὰ πνεύματα, *who has the seven spirits*. Christ has the gifts of the Holy Spirit in His hand and distributes them to whomever He wishes (v. 4). Those spirits are before the throne of God. Also according to His human nature, Christ received the Holy Spirit "without measure" (John 3:34). "From His fullness we receive" (John 1:16). Τὰ ἔργα, *your works*, how things have gone with you.

Τὸ ὄνομα ἔχεις ὅτι ζῇς, *you have the name that you live*, that you have a share in the spiritual life that is from God (Eph. 4:18), that you live by faith and works of godliness.

Καὶ νεκρὸς εἶ, *and you are dead*, dead in sins and toward every good work (Luke 9:60, 1 Tim. 5:6, James 2:17). You have abandoned the true faith by which alone a person can be made a partaker in spiritual life (Gal. 2:20). Observe the following against the papists: (1) A firm argument is not deduced from one's name. (2) Love is not the cause, but the effect and sign of spiritual life. 1 John 3, "We know, etc."

v. 2 Γίνου γρηγορῶν, *be watchful*, in the administration of your office, wake up, snap out of your stupor of idleness and security.

Στήρισον τὰ λοιπὰ ἃ μέλλει ἀποθανεῖν, *strengthen the remaining things that are about to die*, a reference to weak Christians who are like dying sheep (Eze. 34:16), in whom faith and love are nearly extinct, who are beginning to doubt and waver through your negligence.

Πεπληρωμένα, *perfect,* sincere and free of hypocrisy, because you serve with words and appearances rather than with the heart (1 Kings 11:4). You give in to sleep. There is a twofold sense in the phrase, "with all one's heart."

v. 3 Πῶς εἴληφας καὶ ἤκουσας, *how you have received and heard.* The latter explains the former, how you were instructed by the apostles to conduct yourself (Gal. 3:3, Eph. 4:2), how the ministry was entrusted to you with the deposit of doctrine, namely, that you might faithfully guard it and propagate it to others. Τήρει, *keep,* persevere in it.

ἥξω ἐπὶ σέ, *I will come against you.* I will come quickly with punishment.

ὡς κλέπτης, *like a thief,* who comes unexpectedly and secretly (Mat. 24:42, Luke 12:39, 1 The. 5:2, 2 Pet. 3:10, Rev. 16:15).

ὀλίγα ὀνόματα, *a few names.* In some manuscripts an adversative has been added which the Latin also expresses. "Meanwhile you have a few names." Some interpret this as "leaders or members of your congregation." Better, people whose names are written in the book of life (Acts 1:15, Phi. 4:3).

ἃ οὐκ ἐμόλυναν τὰ ἱμάτια αὐτῶν, *that have not soiled their robes* with fornication, idolatry and other shameful deeds (2 Pet. 2:20, Jude 23). They have not fornicated according to the custom of the Nicolaitans.

Περιπατήσουσι μετ' ἐμοῦ, *they will walk with Me,* they will live with Me in heavenly joy and glory, ἐν λευκοῖς, *in white robes.* White robes are a symbol: (1) of perfect holiness and purity; (2) of royal and priestly dignity; (3) of happiness; (4) of triumph over one's foes; (5) of glory. (Cf. Rev. 4:4, 6:11, 7:13.)

ἄξιοί εἰσι, *they are worthy.* God has rendered them worthy of heavenly glory in Christ (Luke 20:35, Phi. 1:27, 2 The. 1:5, 11). They have walked in a manner worthy of the Gospel.

v. 5 οὐ μὴ ἐξαλείψω τὸ ὄνομα αὐτοῦ, *I will never blot out his name* (Exo. 32:32; Psa. 69:29; Phi. 4:3; Rev. 20:12, 21:27). I will not exclude him from the number of the sons of God and heirs of eternal life.

Ἐξομολογήσομαι, *I will confess* (Mat. 10:32).

v. 7 ὁ ἅγιος, *the holy One.* According to His divine nature, He is holiness itself; according to His human nature, He is innocent and immaculate (Heb. 7:26).

ὁ ἀληθινός, *the true One*. According to His divine nature He is truth itself; according to His human nature, "no deceit was found in His mouth." He is truthful both in His promises and in His threats.

ὁ ἔχων τὴν κλεῖν Δαυίδ, *the One having the key of David*.

1. Ambrose understands the key to be Christ Himself, who is the Door (John 10:9), and the Key, and the Door-Keeper, and therefore it follows: "Behold, I have set before you a door."

2. Some understand David, by way of synecdoche, to represent all the prophets. Christ holds the key of all the prophets. He is the One who can fully impart the understanding of the prophets to whomever He wishes (Luke 11:25), the key of knowledge.

3. Bede takes the key as the royal authority that belongs to David, since Christ is in the royal line of David and traces His origins to the tribe of Judah.

4. The phrase "of the house" is understood. He has the key of the house of David, that is, the Church (Luke 1:32). Isaiah 22:22 is referring to Shebna, "I will give the key of the house of David upon his shoulder." As the heir of David, He has full authority in the Church, which is the house of God (1 Tim. 3:15), symbolized by the house of David.

Only David is named as representing everyone, because, more than the rest, he vividly portrayed the mysteries of Christ in his birth, his actions, his reign, and his prophecies.

ὁ ἀνοίγων καὶ οὐδεὶς κλείσει, *who opens and no one will shut*. (1) Since He has full authority, no one can impede or resist Him as He rules the Church; all things are subject to His authority. (2) He commands and He forbids. (3) He remits sins, and thus He opens heaven by His own absolute authority. He receives into the Church Militant and the Church Triumphant whomever He wishes. (4) "He has the keys of heaven and hell" (Rev. 1:18).

v. 8 Τὰ ἔργα, *your works*, your works of faith and love, and of your office.

Θύραν ἠνεῳγμένην, *an open door*. This door signifies: (1) the understanding of the Scriptures; (2) especially the office of preaching. An open door thus signifies a convenient opportunity to preach the Gospel and to gain men for Christ which that bishop was supposed to use (1 Cor. 16:9, 2 Cor. 2:12, Col. 4:2). Some apply it to the whole Church, in this sense: By the preaching of the Gospel and the working of the Holy Spirit, I have given you free access to the grace of God and the possession of the heavenly goods (Rom. 5:2; Eph. 2:18, 3:12; 1 John 2:28). Both explanations can be combined, the first with respect to the teachers, and the second with respect to the hearers.

Οὐδεὶς δύναται κλεῖσαι αὐτήν, *no one is able to shut it.* No tyrant is able to hinder the course of the Gospel or deprive believers of their salvation or impede access to God.

Μικρὰν ἔχεις δύναμιν, *you have little power* (1) in comparison with the power of your persecutors; you have little power to resist them. (2) Of yourself you can do little, and so, unless I open the door, you can do very little to open it with your own powers. (3) The church that has been entrusted to you is a "little flock" (Luke 12:32).

ἐτήρησας, *you have kept.* This should be taken adversatively. Nevertheless, you have kept My Word.

v. 9 Δίδωμι, *I give.* I will cause it to work out that some from that diabolical congregation of those who claim to be the true descendants of the patriarchs and the true Church will come and worship before your feet, (1) so that they humble themselves before you and seek forgiveness for the crimes they committed against you; (2) so that they join themselves to the true Church and call upon the true God together with you (Isa. 49:23, Acts 16:19).

ὅτι ἐγὼ ἠγάπησά σε, *that I have loved you.* They will publicly admit that you are My faithful minister and steadfast confessor.

v.10 Τὸν λόγον τῆς ὑπομονῆς, *the word of patience,* (1) because the Gospel demands perseverance. (2) Patience is required, because those who confess the Gospel are subject to the cross in this life (Rev. 1:9, Luke 8:15).

Ὅτι ἐτήρησας τὸν λόγον τῆς ὑπομονῆς μου κἀγώ σε τηρήσω, *because you have kept the word of My patience, I also will keep you.* An elegant example of antanaclasis.

Τηρήσω σε ἐκ τῆς ὥρας τοῦ πειρασμοῦ, *I will keep you from the hour of trial.* I will keep you so that, in the imminent universal persecutions that the pagan rulers will stir up, you do not suffer damage to your soul. Instead, I will see to it that those things serve you for good.

v. 11 Ἔρχομαι ταχύ, *I am coming soon,* that is, for judgment, so that I may free you through death.

Κράτει ὃ ἔχεις, *hold onto what you have,* namely, the purity of the Word and the truth of the faith (Rev. 2:25).

ἵνα μηδεὶς λάβῃ τὸν στέφανόν σου, *so that no one may take your crown,* the crown of glory that is to be given in eternal life to the steadfast confessors of the Word.

So that you may not lose the crown of life, which is given only to those who persevere until the end; your crown that is destined for you. In order to obtain it, it is necessary that you fight valiantly until the end.

v. 12 Ποιήσω αὐτὸν στῦλον ἐν τῷ ναῷ τοῦ Θεοῦ μου, *I will make him a pillar in the temple of My God.* I will make him an immovable pillar in the Church Triumphant and Militant. A pillar is a symbol (1) of the stability of the elect in the grace of God; (2) of immovability in the state of heavenly glory, so that there is no danger of falling away (1 Kings 7:21, Gal. 2:9). Richard: "I will cause him to be like a pillar, firm through faith, straight through equity, upright through intention, sublime through contemplation, who also sustains others by the word of consolation, by devotion to prayer, by example of action."

Καὶ ἔξω οὐ μὴ ἐξέλθῃ ἔτι, *and He will never go out.* Just as pillars are not removed from a house, so the one who overcomes will not be cast out of the Church, nor will he lose his salvation. He will be a triumphant pillar, inviting others to steadfastness.

Καὶ γράψω ἐπ᾽ αὐτὸν τὸ ὄνομα τοῦ Θεοῦ μου, *and I will write on him the name of My God.* On the pillars of kings and rulers they used to inscribe the names of those who erected them. *I will inscribe the name of My God,* namely, that He may be called a son of God.

The name of God is written on the saints, who, here by grace and there by beatific vision, are called the adopted sons of God. Since this is a supernatural name, it is said to be written, not in them, but upon them.

Conquerors used to inscribe their names on pillars. Christ will confess before the heavenly Father and the angels that those who overcome are true sons of God.

Καὶ τὸ ὄνομα τῆς πόλεως τοῦ Θεοῦ μου, τῆς· καινῆς Ἰερουσαλήμ, *and the name of the city of My God, the new Jerusalem*. I will testify that the city of Jerusalem is spiritual and heavenly, that it is the city of the Church and of heaven (1 John 3:2). (Gal. 4:26 and Heb. 12:22 treat of this heavenly Jerusalem.) "Coming down out of heaven," (Rev. 21:2) that is, whose architect is God (Heb. 11:10, 16).

Καὶ τὸ ὄνομά μου τὸ καινόν, *and My new name*. That he may be called a true Christian, not in name only, but also in fact. Likewise "heavenly King," the name that I attained through suffering.

The new name of Christ is written on him, that is, it will be manifest that those pillars in heaven were erected by Christ through His suffering and death, by which He obtained that new name, as a memorial of His victory. The glory that Christ received from all the saints is to be conferred on him.

v. 14 ὁ Ἀμήν, *the Amen*. The explanation is immediately added. "In Him all the promises are 'yes' and 'amen'" (2 Cor. 1:20); "the faithful witness" (Rev. 1:5).

ἡ ἀρχὴ τῆς κτίσεως τοῦ Θεοῦ, *the beginning of God's creation*. The Photinians translate, "the first creation of God" (Job 40:2). Some Calvinists claim that this refers to "the new creation and the new state of the Church, that Christ renews it in this life by His Spirit and will glorify it in the future, Isa. 65:17, 2 Cor. 5:17, Rev. 21:1."

But it is better to say that He is the efficient beginning, just as the architect is said to be the beginning of the house. "All things were made through Him" (John 1:3, Col. 1:16). He (together with the Father and the Holy Spirit) created all things. In a secondary way, this has in view the fact that He brought us forth by the word of truth, that we may be "the beginning of creation" (James 1:18).

v. 15 οὔτε ψυχρὸς εἶ οὔτε ζεστός, *you are neither cold nor hot*, that is, you are not at a level of excellence. Therefore Andreas Caesariensis adds, following the interpretation of Gregory Nazianzus, "to be notably hot or notably cold."

1. Ambrose, *Sermo in Psa. 118*, Bede and Aretas take *cold* to refer to "an unbeliever who has some excuse for his sins on account of the ignorance in which he lives." They take *lukewarm* to refer to "a believer who is considered to be worse than cold, because with the same kind of sin he sins more gravely than the unbeliever because he knows the truth and has received greater benefits from God (Luke 12:17)."

2. Oecumenius: "He is cold who is devoid of the efficacy and outpouring of the Holy Spirit. He is hot who burns with the Spirit. But he is lukewarm who is fickle in both respects, wavering and duplicitous, someone who, although he was given a share of the Holy Spirit through Baptism, has extinguished the gift of those things that were keeping his soul alive, setting it aside out of concern for present things."

3. Some take *cold* to refer to one who, although he has committed mortal sin, acknowledges his guilt. They take *hot* to refer to one who has love. They take *lukewarm* to refer to one who, since he lacks grace, hypocritically pretends to be approved and places true holiness and confidence of salvation in performing external works.

4. Joach. Abbas: "He is hot who rejoices in the Lord on account of His mercy. He is cold who mourns over his sins. But he is lukewarm who is neither penitently sorrowful nor glad to serve God."

5. Gregory, Book III, *Cur. Pastor. Adm* . 35: "Since *lukewarm* refers to two different conditions, one in which someone is going from cold to hot and the other in which someone is returning from hot to cold, in this passage we must understand the latter—someone who is called worse than cold because the one who is cold before he is lukewarm has hope, but the one who is lukewarm after he has been cold is hopeless. In other words, the person who is still in his sins does not lose the hope of conversion. But the one who has become lukewarm after conversion at the same time has lost the hope that belongs to the sinner." And he adds this on the same passage, Book XXXIV, *Moral.*, ch. 2: "Everyone is required to be either hot or cold, lest he be spit out as one who is lukewarm. That is, a person who has not yet been converted still has the opportunity to be converted, while the one who has already been converted burns with virtues. But the one who is lukewarm will be spit out, because he has returned from the heat he once displayed to the deadly cold."

6. Augustine, *Homil. 3. in Apoc.*, explains this passage to be about "the rich, who are devoid of compassion."

7. The simplest explanation is this: 'I know that you have no zeal for religion and godliness. It would have been better for you never to have received the knowledge of heavenly truth than, having received it, to cease to burn with spiritual zeal (2 Pet. 2:21). Therefore, since you neither burn with the Spirit (Rom. 12) nor are you hot in faith and love, therefore I will spit you out of My mouth. Just as the belly cannot retain a lukewarm drink, so I will cast you out of My Church; I will not acknowledge you as a genuine disciple of Mine.'

Therefore, lukewarmness is condemned and is described, on the one hand, as being halfway on the path to virtue, which is hotness, and on the other hand, as being halfway on the path to the other extreme vice, which is coldness. A similar proverb can be found with Irenaeus, Book I, ch. 9: "Neither outside nor inside."

v. 17 ὅτι πλούσιός εἰμι καὶ πεπλούτηκα, *that I am rich and have become wealthy*. You falsely think that you are rich and perfect in the knowledge of God and in good works (1 Cor. 4:8), not "hungry or thirsty for righteousness" (Mat. 5:6). You do not acknowledge your poverty, your defects.

οὐκ οἶδας ὅτι σὺ εἶ ὁ ταλαίπωρος, *you do not know*, that is, you do not acknowledge, *that*, with respect to your soul, *you are miserable, poor, blind, naked*, that is, that you are devoid of spiritual and heavenly goods, of the saving knowledge of God, of the robe of righteousness with which you are able to stand before God.

Gregory, Book XXXIV, *Moral.*, ch. 2: "He claims to be rich who is puffed up with arrogance, but proves to be poor, blind, and naked. Poor, because he does not have the riches of virtue; blind, because he does not see the poverty that he suffers; naked, because he has lost his primary garment, but worse, because he does not even know that he has lost it."

He is *miserable* who does not acknowledge his misery. He is *poor* who is not rich in God. He is *blind* who is devoid of heavenly wisdom. He is *naked* who lacks righteousness.

v. 18 χρυσίον πεπυρωμένον ἐκ πυρὸς, *gold refined by fire*. Gold is a symbol of the spiritual wisdom and godliness gained from God's Word (Psa.

12:7; Psa. 19:11; Psa. 119:127; 1 Pet. 1:7). I urge you to obtain for yourself, from Me, the true knowledge of God and faith through true repentance and prayer, so that you may become rich in all doctrine and knowledge (1 Cor. 1:5).

Primasius on this passage and Gregory, Book IV, *Moral.*, ch. 34, take the gold to symbolize wisdom and fire to symbolize love, so that "gold refined" signifies wisdom combined with love.

ἱμάτια λευκὰ, *white garments*, are a symbol of holiness and righteousness. In Rev. 19:8, fine linen refers to righteousness, that is, the righteousness of Christ that is imputed to believers by faith (Isa. 61:10, Gal. 3:27).

The shame of nakedness, that is, your shameful nakedness, because of which you should rightfully be ashamed before God.

Κολλούριον ἔγχρισον, *rubbed-in eye salve*. Stephanus, *Append. Thesauri*, f. 1257, explains what this κολλούριον properly is.

(1) Bede and Ansbertus understand it to refer to "the contemplation of divine utterances, combined with the working thereof." (2) Rupert interprets it as "humility that arises from a knowledge of proper worthlessness." (3) Richard interprets it as "the bitterness of repentance, which clarifies the senses of the heart through remorse." (4) Others interpret it as the memory of Christ's suffering. (5) It is most simply explained in this way: Cry to God that, through His Word and Holy Spirit, He may give you enlightened eyes of understanding (Eph. 1:18), so that, having been freed from spiritual blindness, you may, for your own good, acknowledge Me as the Savior and Physician of your soul.

v. 19 Ἐγὼ ὅσους ἐὰν φιλῶ, ἐλέγχω καὶ παιδεύω, *As many as I love, I rebuke and discipline.* (Cf. Job 5:17; Pro. 3:11–12; Heb. 12:5–6; James 1:12.) He disciplines (1) through the Word, and (2) through the fatherly rod of the cross.

Ζήλευε οὖν καὶ μετανόησον, *be zealous, therefore, and repent.* May you possess the zeal of faith and good works that has been commended to you (Titus 2:14).

v. 20 ἕστηκα ἐπὶ τὴν θύραν καὶ κρούω, *I stand at the door and knock.* Christ knocks (1) with the hammer of the Law; (2) with the hammer of the cross; (3) with the hammer of death.

He knocks (1) with the external call; (2) with the internal utterance and impulse. It means that He awaits the conversion of men and offers them His grace and heavenly benefits through the preaching of the Word (Isa. 65:2).

Ἐάν τις ἀκούσῃ τῆς φωνῆς μου καὶ ἀνοίξῃ τὴν θύραν, *if anyone hears My voice and opens the door*. He requires (1) listening, and (2) the opening of the door. The door of the heart is meant. This opening is not a work of one's natural powers; the Holy Spirit takes a heart of stone and makes it into a heart of flesh. Just as He opened the heart of Lydia, so He still opens hearts today (Acts 16:14). This means that listening is His means of opening. In those who do not resist with voluntary malice, nor put up the barrier of obduracy, He wishes to work to enable them to open their heart.

εἰσελεύσομαι, *I will come in*. He promises (1) a gracious entrance (John 14:23), I will dwell by faith in his heart (Eph. 3:17); (2) the use of the mystical supper. This is a symbol (i) of familiarity; (ii) of the communication of heavenly goods; (iii) of spiritual joy. I will satisfy his soul with the bread of life in this age and in the next (Luke 22:30).

v. 21 καθίσαι μετ' ἐμοῦ, *to sit with Me*. The Calvinists conclude from this passage that "it is not possible to deduce Christ's infinite majesty from His session at the right hand of God, since that session is common to Christ and the elect."

We reply: (1) This is not a reference to equality of honor between Christ and the blessed, but only to their association as a definite level and measure. (2) There is a difference between "the throne of God" on which Christ has been placed and "the throne of Christ, etc.," on which the elect are placed. (i) On the throne of God the Father, not the saints, nor even the angels, but Christ sits (Heb. 1:13). On the throne of Christ, the saints are seated, as Scripture puts it. (ii) The throne of God is His immeasurable majesty; the throne of Christ on which He has placed His saints is eternal blessedness (John 14:2). (iii) The throne of God is infinite and everywhere; the throne of Christ is finite and located in Paradise. (iv) The throne of God is unique, but there are many thrones of the saints (Rev. 4:4). (v) God's throne is eternal and uncreated, but these thrones of the saints have been prepared (Mat. 25:34). Therefore, the sense is this: After he overcomes, I will give him to reign with Me in heaven (2 Tim. 2:12, Rev. 2:26), just as I overcame by suffering and resurrection and sat down with the Father (Mat. 28:18; Eph. 1:20, 4:10).

44

Chapter 4

There are two parts to this chapter:
I. Preparation for the second vision, v. 1;
II. *Thronography*, a description of that throne on which Christ is seated with the Father, where He who sits on the throne and those who stand before the throne are also described, v. 2 to the end.

v. 1 Μετὰ ταῦτα εἶδον, *after these things I saw*, namely, in a vision, not with physical, but with spiritual eyes.

Θύρα ἠνεῳγμένη ἐν τῷ οὐρανῷ, *an open door in heaven*, signifying that heavenly and hidden mysteries were about to be revealed to John.

ἡ φωνὴ ἡ πρώτη ἣν ἤκουσα, *the first voice that I heard* (Rev. 1:10,12).

ἃ δεῖ γενέσθαι μετὰ ταῦτα, *the things that must take place after these things*, what will take place in the Church, and also outside the Church, in the world. Until this point, the present state of the Church had been revealed to John.

v. 2 ἐγενόμην ἐν πνεύματι, *I was in spirit* (Rev. 1:10).

Θρόνος ἔκειτο ἐν τῷ οὐρανῷ, *a throne was placed in heaven*. Compare with this vision Isa. 6:1; Eze. 1:26, 10:1.

"Throne" is understood (1) by some as the angels; (2) by others as the saints; (3) by others as the Church. (4) The ordinary interpretation is the authority and power of God as He governs the Church.

Καὶ ἐπὶ τοῦ θρόνου καθήμενος, *and seated on the throne*. (1) Some think this is a reference to God, and that Christ cannot be meant here, because in the next chapter, the Lamb (who represents Christ) accepts the book sealed with the seven seals from the hand of the One seated on the throne. (2) But it is better to say that the One sitting on the throne is Christ, (i) because John said at the end of the preceding chapter that Christ was seated with the Father on the throne, which is the throne of majesty and glory, on which He rules over all things in heaven and earth, especially in the Church Militant and Triumphant. (ii) Isaiah saw the glory of Christ (John 12:41). (iii) The glory to which Christ was exalted after His resurrection and ascension is often symbolized in Scripture by a throne.

Therefore, He who sits on the throne was like "a Son of Man" (Rev. 1:13). According to His human nature, He was placed on the throne of divine majesty at the time of His ascension. He was placed there and now is present for the Church.

Λίθῳ ἰάσπιδι καὶ σαρδίνῳ, *a jasper and sardius stone.*

(1) Abbas: "The Person of the Father, who is the beginning of all life, is expressed with the jasper, for the life of trees and vegetation is perceived in the color green. The Son is represented by the sardius, whose color is blood-red, for the Son, in the humanity He assumed, appeared red in His suffering. The Holy Spirit is signified by the emerald, which displays the most excellent shade of green, for He stirs up the hearts of men to hope by means of His gifts of grace." But the entire vision is dealing with Christ.

(2) Ansbertus concludes that "the green jasper gem refers to the divinity of Christ, for the greenness of unfading glory consists in contemplating and enjoying Him. Sardius, a red gem, shows His humanity, which turned red at the time of His suffering."

(3) Bede, Primasius, and Rupert say that "jasper, which is the color of water, represents the flood of water that already took place, while sardius, with its fiery color, represents the flood of fire that is still to come."

(4) Richard of St. Victor says: "The green of the jasper represents unfading glory. The red of the sardius stands for the fire of hell. And so both colors refer to God, because green sooths the elect with grace while red frightens the reprobate with the threat of hellfire."

(5) Jasper, which is green and in some parts has a bluish color, signifies that God shows Himself to be friendly toward to elect. Sardius has a ruby-red color, and thus denotes vengeance against His foes.

(6) Jasper, on account of its green color, is a symbol of good hope, the

mercy of God. Sardius, on account of its fiery color, represents the justice of God.

The second explanation above is the most suitable. Christ's divinity is represented with jasper, because jasper is a very precious gem. It shines brilliantly. It resists corruption. It is pleasing to the eye. Sardius represents Christ's humanity, because sardius has a reddish hue and thus symbolizes the human nature of Christ, which was reddened with blood at the time of His suffering (Gen. 49:11, Isa. 63:2, Luke 22:44). Sardius makes a person bold. It depicts blood.

ἶρις κυκλόθεν τοῦ θρόνου, *a rainbow encircling the throne*. The rainbow signifies our reconciliation with God through Christ (Gen. 9:13, Rom. 5:10), the mercy of God in Christ.

Emeralds are green in color, and the green in a rainbow is very beautiful and visually gratifying. Emerald also sooths the eyes. Thus it signifies that the grace of God in Christ is always green (Lam. 3:23). It is exhilarating and invigorating to the heart when one meditates upon it.

v. 4 εἴκοσι τέσσαρας πρεσβυτέρους, *twenty-four elders*. (1) Some understand the twelve patriarchs and the twelve apostles. (2) Others take it to be the twelve prophets and the twelve apostles. (3) Still others understand all the faithful teachers of the Church. (4) Augustine and Primasius apply it to all the saints of the Old and New Testaments. David divided the Levitical priests, whom God had consecrated for ministry in the stead all His people, into twenty-four orders (1 Chr. 25:7). From the twelve sons of the patriarch Jacob, the whole Israelite people in the Old Testament was propagated (Gen. 49:28). The twelve apostles gave birth to all the believers of the New Testament through the word of the Gospel (1 Cor. 4:15). Therefore, these twenty-four elders represent all the believers in the Old and New Testaments, because in Rev. 5:9–10 they proclaim, "You purchased us with Your blood from all the nations." Not only the members of the Church Militant are included, but also and especially the citizens of the Church Triumphant, for they all praise Christ.

Of the white robes (mentioned above in Rev. 3:5): White robes are a sign of holiness, purity, joy, and gladness (Rev. 6:11, 7:13). Crowns stand for royal dignity and also victory against one's foes. They stand for the adornments of virtue and the glory of the soul. Kings wear crowns; priests wear white garments (Rev. 5:10).

v. 5 ἐκ τοῦ θρόνου ἐκπορεύονται ἀστραπαὶ καὶ βρονταὶ καὶ φωναί, *from the throne proceed lightning and thundering and voices.* (1) Some maintain that these refer to God's majesty and power, which He exerts in punishing the ungodly. (2) Others take it to refer to the office and gifts of the Holy Spirit. (3) They are most simply understood as the penetrating power of the Gospel (Mat. 24:27); the thunder and strong voice of the heavenly Word (Psa. 68:34, Mark 3:17), which sound throughout the entire world by the command of Christ, by which He gathers the Church to Himself from all kingdoms and peoples and overthrows all human and worldly wisdom and power (2 Cor. 10:5).

Καὶ ἑπτὰ λαμπάδες πυρὸς καιόμεναι ἐνώπιον τοῦ θρόνου, *and seven lamps of fire burning before the throne.* The explanation is immediately added, αἵ εἰσι ἑπτὰ πνεύματα τοῦ Θεοῦ, *which are the seven spirits of God,* that is, the Holy Spirit with His seven—that is, His multiple—gifts, virtue, and work, inasmuch as He converts men by the Word of the Gospel, kindles the fire of faith and divine love in men's hearts, leads men to the kingdom of Christ, saves, etc. This interpretation agrees with what some maintain, that those lamps of fire are a symbol of the illumination of the mind for the purpose of rightly acknowledging God and the inflammation of the heart for the purpose of loving God and neighbor.

(Cf. Acts 2:3, tongues of fire; Mat. 3:11, "He will baptize with fire.")

v. 6 ἐνώπιον τοῦ θρόνου θάλασσα ὑαλίνη ὁμοία κρυστάλλῳ, *before the throne a sea of glass like crystal.* The sea of glass is understood by some as (1) the world, that is, the human race, which is like the turbulent and restless sea. It is of glass because of the fragility of man, and also because the innermost thoughts of the heart are clear to God, so the phrase "like crystal" is added.

(2) Joach. Abbas explains it concerning Scripture, in which all kinds of faces can be contemplated, so that each one may know for himself what he looks like.

(3) Bede, Rupert, Primasius, and others explain it as referring to Baptism. For Christ, as He sits on the throne of majesty, gathers the Church to Himself from the world by means of the Word and Sacraments. Baptism (i) is the "washing with the word" (Eph. 5:26); the washing of regeneration (Titus 3:5); that sea into which our sins are hurled (Micah 7:19). It was prefigured in the Red Sea in which Pharaoh's army was drowned (Exo. 14:27). (ii) Baptism is implied by crystal, because through this Sacrament the hearts of men are illuminated. (iii) It is before the throne of Christ, because Baptism is the saving means by which entrance into the kingdom of grace and of glory is given (Eph. 5:5). Everyone who desires to approach the throne of God should cross over the sea of Baptism.

ἐν μέσῳ τοῦ θρόνου καὶ κύκλῳ τοῦ θρόνου, *in the midst of the throne and around the throne*. The latter phrase explains the former.

Τέσσαρα ζῷα, *four animals*. These are described (1) by number: there were four of them; (2) by abundance of eyes: they were full of eyes in front and behind; (3) by their form: one was like a lion, the second like a calf, the third like a man, the fourth like an eagle; (4) by their wings: each one had six wings all around, and inside, that is, under the wings, they were full of eyes; (5) by what they were doing: they did not rest from divine praise.

These four animals are interpreted by most interpreters as (1) the four Evangelists. (Cf. Augustine, Book I, *De Cons. Evang.*, ch. 6; Jerome, in the introduction to his commentary on Matthew; Bede; Primasius.) All the Evangelists treat of Christ, who was a man in His incarnation, a calf in His suffering, a lion in His resurrection, an eagle in His ascension. Jerome and Augustine disagree on how this fits together. In Rev. 6:1, one of the animals says to John: "Come and see!" The second, third, and fourth likewise speak with him. It would therefore be serving double duty in also representing the person of John.

(2) Some say they refer to the four angels as they serve God in the four corners of the earth (Isa. 6:2-3). The Seraphim also have six wings and sing the same song. They are said to be full of eyes as a sign of their vigilance. The lion is a symbol of strength, the calf of labor, the man of wisdom, the eagle of keen eyesight. But in Rev. 7:11, the angels are distinguished from these

four animals. These animals say that they were purchased with the blood of Christ, which does not apply to angels (Rev. 5:9).

(3) Others, therefore, suggest they refer to the archangels, who are distinct from the angels of the lower class (cf. Piscator). But in the passage just cited, all the angels are distinguished from the four animals.

(4) Some claim that they symbolize the four estates, namely, the ecclesiastical estate, represented by the calf; the political estate, represented by the lion; the domestic estate, represented by the man; and the scholastic estate, represented by the eagle. But the scholastic estate can be included in the ecclesiastical.

(5) Others interpret them as the four seasons of the year, just as they interpret the twenty-four elders as the twenty-four hours of the day.

(6) The simplest interpretation is that they refer to all the faithful teachers of the Church, who are called animals (Psa. 68:10) because they are to select whatever they preach about the person, office, and benefits of Christ from the writings of the four Evangelists.

1. They are full of eyes in front and behind, because they should tend the flock (Acts 20:28; 1 Pet. 5:2) and because they lead men to the knowledge of God (Mat. 5:14).

2. They are referred to as a lion, because they should have a fearless spirit in the midst of adversities; as a calf, because they should be hard-working and industrious in their office (1 Tim. 5:18); as a man, because they are humane (2 Tim. 2:24), especially toward the weak (Rom. 14:1); as an eagle, because they should not preach human dreams, but the heavenly doctrine that Christ brought forth from the bosom of the Father (John 1:18). They should preach nothing else but Christ (1 Cor. 2:2), who is "the lion of the tribe of Judah" (Rev. 5:5) and who has overthrown all His enemies; "He offered Himself to God as an sweet aroma" (Eph. 5:2), like the calf offered to God in the Old Testament; He is true God and Man, represented by a man and an eagle.

3. They have six wings for the same reason that the angels appear this way (Isa. 6:3), because the same zeal and diligence in the works of administering their office should also be in them.

4. Inside they are full of eyes, because they should be enlightened by the Holy Spirit, having "the eyes of their heart enlightened" (Eph. 1:18).

5. They have no rest; they sing praises to God. In this way also they are like the angels. Since they praise God, not only with their tongue, but also with their whole life, they will be continually occupied in eternity with praising Him.

They sing: "Holy, etc." In the manuscript of Arias Montanus, it is repeated nine times. But it should properly be repeated no more than three times, as in Isaiah 6:3.

ὁ θεὸς ὁ παντοκράτωρ, ὁ ἦν καὶ ὁ ὢν καὶ ὁ ἐρχόμενος, *God the Almighty, who was and who is and who is to come.* (Cf. Rev. 1:4, 8.)

v. 9 *When the animals gave glory and honor to the One sitting on the throne,* that is, to Christ Jesus, *the twenty-four elders fell prostrate,* because it is necessary for the ministers of the Church to initiate the glorification of God, to stir others up to praise Him.

v. 10 βαλοῦσι τοὺς στεφάνους, *they cast their crowns,* the crowns they had on their heads (v. 4), they cast down out of true humility in order to show that they ascribe the glory of the victory they had attained over the flesh, the devil, death, and hell, to Christ alone.

v. 11 δύναμιν, *power,* the praise, testimony, confession of power. Some explain the phrase "to receive power" as showing power by taking revenge on His enemies.

Some manuscripts read ἦσαν, *they were,* as referring to their preservation. But the better reading is εἰσί, *they are.* Luther: "*Sie haben das Wesen.*"

52

Chapter 5

This chapter deals with the opening of the seals, in three parts:
I. A description of the book with writing inside and out, having seven seals, vv. 1–5;
II. A description of the Lamb, who is equipped with seven eyes and horns, vv. 6–7;
III. The praise of the four animals and the twenty-four elders, accompanied by the angels, v. 8 to the end.

v. 1 Εἶδον ἐπὶ τὴν δεξιὰν τοῦ καθημένου ἐπὶ τοῦ θρόνου, *I saw upon the right hand of the One seated on the throne*. This should be understood as God the Father, the first Person of the Deity. For since Christ sits on one throne with the Father (Rev. 3:21, 7:10), He was seen in the previous chapter sitting on the throne of God. But since He is a distinct Person from the Father and took on human nature in the unity of His Person, He now appears as a Lamb standing before the throne where the Father sits.

Βιβλίον γεγραμμένον ἔσωθεν καὶ ὄπισθεν κατεσφραγισμένον σφραγῖσιν ἑπτά, *a book with writing inside and out, sealed with seven seals*. Concerning this book:

(1) Augustine, Jerome, Ambrose, Origen, Hilary, Eusebius, Bede, Hugo, and, more recently Primasius, Ansbertus, Marloratus, and Barradius take it to refer to Holy Scripture, the Old and New Testaments. Weidner, in the locus on faith, tract. 2, p. 286: "The book of the Law and the Prophets was written on the outside according to the literal sense, and on the inside according to a spiritual and prophetic sense, containing beneath the seven seals seven profound mysteries about Christ and the Church, namely, the mystery of Christ's incarnation, preaching, suffering, resurrection, the sending of the Holy Spirit, the conversion of the Gentiles, and His final glorification. Christ has unsealed these mysteries that were enclosed in the old Law." Hilary, in his preface to the Psalms: "There were seven mysteries of our redemption

hidden in the ceremonies of the Law: (i) incarnation; (ii) nativity; (iii) suffering; (iv) resurrection; (v) ascension; (vi) the sending of the Holy Spirit; (vii) the coming for judgment."

Others claim that the 'writing on the outside' refers to the external preaching of the Gospel which is common to the ungodly and the godly, while the inner writing refers to the saving power that applies only to the godly.

But the apostle's aim is to announce beforehand the future state of the Church (Rev. 4:1), which cannot refer to the Old Testament.

(2) Some suggest this book refers to the suffering of Christ. Bernhard (*Sermo 1, In Fest. Pasch..* f. 167): "Christ is the book written upon inside and out. On the inside with regard to the torments of His soul, and externally with regard to His flogging and wounds. The seven seals represent the seven words."

(3) Andreas Caesariensis and Aretas interpret this book as the all-knowing, irreproachable memory of God, as the book of life in which are written the names of the elect. Lyranus says it is the book of divine knowledge, which is related.

(4) Most simply, this book is interpreted as the book of divine providence (Psa. 139:16) and of the divine decrees concerning the gathering of the Church from the human race; concerning the persecutions that would be brought upon the Church with God's permission; concerning the preservation of the godly in the midst of them; concerning the punishment of the ungodly and the persecutors, etc.

This book has writing *inside and out*. For whatever happens in time, God foresaw from eternity. And what was hidden in God from eternity happens openly in the execution of the divine decrees.

The seven seals signify that the decrees and judgments of God cannot be known by any man, either until their manifestation takes place or until their fulfillment approaches, just as in a closed and sealed book no one can read anything unless it is opened. The judgments of God are sealed with the truth, so that no one can contradict them. The seven seals of this book and the opening of them fit nicely with the seven visions that are noted by John in this book. The things that are spoken after the opening of the seals also confirm this explanation. The wonderful judgments of God are said to flow forth from that book, as described in chapter 6.

v. 2 ἄγγελον ἰσχυρὸν, *a strong angel*, refers to Gabriel, for his name means "strength of God."

κηρύσσοντα ἐν φωνῇ μεγάλῃ, *proclaiming in a loud voice*, crying out, heralding.

Τίς ἐστιν ἄξιός, *who is worthy*, that is, qualified.

To open, Ambrose understands as "to fulfill the things that were predicted in the book." "No one," he says, "appeared who could redeem the human race from the power of the devil. This redemption is the opening of the Old Testament." But it actually refers to the manifestation of God's decrees, that is, of those things that were to come and that would happen, both for the Church and for the ungodly.

v. 3 ἐν τῷ οὐρανῷ, *in heaven*, among the angels; οὐδὲ ἐπὶ τῆς γῆς, *nor on earth*, among living men. Ὑποκάτω τῆς γῆς, *under the earth*, among the dead. The papists apply this to purgatory.

No one could open it, much less could anyone read or understand the things written in this book. For apart from the special revelation of God, no one can seek and discover God's decrees or future matters by his own natural powers.

v. 4 ἔκλαιον πολύ, *I was weeping much*, I was pouring out long tears. Οὔτε βλέπειν αὐτό, *nor see it*, that is, the things in it.

v. 5 καὶ εἷς ἐκ τῶν πρεσβυτέρων, *and one of the elders*, undoubtedly one of those who were resurrected together with Christ and ascended into heaven (Mat. 27:52). It seems to be the patriarch Jacob, for it was from his prophecy that the title "Lion" is ascribed to Christ (Gen. 49:9).

ἐνίκησεν, *He overcame*. By His merits, He obtained from the heavenly Father the right to open the book; that is, to reveal its decrees. He also overcame death, the devil, and hell.

ὁ λέων ὁ ὢν ἐκ τῆς φυλῆς Ἰούδα, *the Lion who is of the tribe of Judah*. Christ is compared to a lion: (1) because of His surpassing strength (Pro.

30:30); (2) because of His heroic spirit; (3) because of the lion's axiomatic kingship—the lion is the king of beasts; (4) because of the efficacy of His voice, for a lion rouses its cubs with its voice.

He is called a lion: (1) because of His strength; (2) because of His rule; (3) because of His fearless nature; (4) because of His watchfulness. Augustine: "Who could escape the teeth of the lion—the devil—if the Lion of the tribe of Judah had not conquered Him?" From the same sermon, *Sermo 46, De Diversis*, ch. 2: "Christ is a lion on account of His strength; the devil, on account of his ferocity. Christ is a lion who conquers; the devil is a lion who harms."

But Christ especially shows Himself to be a lion in the resurrection: (1) Because there He demonstrated the infinite power of His divinity (Rom. 1:4); (2) "The lion, with its voice, instills terror in other animals, so that, dazed and smitten, they nearly faint from its power" (Ambrose, Book VI, *Hexaem.*, ch. 3). Thus Christ draws the nations forcibly to Himself through the preaching of His apostles. (3) "The chief nobility graces the lion, when his neck and shoulders are clothed with his mane" (Pliny, Book VIII, *Nat. Hist.*, ch. 16). Thus the majesty of Christ shone chiefly through His resurrection, when He was clothed with the robe of immortality. (4) Lion cubs sleep for three days and three nights when they are first born. Then they are awakened by their father's roar. Origen (*Homil. 17 in Gen. 49*) applies this to Christ, who was awakened by His Father on the third day.

The Lion of the tribe of Judah, because, according to the prophecy of the patriarch Jacob (Gen. 49:10), He was born of this royal tribe (Heb. 7:14). The tribe of Judah had the figure of a lion on its banner.

ἡ ῥίζα Δαυίδ, *the Root of David*, which sprang up from David, according to the promise, like a root from a seed: "the Lion of the tribe of Judah" with regard to His humanity, "the Root of David" with regard to His divinity. Bernhard, *Sermo 1, In Die Pasch.*, col. 130: "It does not say that David was His root, but that He was the root of David, because He is the One who bears and is not borne. O holy David, rightly do you call your Son your Lord, for you do not bear the root, but the root bears you."

If the root compared with a seed, He is called the Root of David also according to His human nature. But if it is compared with a tree, then He is the Root of David according to His divine nature.

ἀνοῖξαι τὸ βιβλίον καὶ τὰς ἑπτὰ σφραγῖδας, *to open the book and its seven seals*. Just as on account of Christ all the mysteries that were hidden in the Old Testament under figures were fulfilled in the New Testament, so also God revealed through Christ the future things to John in the New Testament on account of the merit and victory of Christ, namely, what the state of the Church would be until the end of the world, "for in Him lie hidden all the treasures of wisdom" (Col. 2:3). He knows all things that are hidden and that will be, and He reveals as many of those things as are beneficial to the Church.

v. 6 ἐν μέσῳ τοῦ θρόνου, etc., ἀρνίον ὡς ἐσφαγμένον, *in the midst of the throne, etc., a lamb as having been slain*. (Cf. Isa. 53:7; John 1:29, 36; 1 Pet. 1:19.) The paschal lamb and all the Old Testament sacrifices prefigured this Lamb. Just as Christ was compared earlier to a lion on account of His strength and might which He demonstrated most powerfully in His resurrection, so He is represented here by a lamb—a lamb that was slain (1) because He was slaughtered on the cross; (2) because of His gentleness and patience (Isa. 53:6); (3) on account of His innocence; (4) on account of His beneficence. We are clothed in Christ's merits like wool.

Augustine, *Sermo 174, De Temp*.: "Christ is a lion because of His strength, a lamb because of His innocence; a lion because He was invincible, a lamb because He was tame." Bernhard, *Sermo 1, In Die Pasch*., col. 130: "The lamb was killed, but the lion conquered."

Ὡς, *as*, is used here for the Hebrew כ, which expresses truth. (Cf. John 1:14, ὡς μονογενοῦς, *as an only-begotten*.)

This lamb is standing (1) because He rose again to immortal life; (2) He stands as One who is prepared to perform the work of redemption; (3) to help; (4) to judge; (5) to intercede.

ἔχων κέρατα ἑπτὰ καὶ ὀφθαλμοὺς ἑπτά, *having seven horns and seven eyes*. The seven horns denote an eminence of power (Lam. 2:3). The seven eyes denote wisdom, omniscience, providence in governing the Church

(Zec. 3:9, 4:10). The seven eyes are over the plumb line. According to His human nature, He received from the Father infinite power and wisdom. He has seven horns; therefore He is strong to strike down the enemies of the Church. He has seven eyes; therefore He is vigilant in caring for the Church.

οἵ εἰσι τὰ ἑπτὰ τοῦ θεοῦ πνεύματα, *which are the seven spirits of God.* The seven eyes represent the manifold gifts of the Holy Spirit which this omnipotent Lord has in His hand, not only according to His divine, but also His human nature, according to which He has been placed on the throne of paternal majesty. He distributes these gifts to the faithful, dispersed throughout the whole world.

v. 7 εἴληφε βιβλίον ἐκ τῆς δεξιᾶς, *He took the book from the right hand, etc.* This expresses (1) the mystery of the personal union (1 Tim. 3:16); (2) and thus of the resulting communication of attributes that were bestowed on Christ according to His human nature; namely, that Christ sits and reigns on the throne of majesty and glory as both God and Man after His exaltation in the unity of person, yet in such a way that, according to His divine nature, together with the Father and the Holy Spirit, He held in His hand from eternity the sealed book of divine decrees, mysteries, and judgments, but according to His human nature, He received in time divine power to open the book, and full dominion through the union and exaltation of His human nature.

The Lamb opened the book; that is, He fulfilled the truth of the Scriptures by His suffering. "Every knee in heaven, earth, and hell bowed to Him" (Phi. 2:9).

v. 8 The four animals and twenty-four elders fell down prostrate before the Lamb. They were in awe of the sublime mystery of the personal union and communication of attributes, that the human nature in Christ had been exalted to so lofty a height of dignity and power, and thus they worshiped Him according to both natures.

ἔχοντες κιθάραν καὶ φιάλας χρυσᾶς, *having a harp and golden bowls.* Harps are a symbol (1) of divine praise; (2) of thanksgiving; (3) of gladness (Psa. 33:2; Psa. 149:3; Psa. 150:3).

The text explains what the bowls full of incense mean. Incense rises upward and emits a pleasing aroma. Thus prayers convey a very sweet aroma to God (Psa. 141:2, Rev. 8:3).

Faith in Christ, from which prayers proceed, is precious like gold. The prayers themselves are pleasing to God, just as the scent of aromatic spices is pleasing to man.

v. 9 ᾠδὴ καινὴ, *a new song* is here a notable or special song combined with particular gladness, the kind of song that is normally composed on account of some new benefit (Psa. 33:3, Psa. 40:4, Psa. 96:1, Psa. 98:1). Although the promise of such benefits was very old, nevertheless, since its fulfillment and manifestation pertain to the New Testament, it was new. "New" can also be understood as extraordinary.

ἠγόρασας τῷ Θεῷ ἡμᾶς ἐν τῷ αἵματί σου, *You purchased us for God by Your blood.* The blood of Christ is the dear price of our redemption. He holds us dear, because He paid dearly for us.

Since You redeemed us with Your own blood, it is fitting for us to say that also according to Your human nature You have been given power to govern Your Church and knowledge to manifest to others the future state of the Church.

v. 10 βασιλεῖς καὶ ἱερεῖς, *kings and priests.* We will reign over the new earth, where we will rule perfectly (2 Pet. 3:13, Rev. 21:1).

v. 11 εἶδον, καὶ ἤκουσα, *I saw and I heard*, that is, I heard in a vision.

Κυκλόθεν τοῦ θρόνου, *encircling the throne*, because the angels stand before the throne of God, ready to execute His commands (Psa. 103:20, Dan. 7:10, Heb. 1:14).

καὶ τῶν ζῴων καὶ τῶν πρεσβυτέρων, *and of the animals and the elders*, because the angels encamp around the faithful teachers of the Church, and around all those who fear God in this life (Psa. 34:8). They also have a sweet association with the blessed in eternal life.

ἀριθμὸς αὐτῶν μυριάδες μυριάδων καὶ χιλιάδες χιλιάδων, *their number was a thousand times a hundred thousand and ten times a hundred thousand*, indicating infinite classes of the highest numbers.

Alcazar, in his commentary on this passage, p. 395: "It should be pointed out that to be in a circle can be understood in two ways. First, that they are like a wall and a rampart. The second explanation is not that of a wall and defense, but of their presence and prompt readiness to serve and attend. This meaning is, in the present passage, if I am not mistaken, very much to the point and fits together well with the first meaning. For in the worship of the animals and elders, the sacrifice of the Mass is understood. Furthermore, we may draw the conclusion that, for the purpose of defense, angels regularly attend the sacrifice of the Mass in order to accompany those who venerate the most holy body of Christ."

We reply: (1) The presence of the angels at the Mass cannot be concluded from the fact that Christ rules in the Church with His gracious presence. (2) Much less can it be concluded that they bear the body of Christ into heaven, as the canon of the Mass claims. (3) Thus Cornelius a Lapide, in commenting on this passage, refutes Alcazar by name and says: "All these things were seen in heaven, not on earth, and they denote the praise of those in heaven, not of those on earth."

v. 12 Λαβεῖν τὴν δύναμιν, *to receive power*. "The Lamb who was slain," that is, Christ according to His human nature, since He suffered and died, "is worthy to receive power, etc." All of this was conferred upon Christ as the Son of Man in His exaltation after His suffering. When the Church honors God by confessing that these things were given to Christ by the Father, then Christ is said to receive these things.

v. 13 καὶ πᾶν κτίσμα, *and all creation*. After Christ was exalted to the right hand of the Father and placed on the throne of the divine majesty, "every knee bows to Him, etc." (Phi. 2:10–11). The irrational creatures praise Him; that is, they supply men and angels with the material for praising Him.

Andreas Caesariensis on this passage: "God is praised as the Creator of all, together with His only-begotten and consubstantial Son, by the natural voices of all creation: creatures with intellect and creatures with senses, living things and simply things that exist."

Rupert on this passage: "The rest of the creatures that are in heaven and above earth and under the earth and in the earth—sun, moon, and stars, the waters that are above the heavens, and all other things that the Psalmist incites to praise the Lord."

v. 14 τέσσαρα ζῷα ἔλεγον· ἀμήν, *the four animals would say, Amen*.

The teachers of the Church prefigured by these animals confirm this praise and testify that it does, in fact, belong to Christ. It also means that the praise of Christ is most greatly propagated through the ecclesiastical ministry.

Chapter 6

Six of the seals are opened in this chapter. Thus there are six parts:
    I. After the opening of the first seal, a rider on a white horse appears, having a bow and a crown;
    II. After the second seal is opened, a rider on a red horse appears, having a sword;
    III. A black horse, with a rider holding a scale;
    IV. A pale horse, with a rider who is called Death;
    V. The souls under the altar;
    VI. An earthquake, the sun is darkened, the moon turns red, the stars fall, etc.

v. 1 Since it was said in the previous chapter (v. 5) that the Lamb had been found worthy, on account of the victory He had achieved, to open the book and to break its seals, and then it said in v. 8 that He had taken the book, now follows the opening of the seals. These things prefigure what was about to follow in the Church and in the world immediately after the days of John.

ἤκουσα ἑνὸς ἐκ τῶν τεσσάρων ζῴων, *I heard one of the four animals.* This is repeated at the opening of the first four seals, because it corresponds to the same number of animals. This first animal is the one that was like a lion.

v. 2 There appears: (1) the rider on the white horse, (2) having a bow, (3) with a crown on His head, (4) who went out conquering and to conquer. The former is shown by the crown, the latter by the bow.

(1) Petrus Aureolus maintained that every one of these four horses must be understood as the Roman Empire under various emperors, who are to be understood as the riders and horsemen. He takes the rider on the white horse to be "Gaius Caligula, who in no way harassed the Church. For under the reign of this emperor many were led to the Christian religion."

(2) Luther takes it as the persecution of tyrants. Osiander and Dr. Hoehe follow him in this. "This rider signifies those magistrates who persecute the Gospel. They abuse their crown to oppress the confessors. They are carried by a white horse, because they actually persecute the godly in times of peace. The bow signifies that he strikes down, now this one, now that one. He is said to conquer by the judgment of the world. He went out to conquer, because the effort of the tyrants is greater than the effect."

(3) It is most simply understood as representing Christ Himself, who rides a white horse, because He has seen to it that peace is proclaimed in the world through the Gospel (Isa. 52:7). It also signifies His triumph, because conquerors would enter Rome riding a white horse. The bow represents the efficacy of the Gospel, for it penetrates hearts like arrows (Psa. 45:6, Heb. 4:12). The crown is given as a sign of dominion and victory. He goes out to conquer, because as a mighty hero He conquers all the wisdom and power of the world, especially the idolatry of the Gentiles, so that the peoples fall down prostrate before Him (Psa. 45:6) as they are led to acknowledge the truth. (Cf. 2 Cor. 10:45.)

It symbolizes the preaching of the Gospel which Christ propagated in the world through the apostles after His ascension to heaven and His exaltation to the right hand of the Father. For since the Word of the Gospel obtains the victory and gives the Church solace in the midst of the spiritual and physical plagues that are hereafter described in this chapter, it is mentioned here at the beginning, just as Christ also appears before the plagues in chapter 8.

v. 3 Δεύτερον ζῶον, *the second animal*, which was like a calf. Patience is required in the midst of persecutions.

v. 4 There appears: (1) a rider on a red horse, (2) who was given power to take peace away from the earth; (3) a sword was given to him.

(1) Aureolus thinks this refers to "the Roman Empire under the rule of Nero, under whom the Church first suffered general persecution by public edict, under whom many Christians sweat their blood."

(2) Some think it refers to angels who incited wars in the world on account of contempt for the Gospel.

(3) It signifies the wars, persecutions, and bloodshed that normally follow the preaching of the Gospel in the world. By means of these things, God punishes the contempt of His Word and the ingratitude of men. The devil is represented by the rider, for he is "a murderer from the beginning" (John 8:44). With God's permission he incites persecutions, wars, and bloodshed.

v. 5 Τρίτον ζῷον, *the third animal*. This one had the face like a man. With regard to the black horse, (1) Aureolus understands it to be the Empire under Emperor Titus, the son of Vespasian, who surrounded Jerusalem with a blockade and assaulted it at the same time.

(2) Some take this black horse to be heretics and heresiarchs. They take the rider to be a demon who incites the heretics like horses against the Church. They have in their hand a deceitful scale, that is, a false interpretation of Scripture.

(3) Some take it to refer to angels, who assault the earth with a lack of provisions and with famine because of man's contempt of the Gospel.

(4) The lack of provisions and famine are symbolized here, for famine makes the faces of men sallow and dark (Lam. 4:8). The rider of this horse has a scale in his hand, for in times of famine, provisions are not sold in dry measures, but using the kind of scales on which spices are normally weighed and sold (Lev. 26:26, Eze. 4:10).

v. 6 A *Choenix* is a measure that is the equivalent of two pints or four cups: 22 ounces. Laertius and Suidas translate it with "daily measure." For at that time, the daily food allotment was distributed to slaves by the quart so that they, in turn, might pay off their allotment with their labors. Luther: *"Das Mass Choenitz hält bey uns eine Kanne oder zwei Nösel, das ist, eine halbe Messe."*

Δηνάριος, *a denarius*. The response is essentially an angelic penny. Luther: *"Dreisig Löwenpfennig."*

ὁ ἔλαιον καὶ τὸν οἶνον μὴ ἀδικήσῃς, *do not harm the oil and the wine*. This means that there will be no scarcity of the other fruits, but only of grains and bread. Yet even so, men can suffer very bitterly with regard to their vital sustenance.

v. 7 Τέταρτον ζῷον, *the fourth animal*, was like a flying eagle. Let us meditate on heavenly things in times of pestilence!

v. 8 *The pale horse*, (1) according to Aureolus, represents the Roman Empire under Domitian, who mounted the second persecution against the Church. He is compared to a pale horse, because Domitian inspired incredible fear, both for the Romans and especially for the Christians. He is called "death," because he exercised terrible cruelty.

(2) Some understand the pale horse to be false prophets and hypocrites, especially the Muhammadans, whom the demon stirred up against the Church like unrestrained horsemen.

(3) Some take it to refer to angels, who afflicted the world with various kinds of death.

(4) It refers to pestilence, because death renders men pale, which is why it is even called "the pale one" by the poets. Hell is said to follow death, because the death of the wicked is the beginning of eternal damnation for them. But it is better to understand it as the grave, because this message has to do with physical death.

Αὐτοῖς, *to them*. The Vulgate translates poorly with a singular, "to him." Better, "to them," namely, to the three horsemen on the red, black, and pale horses.

The fourth part should be understood as a great multitude of men, for a definite number is being used for an indefinite number.

Θάνατος, *death*, is pestilence. Τὰ θηρία τῆς γῆς, *the beasts of the earth*, are lions, bears, wolves. This is the fourfold family of plagues that God threatens to send upon the world (Lev. 26:22; Eze. 14:21).

v. 9 *The souls beneath the altar*. (1) According to Aureolus, the opening of this fifth seal represents "the time of Trajan, who succeeded Domitian until Diocletian. This period included many persecutions of the Church, namely, the third, fourth, fifth, sixth, seventh, eighth, ninth, and tenth, all of which preceded that most serious persecution of all under Diocletian and Maximian, which relates to the sixth seal."

(2) It stands for the persecutions of the confessors of the Gospel, for which those plagues on the world, signified by the three preceding seals, fur-

nished the occasion, because wicked men would ascribe the cause of those plagues to the doctrine of the Gospel and its confessors.

(3) The state of the Church Triumphant is prefigured—what the souls of the blessed are doing in heaven while the Church Militant is experiencing these plagues.

Lorinus, commenting on 2 Pet. 3:8, and Baronius, Vol. I, *Annal. Ann.*, 55, n. 15, understand the souls under the altar to be the bones of the martyrs concealed under the altars. Therefore they are forced to conclude that the Greek noun ψυχῆς, *soul*, should be understood as parts of a dead body.

The altar is better understood as Christ Himself, who "offered Himself as a sweet-smelling aroma" (Eph. 5:2), to the heavenly Father on the altar of the cross, of which it says in Heb. 13:10, "we have an altar," on which "we offer our spiritual sacrifices" (1 Pet. 2:5).

The testimony is the Gospel, which is the testimony of Christ (Rev. 1:9), which they so steadfastly embraced that they did not hesitate to meet death for it, and they became martyrs, that is, witnesses who confirmed the truth of the Gospel with their blood.

That the souls of the martyrs are those who appear under the altar is indicated by the fact that the souls of the godly who died, especially the martyrs, are in the hand of Christ, under the protection and shade of Christ until the Day of Judgment, safe from all perils and adversities (Wisdom 3:1, Acts 7:59, 1 Pet. 4:19).

v. 10 ὁ δεσπότης ὁ ἅγιος καὶ ἀληθινός, *the holy and true Lord*. By virtue of the divine and true threats You have made, You cannot let the malice of the persecutors go unpunished.

οὐ κρίνεις καὶ ἐκδικεῖς τὸ αἷμα ἡμῶν, *will You not judge and avenge our blood* (Psa. 9:13). How can You put up with the violence of our enemies for so long? Why do You put off the liberation of Your Church for so long? Yet the souls do not say these things out of impatience or lust for revenge, but out of their sincere desire, both for the final and complete liberation of the Church, and to be united with their resurrected bodies. Gregory, Book II, *Moral.*, ch. 6: "Great is their cry, great is their desire, both for the resurrection, and for judgment. The less one cries out, the less one desires; and the more loudly one raises his voice, the more fully he pours himself into what he desires." Chrysostom on Psalm 9: "They cry out, meanwhile, for God to break the power of their adversaries, so that they may acknowledge the power and divinity of Christ."

v. 11 ἐδόθησαν ἑκάστοις στολαὶ λευκαί, *white robes were given to each of them.* (1) These are commonly understood as the glorification of the soul which is attributed to the saints before the resurrection of the body. (2) White robes are a symbol of holiness, purity, and joy. (3) Primasius takes it "as the highest joy, which they received from this revelation, since it was said to them that there would still be many martyrs and saints." These things can be combined. It signifies the purity and perfect righteousness of those souls, especially the gladness they enjoy also before the resurrection (Dan. 7:9, Mark 16:5). This joy grows out of the revelation of the number of martyrs, and from the fact that they are assured that their bodies were to be glorified in the resurrection (Rev. 3:5, 7:13).

ἵνα ἀναπαύσωνται, *that they should rest,* that they should wait with a quiet spirit, ἕως οὗ πληρώσωσι, *until* the number of martyrs *is fulfilled,* by the persecution of those who would put them to death.

v. 12 The horrible scene depicted here (1) is understood by some to refer to that great disturbance of all things which will come right before the day of final judgment. They reach this conclusion from v. 17 and from the prophecies of Christ. (2) Some understand it to refer to the period under Emperors Diocletian and Maximian, under whom the Church suffered the eleventh persecution. The earthquake signifies the brutality and the long duration of the persecution. *The sun was made black like sackcloth,* because Christ is denigrated and treated harmfully in His members. *The whole moon was made like blood,* that is, the universal Church was reddened with the blood of the martyrs. *The stars fell from the sky,* that is, men of surpassing dignity faltered in their confession of the faith for fear of death. (3) This scene fits best with the times of the Antichrist.

The *earthquake* represents great disturbances and confusion in the world, especially in the Church, at the time of the coming reign of the Antichrist, through heresies, corruptions of doctrine, sects, and dissensions.

The *blackening of the sun* represents the corruption of the doctrine of the person, office, and benefits of Christ, who is the Sun of Righteousness (Mal. 4:2, Luke 1:78).

The *moon made like blood* prefigures notable persecutions, in which the Church is colored with blood. The Church is pictured by the moon, because she receives her splendor from Christ. She also sometimes waxes and sometimes wanes (Song of Solomon 6:10).

v. 13 *The stars fall from the sky* (Mat. 24:29). This means that many teachers of the Church will abandon the truth, some of whom will resign from their ecclesiastical office and move over to the political realm. Others, moved by the fear of persecution and influenced by the promises of reward, will deny the truth of the Gospel. The teachers of the Church are referred to as stars (Dan. 12:3; Rev. 1:20, 12:4).

v. 14 οὐρανὸς ἀπεχωρίσθη, *the sky receded*. This signifies that the Church will diminish and that the confessors will go into hiding on account of the severity of the persecutions.

πᾶν ὄρος καὶ νῆσος ἐκ τῶν τόπων αὐτῶν ἐκινήθησαν, *every mountain and island* (the singular is used for the plural) *were moved from their places*, that is, by the earthquake. This means that the kingdoms of the world, which are represented by mountains (Psa. 65:7; Psa. 68:17; Jer. 51:25; Micah 6:2), are to be shaken and disturbed, and that the inhabitants of the islands are to be moved from their place. Likewise, it means that those who were supposed to be like firm and immovable mountains will be displaced from the confession of the faith (Mat. 24:24).

v. 16 The wars and troubles stirred up by the Eastern Antichrist were so bloody and so horrible that men from both lower and higher orders wished for death. In the kingdom of the Western Antichrist, many who were involved in the dignity of the magistrate deserted their office and holed themselves up in monasteries and cloisters in order to make satisfaction for their sins and merit eternal life. But they were always ordered to doubt the mercy of God and the remission of sins. This time when both Antichrists exercised dominion was a time of wrath, because God permitted it out of His righteous wrath (2 The. 2:10). This calamity was also a prelude to the anguish that the wicked will experience on the Day of Judgment, when they will likewise say to the mountains, "Fall on us!" (Luke 23:30)

Concerning the sequence of events: As long as the white and red horses advanced for the Church, things went well for the Church with regard to faith and godliness under the persecutions. But after the black horse advanced with heresies and the pale horse advanced with the ambition and hypocrisy of the bishops, the Church took on a deathly pallor and began to be mortally ill. While the *woman in labor*, that is, the genuine Church, *was forced to flee into the desert*, it vanished from the appearance of men for a short time, and then the Roman beast rose up out of the sea, ridden by another woman, the great harlot, the Church of Antichrist described in Rev. 17.

Chapter 7

Chapter 7 describes the blessed state of the godly after the opening of the sixth seal:
  I.   The turning away of the evil works of Antichrist, vv. 1–3;
  II. The sealing of the spiritual Israelites, vv. 4–8;
  III. The most blessed condition of the elect, v. 9 to the end of the chapter.

v. 1 Μετὰ ταῦτα, *after those things* that followed the opening of the five seals, for the things described in this chapter also happened after the opening of the sixth seal.

With regard to the four angels standing over the four corners of the earth, holding back the four winds, (1) Aretas understands them literally as four angels who will hold back the wind around the time of the end of the world.

(2) Ansbertus, Primasius, and Haymo suggest that it refers to the period preceding the preaching of the Gospel in the whole world. They take the four angels as four demons who control four empires of the world, namely, the Assyrians, the Persians, the Greeks, and the Romans. They take the four winds as the same four empires (Dan. 7:2). Therefore, those demons held the four winds in their hands, that is, the four empires, so that they would not stand upon the earth, that is, so that no one could acknowledge the doctrine of the truth in them.

(3) Dionysius, Rupert, and Hugo understand the four angels as all the rulers of the earth, who held the four winds, that is, all the heralds of the Gospel, so that they would not dare to instill in mortals even the least bit of sacred doctrine.

(4) Tossanus concludes from v. 3 that they were good angels, whose ministry God used in punishing the ungodly by tormenting them with excessive heat.

(5) Some understand them as evil angels, as is made clear from their actions, namely, that they impeded the effect of evangelical preaching in the hearts of men, lest they should be made alive through it. Cf. v. 2, where it says they are given power to strike the earth.

(6) The four angels represent false teachers and the evil spirits that spur them on, for heresy is "a doctrine of demons" (1 Tim. 4:1). There are four of them, because they stood in the four corners of the earth, that is, they spread their heresies in all four corners of the world. They impede the genuine teachers in their ministry (which is the "ministry of the Spirit" [Gen. 6:3; Eze. 1:20; John 3:8; Acts 2:2; 2 Cor. 3:6]), so that they do not preach the Word of the Gospel purely and without corruption in all the earth, according to God's command, and so that men do not experience from it the life-giving consolation and refreshment of their souls, but would faint because of the heat of divine wrath and anguish of soul.

v. 2 Καὶ εἶδον ἄλλον ἄγγελον, *and I saw another angel*. (1) Tossanus takes this as a created angel who receives a special command to seal the elect, since v. 3 associates him with those who do the sealing.

(2) But it is better to understand it as Christ Himself, "the Angel of the covenant" (Mal. 3:1). He is also called "an angel" elsewhere (Gen. 48:16, Rev. 8:3). Christ was sent by the Father into this world to preach the Gospel and to perform the work of redemption. He descends from the rising sun, because He is the "rising from on high" (Luke 1:78), and "the Sun of righteousness" (Mal. 4:2), who breathes the most wholesome wind from the rising of the sun.

The rising of the sun is a symbol of something joyful, namely, the protection of the elect. Since Christ rose from the dead, He rightfully seemed to rise like the morning sun.

He is in every way distinct from the created angels, which is why He is called ἄλλος, *another*.

ἔχοντα σφραγῖδα, *having the seal*. The heavenly Father has sealed Him (John 6:27) and has publicly testified concerning Him that He is His "beloved Son" (Mat. 3:17). In Him, the Father has elected all who believe and persevere in faith to the end of their life (Eph. 1:4), "who have this seal: the Lord knows who are His" (2 Tim. 2:19). He has also "given Him the Spirit without measure" (John 3:34), so that from His fullness He can give the Holy Spirit to believers (John 1:16). He is the seal with which they are sealed for the day of redemption (2 Cor. 1:21; Eph. 1:13, 4:30).

Those who explain this angel as a created angel take this seal to be a definite command to separate the believing and elect from other men, lest they be struck down together with them (Eze. 9:4).

ἔκραξε φωνῇ μεγάλῃ, *He cried with a loud voice*, which signifies His divine power by which He prevails over the evil spirits.

οἷς ἐδόθη, *to whom it was granted*, by God's permission and on the basis of His righteous judgment.

The *earth and sea* stand for those who live on land and on the islands of the sea.

v. 3 The *trees* stand for men of preeminent power and authority. Think magistrates, kings, rulers, teachers of the Church.

ἄχρι σφραγίσωμεν, *until we seal*, until I, together with the Father and the Holy Spirit, seal them, so that I may discern and separate the true sons of God and the elect from the rest of men, lest they be struck down with other men, just as houses of the Israelites were sealed with the blood of the paschal lamb, lest the destroying angel strike their firstborn (Exo. 12:22); and as the citizens of Jerusalem who groaned over the abominations of Jerusalem were sealed with a mark by him who was dressed in a linen robe and had an inkhorn at his side (Eze. 9:4). But those who were sealed are described later in this book as having the name of the heavenly Father "written on their foreheads" (Rev. 14:1), which signifies that "God knows His own" (2 Tim. 2:19).

ἐπὶ τῶν μετώπων αὐτῶν, *on their foreheads*. This means that they are not ashamed of the name of Christ, but confess it publicly (Mat. 10:32).

The general significance of this is that, in the midst of heresies, God preserves the elect so that they do not assent to them, or that they will again certainly be led out of them before the end of their life.

By those who were sealed (1) some understand all the believers from the Jews and Gentiles, who are the true Israelites and sons of Abraham (Rom. 9:8, Gal. 6:16).

(2) It is better to say that they represent those who have been converted to Christ from Judaism, who are referred to with a definite number in order to express how few they are. For they were very few in comparison with the number of Jews who did not receive Christ, and in comparison with those who believed from among the Gentiles. This explanation is proved (1) because the tribes of Israel are listed; (2) because it goes on: *After these things I saw a great multitude that no one could count*. Yet some say that this should be understood as referring to the same ones who were sealed, since they were sealed for this very reason, that their salvation not be overturned by those angels.

It should be noted (1) that a definite number is used by way of synecdoche for a great number.

(2) That in the enumeration of tribes there is no rationale for the order given, signifying that, in the matter of salvation, God has no reason to consider carnal advantages.

(3) The tribe of Ephraim is indicated with the tribe of Joseph. Blas. de Viegas, p. 330: "Instead of Ephraim, he uses the name of Ephraim's father. For Jeroboam was from the tribe of Ephraim, and he was the first to introduce idolatry into the ten tribes, 1 Kings 12." For the tribe of Joseph was split in two, namely, Manasseh and Ephraim. But the tribe of Manasseh was also listed in v. 6. Ephraim was placed in front of Manasseh by his grandfather.

(4) The tribe of Dan is omitted. The papists claim that the reason for this is that the Antichrist would be born from that tribe. But it is asserted in vain that the Antichrist would be a Jew. Others offer this reason, that the Danites had long ago abandoned the worship of God and thus had gone over from their portion among the people of God to a portion among the Gentiles. Practically all the adults in this tribe perished, and therefore John did not want to mention it as a reprobate tribe. They were not overlooked because none in that tribe were believing and elect, but because this tribe was to be attached to one of the other tribes, just as Moses also omits the tribe of Simeon in his benediction, since it was attached to the tribe of Levi (Deu. 33:8).

(5) The tribe of Judah is listed in first place, because Christ was born from it (Gen. 49:10, Heb. 7:14).

Therefore, just as the twenty-four elders (Rev. 4:4, 5:8) represent all the believing and elect of the Old and New Testaments, so the six-times-twenty-four thousand, that is, the 144,000, represent all the believing and elect from the descendants of Israel.

v. 9 Since Christ gathers His Church not only from among the Jews, but also from among the Gentiles, therefore from this point on in this prophetic vision John sees the believing and elect from among the Gentiles.

ὄχλος πολύς, ὃν ἀριθμῆσαι αὐτὸν (a Hebraism) οὐδεὶς ἐδύνατο, *a great multitude which no one could number*, because to God alone is known the number of the believing and elect. But the elect are called "few" in Mat. 20:16. We reply: that is said in a comparative, not in an absolute sense. (Cf. Augustine, *De Unit. Eccles.*, ch. 3.)

ἐκ παντὸς ἔθνους καὶ φυλῶν, *from all nations and tribes*. Luther omitted the latter in his German version and simply translated: "*aus allen Heyden.*"

ἐνώπιον τοῦ θρόνου καὶ ἐνώπιον τοῦ ἀρνίου, *before the throne and before the Lamb*, that is, before the Lamb who was sitting on the throne.

περιβεβλημένους στολὰς λευκάς, *clothed with white robes*, (1) because they put on the robe of Christ's righteousness in this life by true faith; (2) because they are clothed with heavenly splendor, purity, and sanctity in eternal life (Rev. 3:18, 6:11, 7:14).

They are clothed with robes, like priests. The robes are white, that is, they have been whitened in the blood of the Lamb.

καὶ φοίνικες ἐν ταῖς χερσὶν αὐτῶν, *and there were palm branches in their hands*, (1) because in this life they obtained the victory over all their enemies by faith; (2) because in eternal life they fully triumph over all their conquered enemies. For palms were signs of victory among the Romans and other nations.

v. 10 κράζοντες φωνῇ μεγάλῃ, *crying out with a great voice*, out of joy and exultation, ἡ σωτηρία τῷ θεῷ, *salvation to God*, who gave us His Son, our Redeemer and Savior.

τῷ ἀρνίῳ, *to the Lamb*, to Christ our Redeemer and Savior, who, according to His human nature, has been exalted to the right hand of God and sits on the throne of His majesty. To Him alone belong the honor and the glory of salvation: that He alone can give salvation, since "there is salvation in no one else" (Isa. 43:11, Acts 4:12).

v. 11 ἔπεσαν, *they fell*, out of reverence and as a testimony to their submission.

v. 12 ἡ εὐλογία καὶ ἡ δόξα, *blessing and glory*. To our God alone, the only Redeemer of the human race, belong praise, honor and glory, wisdom and power, which is rendered to Him by us, by the angels, and by all the blessed.

v. 13 ἀπεκρίθη, *he replied*. "To reply" in this passage is a Hebrew phrase used when one starts to speak.

ἐκ τῶν πρεσβυτέρων, *of the elders*, who were standing before the throne. He asks, not out of ignorance, but in order to give John and others an opportunity to be informed in this matter.

v. 14 οἱ ἐρχόμενοι ἐκ τῆς θλίψεως τῆς μεγάλης, *those coming out of the great tribulation*. They sustained grave adversities and persecutions by the enemies of the Church, especially by the Antichrist. But now they have been freed from it all.

μεγάλη, *great*, is said, not with respect to God or to the future glory, but with respect to our experience.

The article τῆς expresses something certain, namely, the persecution by the Antichrist or other persecutors. This describes (1) the state of the cross; (2) the state of light. The state of the cross in general is called "the great tribulation." In particular, the things listed include hunger, thirst, the heat of the sun, tears.

The state of light is described (1) by the whitening of the robe; (2) by the blessed station and vision before the throne of the Lamb; (3) by the glorious cohabitation with God; (4) by the cessation of tribulation; (5) by eternal refreshment.

ἔπλυναν τὰς στολὰς, etc., *they washed their robes*. By true faith they put on Christ, "who was made righteousness by God" (1 Cor. 1:30, Gal. 3:27). They were cleansed from sin by His blood (1 John 1:7, Heb. 9:14, Rev. 1:5), and in Him they obtained the perfect righteousness and purity that avail before God (Psa. 51:9, Isa. 1:16). See, this is the power of the blood of Christ, not to turn red or to stain, but to whiten and to cleanse. Ambrose: "Because the souls of the elect that were formerly wrapped in the blackness of sin have taken on the whiteness of cleanliness through the redemption of the blood of Christ." Haymo: "As if to say that for this very reason they belong to the number of the elect, because they appear to have been cleansed by the blood of the Lamb."

v. 15 διὰ τοῦτό, *therefore*, not the meritorious cause, but (1) with respect to Christ; (3) the instrumental cause; (3) by way of order.

Very rich rewards. (1) εἰσιν ἐνώπιον τοῦ θρόνου, *they are before the throne*, they see Him face to face (1 Cor. 13:12). Inexpressible joy arises in them from this beatific vision of God.

(2) λατρεύουσιν αὐτῷ ἡμέρας καὶ νυκτὸς ἐν τῷ ναῷ αὐτοῦ, *they serve Him day and night in His temple*. They serve Him without interruption in heaven, the type of which was the Jerusalem temple (Heb. 9:24). They serve Him as priests. They praise, they give thanks, because they serve together with the angels, with whom they are in fellowship.

(3) ὁ καθήμενος ἐπὶ τοῦ θρόνου σκηνώσει ἐπ' αὐτούς, *the One seated on the throne will have His tent upon them*. He will protect them with shelter against the heat of the sun, that is, against the persecutions and against any and all adversaries (Isa. 4:5–6). He will shine upon them with the light of heavenly glory. He will dwell with them in a familiar way, as those who live in the same house.

v. 16 οὐ πεινάσουσιν ἔτι οὐδὲ διψήσουσιν ἔτι, *they will not hunger anymore nor will they thirst anymore*. (Cf. Isa. 49:10.) For they will be satisfied with heavenly good things. They will be free from famine and thirst, from poverty, from the things to which they were subject in this life. They will not have any desire for earthly things, for they will have in God the fullness of all good things.

οὐδὲ μὴ πέσῃ ἐπ' αὐτοὺς ὁ ἥλιος οὐδὲ πᾶν καῦμα, *nor will the sun fall upon them nor any heat*. The heat of temptation and persecution (1 Pet. 4:12, Psa. 121:6, Song of Solomon 1:6); the heat of a restless conscience, divine wrath, the fire of hell.

v. 17 τὸ ἀρνίον ποιμανεῖ αὐτούς, *the Lamb will shepherd them*. He will provide for them from the heavenly pastures. He will satisfy them with the fullness of heavenly good things (Psa. 23:2, John 10:9, 11).

ὁδηγήσει, etc., *He will lead, etc.* He will grant them the fullness of all the gifts of the Holy Spirit (Rev. 22:1). He will lead them to the perpetually flowing springs of consolation and joy (Psa. 36:11–12).

ἐξαλείψει, *He will wipe away*, etc. (Cf. Isa. 25:8, Rev. 21:4.) He will wipe away all the tears they shed in this life—a metaphor from a mother who wipes away the tears of her little children (Isa. 66:13). "There will be no more sorrow" (Rev. 21:4).

Chapter 8

There are five parts to this chapter:
  I. There is added to the introduction, which includes the opening of the seven seals and the third vision, a description of an angel with a censer, vv. 1–6;
  II. The first angel's trumpet;
  III. The second angel's trumpet;
  IV. The third angel's trumpet;
  V. The fourth angel's trumpet.

The trumpet of the first angel is followed by hail and fire mixed with blood, falling on the earth. After the trumpet of the second angel, a huge mountain burning with fire is thrown headlong into the sea. After the trumpet of the third angel, a star resembling a little burning torch falls from heaven. After the trumpet of the fourth angel, a third of the sun, moon, and stars is darkened, after which an angel proclaims with a loud voice that a greater woe is yet to come.

v. 1 ἐγένετο σιγή, *there was silence*. (1) Some think this silence refers to respite for the Church, granted at a time after the persecutions. (2) But others think it was a sign that something great and unique was about to be revealed to John, which would properly be done in silence.

It is as if the angels and elect were dumbstruck at those disturbances which were about to happen in the Church.

εἶδον τοὺς ἑπτὰ ἀγγέλους, *I saw the seven angels*. Some see the apostles represented by the seven angels sounding their trumpets—indeed, all preachers and heralds of the divine Word, who filled the whole world with sound of the Gospel, proclaiming the merit of the sacrifice Christ made on the cross, which is expressed in this passage with the censer filled with fire and incense.

Others suggest that these seven angels refer to the good angels, and that all of them are signified with the number seven, being a perfect number, because what is said about them—that they stand before God—is the common office of all of them. Trumpets are given to them, because they were supposed to announce the judgments of God to the world, and also carry them out.

But it is better to say that the evil angels are indicated, whose work God uses in carrying out His judgments and in executing His punishments. (Cf. 1 Kings 22:21, Job 1:6.) The trumpets are heretics who disturb the Church with the sound of their false doctrine. These trumpets are given to the evil angels, because God, by His just judgment, permits the evil angels to stir up heretics in the Church. (Cf. 1 Tim. 4:1, 2 The. 2:9–11.)

The sound of the trumpets indicates the time, not when a certain heresy sprang up, but when it was most forcefully advanced.

v. 3 Καὶ ἄλλος ἄγγελος, *and another angel*. Christ is the angel of the covenant (Mal. 3:1). Ἐστάθη ἐπὶ τὸ θυσιαστήριον, *he stood upon the altar*. (1) Some understand this as the altar of incense. (2) Others take it to be the altar of burnt offering. If the latter is accepted, then Christ's standing upon the altar signifies that Christ is at the same time priest and victim, who offered Himself on the altar of the cross. But the former explanation is confirmed by the fact (i) that He is said to have stood with a censer, as if He were about to offer incense, for frankincense and incense were burned on the altar of incense; (ii) that this altar is said to be made of gold, for the altar of burnt offering was made of bronze.

(3) This vision deals with the altar that John saw in heaven, but it represents the fact that Christ, as the only New Testament priest, fulfills His priestly office also in heaven (Heb. 7:22, 27).

ἔχων λιβανωτὸν χρυσοῦν, *having a golden censer*. This censer was prefigured by the altar of incense on which the Old Testament priest would offer incense every day (Exo. 30:1, 7). It was also prefigured by the censer into which the Old Testament priest would place the live coals from the altar of incense and then insert a handful of incense when he wanted to enter the Holy of Holies, so that the smoke of the incense would cover the Mercy Seat (Lev. 16:12–13).

καὶ ἐδόθη αὐτῷ θυμιάματα πολλά, *and He was given much incense*. The incense given to Christ indicates that Christ did not only offer Himself to His heavenly Father once on the altar of the cross as a sweet-smelling aroma (Eph. 5:2), but still intercedes for believers with His heavenly Father by virtue of His merit, offering their prayers to God. That is, He renders them favorable and acceptable to God the Father, as the following words demonstrate. Surely the intercession of Christ makes the prayers of believers acceptable to God, so that they are heard by Him (Heb. 9:24, 1 Pet. 2:5).

The intercession of Christ and the prayers of the saints are mentioned here, because the prayers that rely on Christ's intercession and merit are the best fortification against persecutions.

ἵνα δώσῃ ταῖς προσευχαῖς τῶν ἁγίων πάντων, *so that He may add it to the prayers of all the saints.* Christ's merit and intercession add weight to our prayers.

v. 4 καὶ ἀνέβη ὁ καπνὸς τῶν θυμιαμάτων, *and the smoke of the incense ascended, etc.*, from the hand of the angel, as the one High Priest, Mediator, and Intercessor for all believers.

Just as in chapter 6 above, the divine Word was mentioned first, before the bodily afflictions are listed, so here the prayers are mentioned first, before the spiritual plagues are pronounced, because the Word of God and the prayers that flow from true faith and that rely on the intercession of Christ are a salutary defense in the midst of bodily and spiritual afflictions. Prayers prevent heresies from advancing as far as Satan attempts to sow them.

v. 5 ἐγέμισεν αὐτὸν ἐκ τοῦ πυρὸς, *He filled it from the fire,* just as the Old Testament priest would take fire, that is, burning coals, from the altar when he wanted to offer incense before God. This signified, not only that Christ makes our prayers acceptable to God by His merit so that they are heard by Him, but also that He would pour out the Holy Spirit on the apostles on the Day of Pentecost in the form of tongues of fire, for He Himself is the heavenly fire taken from the heavenly altar. He also still sends the Spirit today into the hearts of believers, so that they may have solace and endure in the midst of all adversities.

Some wish to understand the fire as God's wrath which Christ will pour out on the ungodly, for He is the Savior and Mediator of believers, but the Judge of unbelievers. But the former explanation agrees better with the text.

Blasius de Viegas, p. 340: "Most interpreters confess that this angel is Christ the Lord. For the things that are said in this passage cannot be aptly applied to anyone else. For to whom else does it belong to offer the incense, that is, the prayers of the universal Church, in a golden censer with such great majesty? To whom, besides Christ, does it belong to throw into the earth some of the fire with which the golden censer was filled, and to inflame them with the fire of divine love and with the flaming gifts of the Holy Spirit?"

καὶ ἐγένοντο φωναὶ καὶβρονταὶ, *and there were voices and thunderings, etc.* After the apostles received the fire of the Holy Spirit sent down from heaven by Christ, "they began to speak with different tongues," which signify voices, to thunder with preaching, to flash with miracles, and to shake the whole earth with the splendor of miracles and with the greatness of doctrine. (Cf. Acts 2:4; Psa. 68:34.) Terrible persecutions also followed by which the whole earth was shaken, and then heresies followed.

This indicates that the preaching of the Gospel sounds very loudly just before heresies arise, so that the elect may be fortified with sound doctrine, lest they be seduced by the heresies.

v. 7 ἐγένετο χάλαζα καὶ πῦρ, *there was hail and fire*. It is certain that the seven trumpets of the angels represent heresies. But which heresy is signified by the trumpet of each angel cannot be precisely known, because one heresy was often combined with another, and many heresies followed one right after the other in the first three centuries of the Church.

The sounding of the first trumpet signifies the heresy of the pseudo-apostles: the Nazarenes, the Ebionites, the Cerinthians, the Tatians and the Encratites, who arose in the Church either while the apostles were still living or shortly after the time of the apostles. The pseudo-apostles, the Nazarenes and the Ebionites, taught that we are justified before God by the works of the Mosaic Law. The Ebionites and the Cerinthians taught that Christ is a mere man. Tatian and the Encratites taught that marriage is an impure and detestable way of life.

Yet some interpret it to be about Manes, from whom the Manichaeans arose. But they are later than the heretics listed above.

Those heretics, with the hail of their false doctrine, crushed the seed of the divine Word in the hearts of men. Fire and blood were mixed with the hail, because they boasted of special revelations and of the great number of their martyrs.

Hail and fire mixed with blood are three symbols of the heretical doctrine by which the crops of orthodox doctrine that spring up in the hearts of men are devastated, burned up, and contaminated. Some take the blood to refer to the cruel wars and the bloodshed incited by the heretics.

καὶ τὸ τρίτον τῶν δένδρων κατεκάη, *and a third of the trees were burned up*. The *trees* signify famous and powerful men; likewise the teachers of the Church, humble and common, are represented by the *grass*. No longer are they "trees of righteousness" (Isa. 61:3) and verdant green, but unfruitful trees and dried up grass, dead to any good purpose.

A *third* signifies a great multitude. At the same time, it also indicates that we are not yet dealing with universal apostasy, which is still to come under the Antichrist.

v. 8 After the trumpet of the second angel, *a great mountain burning with fire was cast into the sea, and a third of the sea was turned to blood.*

(1) Some take this to refer to Arius, who is compared to a great mountain on account of his arrogance, and because he was a great authority in the Church. He was a mountain burning with fire, because the fire of this heresy grew slowly over time.

(2) It is better to take it to refer to the Montanists, Marcionites, Manichaeans, Cataphrygians, and Peputians, who claimed to have special revelations and who held positions of great authority, which is why they are compared to a great mountain.

(3) Others interpret the *great mountain* as the devil, who is so called on account of his arrogance; burning, because he is inflamed with the firebrands of envy. He is called a mountain because, through tyrants and the august emperors of Rome, he towered over the Church like a great mountain and seemed to crush it with his mass. But we are dealing here with heretics, not with persecutions.

The *sea* represents the world.

(1) *Blood* is a symbol of heretical dogma. The next verse declares that, just as men who drink deeply of the heretical dogma subsequently die an eternal death, so the living things that swim in the sea will die when they drink the bloody sea (Exo. 7:24).

The Manichaeans incited persecutions and bloodshed.

(2) A third of the sea was turned to blood, because many were made martyrs, who shed their blood for their faith in Christ.

v. 9 καὶ ἀπέθανεν, *a third of the creatures that lived in the sea died*, that is, many believers who lived in the sea of the Church like fish, were frightened by the severity of the persecution, abandoned the faith, and died miserably. At one time they were partakers of spiritual life, but through these heresies they were cast headlong into eternal death.

A third of the ships perished, (1) because many who stood out among others like ships due to their understanding of doctrine and holiness—who should have transported others in the sea of the Church into the port of salvation—were carried away by the power of the storm, dashed against the rocks of persecution, and consequently made shipwreck of their faith.

(2) Many individual churches that at one time were little ships of Christ have been attacked by these heresies and have made shipwreck of their faith (1 Tim. 1:19).

v. 10 With regard to the *star burning like a torch*, (1) Aretas understands it to be the devil. (2) Lyranus thinks it refers to Pelagius. (3) Szegedinus and Chytraeus interpret it as Samosata and Arius. (4) Artopaeus and Brightman think it is the Antichrist Pope. (5) Tossanus thinks it is the rulers who stray from the norm of godliness, and perhaps Julian the Apostate in particular. (6) Eglinus and Napirus understand it to be Muhammad. (7) Aretius and Marloratus take it to be the heretics of later times and of our times. (8) Some understand it to be heresiarchs in general. The star is a symbol of any notable teacher. The torch is a symbol of pernicious but attractive dogma, or also of outstanding authority. The star is called wormwood, because heresiarchs bring the bitterness of death to men. The springs and rivers are turned into wormwood, because the heretics corrupt the divine Scriptures and the books of the fathers. (9) Luther takes it to be Origen, who was an especially notable teacher of the Church. He left behind many writings and was endowed with great authority, which is why he is referred to as a torch. But afterwards, he corrupted the salutary springs of Israel (Psa. 68:27, Isa. 12:3), that is, the prophetic and apostolic books, by rendering them bitter and tasteless with his unfortunate allegories, so that thirsty souls could not draw life-giving consolation from them. Through his writings he prepared the way for the heresiarch Arius.

v. 12 After the fourth angel's trumpet, a third of the sun, a third of the moon, and a third of the stars, etc., were struck.

(1) Some understand this in general of the plague of false prophets and hypocrites.

(2) It is better understood specifically concerning the heresy of the Novatians, who denied that those who fall after Baptism were to be received into grace; of the Pelagians, who denied original sin and ascribed too much to the free will of man; but especially of the Arians, who denied the deity of Christ. Their heresy was disseminated far and wide throughout the Church of Christ. By these heresiarchs, and especially by the Arians, the doctrine about Christ, the Sun of Righteousness, was obscured; the moon, that is, the Church, and the stars, that is, the teachers of the Church, were partially seduced and obscured. But some of them were driven into exile by their persecutors so that they were forced into hiding. Spiritual blindness and ignorance dominated in the hearts of many.

This deprivation of light denotes an ignorance of divine things, of things that pertain to the worship of God and the salvation of men.

The fact that a *third* is mentioned so many times in the description of these four trumpets implies that we are not yet dealing with the universal apostasy that will follow under the Antichrist, but with the heresies that arose before the kingdom of Antichrist and that, in a way, prepared the way for him.

v. 13 Καὶ εἶδον καὶ ἤκουσα ἑνὸς ἀγγέλου, *and I saw and I heard one angel.* The Vulgate reads, "one eagle." In many Greek manuscripts we read, not "eagle," but "angel." Nevertheless, the older manuscripts have "eagle," and thus Bede, Aretas, Ticonius, and the translators commonly also read it. They understand the eagle to represent the preachers of the last days, who will announce divine threats and punishments to men. This angel was a good and holy angel.

Three woes represent three general plagues, as understood from v. 12 of the following chapter.

Those who dwell on the earth represent ungodly men, ἐπίγεια φρονοῦντες, "who have their mind set on earthly things" (Phi. 3:19), who have no place among those sealed by the angels (Rev. 7:3).

ἐκ τῶν λοιπῶν φωνῶν, *from the rest of the voices,* because of the rest of the plagues that will follow the sounding of the trumpets of the three remaining angels. And since those plagues are said to be three in number, therefore also the angel proclaimed three successive woes.

Chapter 9

This chapter has two parts:
I. The fifth angel's trumpet;
II. The sixth angel's trumpet.

v. 1 εἶδον ἀστέρα ἐκ τοῦ οὐρανοῦ πεπτωκότα, *I saw a star fallen from heaven.*

(1) Some take this star fallen from heaven to be some important bishop and his heretical successors.

(2) But it is better to interpret it as the Roman Pope. The star falling from heaven is a symbol of a bishop casting aside his care for heavenly things and taking up concern for earthly things, coveting riches, honor, dignity, and pleasures. For the Roman bishops in the early days were Christians, godly and holy teachers, some of whom sealed the doctrine of Christ with their blood. But afterward, their successors abandoned the ecclesiastical ministry and turned to earthly things, namely, riches, honor, pleasures, and dignity in this world.

Some oppose this explanation, claiming that we are not yet here dealing with the Antichrist. But the order of events in the text demonstrates otherwise, because after the heresies enumerated in the previous chapter, the kingdom of the Pope followed, which is the sewage of all heresies.

ἐδόθη αὐτῷ ἡ κλεὶς τοῦ φρέατος τῆς ἀβύσσου, *the key of the pit of the abyss was given to him.* Aretas says that ἄβυσσον, *abyss*, is the great deep of the primordial elements, either because of a lack of τοῦ βεβύσθαι, *of being covered*, which is said of things that have not been covered, not stopped up, but always lie open with a great chasm; or because it has great depth, so that the prefix α is understood intensively.

The key of the pit of the abyss represents the power to open the abyss, namely, hell, that is, the power to call forth heresies from the underworld.

The pit of the abyss is purgatory, which is said to be close to hell. The Pope has the key of this pit, because he boasts that he has the power to free souls from the flames of purgatory by means of indulgences. The key of the pit is given to this angel. That is, the Pope is permitted, by the righteous judgment of God, to bring forth from the underworld (2 The. 2:9, 12) the doctrine of purgatory and other erroneous doctrines together with the old, worn-out heresies, which are "doctrines of demons" (1 Tim. 4:1).

v. 2 ἀνέβη καπνὸς, *smoke arose, etc.* Smoke signifies false doctrine, which obscures the sun and the air, namely, the brightness of the sun in the air, that is, the heavenly doctrine in the Church, returning into darkness those who were previously enlightened by the true doctrine. For after the doctrine of purgatory was introduced in the Church, various errors and false doctrines arose, namely, doubt concerning the remission of sins, making satisfaction for one's own sins, the merit of works, works of supererogation, papal indulgences, Masses for the dead, pilgrimages, etc., which provide no solid and firm consolation, but vanish like smoke.

καὶ ἐσκοτώθη ὁ ἥλιος καὶ ὁ ἀὴρ, *and the sun and the air were darkened, etc.* Just as a thick smoke obscures the rays of the sun, so the papal false doctrines obscure the brightness of the true and saving doctrine. This darkness seems to have been caused somehow from the exit of the locusts from the pit.

The sun stands for the saving doctrine of the person, office, and benefits of Christ, for He Himself is the *Sun of Righteousness* (Mal. 4:2) under whose wings along is salvation. Just as the natural life of man consists in the continual breathing of air, so the spiritual life of man consists in the Word of God, which was likewise miserably obscured when traditions and apparitions of spirits were introduced in the Church in order to confirm the doctrine of purgatory. Spiritual life also consists in faith (Gal. 2:29), which is likewise obscured, because the hearts of men that were once enlightened by the light of doctrine have lost the purity of doctrine.

v. 3 καὶ ἐκ τοῦ καπνοῦ ἐξῆλθον ἀκρίδες εἰς τὴν γῆν, *and out of the smoke locusts came upon the earth*. (1) Some interpret these locusts as false teachers who come ahead of the Antichrist, for as soon as peace was bestowed on the Church under Constantine, various heresies arose: of the

Arians, Manichaeans, Pelagians and Nestorians. (2) It is better to interpret them as the various monastic orders which grew strong in the Church after the doctrine of purgatory and the other Antichristian errors were introduced. For these orders led men away to the merits of works, to works of supererogation, to performing one's own satisfactions, to papal indulgences, etc. Likewise the salesmen of indulgences, who circulated and sold letters of indulgence throughout the whole world. Likewise the Sophists, who propagated the papal errors and the Antichristian doctrine with their writings. These are compared to locusts, because they spread out in great numbers far and wide and stripped everything and took it for themselves.

καὶ ἐδόθη αὐταῖς ἐξουσία, ὡς ἔχουσιν ἐξουσίαν οἱ σκορπίοι τῆς γῆς, *and power was given to them, like the scorpions of the earth have power*. By the just judgment of God, who punishes contempt for His Word, they were permitted to wound, stab, and torment the consciences of men with the doctrine of perpetual doubt, just as the sting of the scorpion causes pain.

v. 4 καὶ ἐρρέθη αὐταῖς, *and they were told*, a prohibition was issued to them.

ἵνα μὴ ἀδικήσουσιν τὸν χόρτον τῆς γῆς οὐδὲ πᾶν χλωρὸν οὐδὲ πᾶν δένδρον, εἰ μὴ τοὺς ἀνθρώπους μόνους, *not to injure the grass of the earth, nor any green plant, nor any tree, but the men only*. They were not able to injure and seduce all Christians, but only the hypocrites and the ones who held the divine Word in contempt, who did not have the seal of God on their foreheads (Rev. 7:3), that is, who were not among the number of the elect. The true Christians who were grounded in faith, who were green like grass, who flowered and bore fruit as trees of the Lord and as plants of righteousness (Psa. 1:3, 9:13; Isa. 61:13; Jer. 17:18), were not seduced or corrupted by them. The grass represents in particular those men who remained in the simplicity of their faith. The green plants are baptized infants who died at a very young age, before they could be infected with the venom of Antichristian doctrine. The trees are the confessors and martyrs, who bravely opposed the Antichristian doctrine.

Some say that the grass of the earth stands for commoners; the green plants, for men who occupy the middle class; the trees, for noblemen. But from the antithesis it is clear that the godly and elect are signified, of whatever condition or class, who are green like grass and trees in the garden of God, that is, in the Church.

v. 5 καὶ ἐδόθη αὐτοῖς ἵνα μὴ ἀποκτείνωσιν αὐτούς, *and it was given to them not to kill them*, not to kill those whom they seduced. That is, they were not allowed to inflict physical death on them as scorpions often kill a man.

ἀλλ' ἵνα βασανισθήσονται μῆνας πέντε, *but to torment them for five months*, to torture the souls and consciences of men by a doctrine of perpetual doubt: purgatory, enumeration of sins in confession, one's own merits and satisfactions.

The five months are understood (1) by some to be exactly "150 years, which corresponds to the number of days in five months, using the ancient Egyptian custom of attributing thirty days to each month," Franciscus Junius.

(2) It is better taken generally, as a short time. Locusts last for the five months of summer, which is a short time.

Those who interpret the locusts as heresies claim that "the locusts are said to have lasted a short time, because the heresies were repressed by the synods and teachers of the Church." But we have demonstrated that it properly deals with the kingdom of Antichrist. It has an established length of its duration. It was not long established at the height of its power, but just when it reached its highest peak, it began slowly to decline, and many are again delivered from those Antichristian errors before the end of their lives, namely, those who, in the agony of death, rely solely on the merit of Christ.

καὶ ὁ βασανισμὸς αὐτῶν ὡς βασανισμὸς σκορπίου, *and their torment was like the torment of a scorpion, etc.* Just as the sting of a scorpion causes a fiery sensation in a man's body, so also those who were seduced by the Antichristian doctrine had their conscience cauterized (1 Tim. 4:2).

v. 6 καὶ ἐν ταῖς ἡμέραις ἐκείναις ζητήσουσιν οἱ ἄνθρωποι τὸν θάνατον καὶ οὐχ εὑρήσουσιν αὐτόν, *and in those days men will seek death and will not find it, etc.* The restlessness and anxiety of conscience will be so great that they would rather die than go on living any longer with such anxiety. Therefore they will seek death out of the desperation into which false doctrine cast them. Augustine, *Sermo 252, De Temp.*: "Why is death sought in hell and not found? Because those to whom life is offered in this age and who do not want to receive it, will seek death in hell and will not be able to find it."

v. 7 Καὶ τὰ ὁμοιώματα τῶν ἀκρίδων ὅμοια ἵπποις ἡτοιμασμένοις εἰς πόλεμον, *and the likeness of the locusts was like horses prepared for war*. This signifies that they will rise upon against the truth of the heavenly doctrine with great might, and they will fight against it with their writings, and they will inflame the magistrates to persecute and make war against the confessors of the true doctrine. *Horses prepared for war* are a symbol of the contentiousness of the scholastics.

καὶ ἐπὶ τὰς κεφαλὰς αὐτῶν ὡς στέφανοι ὅμοιοι χρυσῷ, *and upon their heads, like crowns of something like gold*.

(1) Some take the crowns to represent the boasting of the heretics about their supposed triumph over the orthodox teachers.

(2) But since this is specifically dealing with monks and Sophists, it is better to say that the crown stands for the shaved top of the head, which they call a *rasuram coronam*, a "shaved crown."

(3) They fight for the triple crown of their head, that is, the Roman Pontiff.

(4) They persuade themselves that they will receive special golden halos because of the merits of their order and the austerity of their life.

These crowns are said to be *like gold*, which is a symbol of hypocrisy, because clerics and monks wear that shaved crown upon themselves as a sign of holiness, claiming to be priests who are sacred to God. All things glimmer in the papacy, and yet not all is gold, but only like gold.

καὶ τὰ πρόσωπα αὐτῶν ὡς πρόσωπα ἀνθρώπων, *and their faces were like the faces of men*. The faces of men are a symbol of charm, allurement, authority and external wisdom, because with the enticement of words and, as the apostle says, with their "smooth words and flattering speech they seduce the hearts of the innocent" (Rom. 16:18).

v. 8 καὶ εἶχον τρίχας ὡς τρίχας γυναικῶν, *and they had hair like women's hair*. Flowing, womanly hair (1) is a symbol of softness and femininity,

(2) and of seduction. Just as shameless women are able to comb and decorate their hair, and even add color to it, in order to find lovers, so the Antichristian teachers often attract others with their charms and color their dogmas.

καὶ οἱ ὀδόντες αὐτῶν ὡς λεόντων ἦσαν, *and their teeth were like lions' teeth*. Lions' teeth are a symbol of (1) cruelty (Joel 1:6); (2) insatiable avarice. Those whom they are unable to entice with their charms, they terrify with their threats and fires.

v. 9 καὶ εἶχον θώρακας ὡς θώρακας σιδηροῦς, *and they had breastplates like breastplates of iron*. Iron breastplates represent (1) confidence in secular strength. For those who adhere to them trust in the power of men. (2) Being hardened in error. They do not allow the salutary arrows of the divine word to pass through (Psa. 45:6). (3) Conspiracy in evil. They are closely connected to one another, like the rings on a breastplate.

καὶ ἡ φωνὴ τῶν πτερύγων αὐτῶν ὡς φωνὴ ἁρμάτων, *and the sound of their wings was like the sound of chariots*, etc. (1) Since they bear themselves proudly, they arrange everything toward splendor. (2) They have many followers. (3) They are swift and untiring in spreading and fighting for their Antichristian errors. (4) With their writings they incite controversies and wars in the Church.

v. 10 καὶ ἔχουσιν οὐρὰς ὁμοίας σκορπίοις, *and they have tails like scorpions*. Their faces are like the faces of men (v. 7), but their tails are like scorpion tails, because their doctrine at first has a wonderful appearance, but afterwards it becomes clear that it cannot supply firm consolation, but leaves its stingers behind in the conscience. Thus they have stingers in their tails, which represent both the sharp pain of false doctrine and those heretical phrases that were customarily attached by false teachers to proper statements of doctrine.

v. 11 Καὶ ἔχουσιν ἐφ᾽ αὐτῶν βασιλέα τὸν ἄγγελον τῆς ἀβύσσου, *and they have as king over them the angel of the abyss*. That angel to whom was given the key of the pit, the abyss of v. 1, boasts that he is an angel, that is, a bishop. But he is an angel of the abyss, that is, of hell (1 Tim. 4:2).

Ἀβαδδών καὶ Ἀπολλύων, *Abaddon and Apollyon*, that is, "the one who destroys, the one who corrupts."

(1) Some understand it of the devil as the author of all destruction.

(2) Alabaster, a new apocalyptic prophet, suggested a new interpretation of this passage, which Helwig examines in *Append. Disputationis contra Judaeos*.[1]

(3) Others say this angel refers to Saladin, ruler of the Saracens, who laid waste to the kingdom of Jerusalem, which was newly founded by Godfrey of Buillon, together with nearly all of Asia, around the year 1195.

(4) It is better to understand this angel as the Antichrist, whom Paul calls υἱὸν τῆς ἀπωλείας, *son of destruction* (2 The. 2:3)—in common with the betrayer (John 17:12). This name is ascribed to the Antichrist (1) according to Chrysostom, *Homilia 3 in 2 The.*, because he will be destroyed; (2) according to Jerome, *Ad Algas.*, q. 11, because he is the "son of the devil, and in fact, the destruction of all things"; (3) but especially in the active sense, because he destroys others, not only with regard to their souls through depraved doctrine, but also with regard to their bodies through terrible violence. Thus Hugo says that "he is called the son of destruction, because he destroys many, both physically and spiritually." Jerome, commenting on Daniel ch. 11, calls Nero "the precursor of the Antichrist, on account of the violence that he exerted."

The king of both monks and Sophists is called the Antichrist Pope. (1) He is their defender and protector. (2) He confirms the monastic orders by his authority. (3) He boasts that he is the head of the Church, the universal monarch, etc.

v. 12 Ἡ οὐαὶ ἡ μία ἀπῆλθεν, *the one woe passed away*. *One woe*, namely, of those three mentioned in Rev. 8:13. *Passed away*, that is, its fulfillment has been clearly described.

ἰδοὺ ἔρχεται ἔτι δύο οὐαὶ μετὰ ταῦτα, *behold! there are still coming two woes after these things*, which will be ushered in by the sixth and seventh angels sounding their trumpets.

---

1 Translator's note: According to Christoph Helwig, Alabaster wrote that Martin Luther was the "angel of the abyss" referenced in this verse, as the one responsible for breaking apart the Church and causing sects to arise within Christianity. Alabaster arrived at his interpretation—for which Helwig mocks him—by inventing spurious connections between the name "LUTHER" and various root words in Hebrew, Greek, and Latin.

v. 13 ἤκουσα φωνὴν μίαν ἐκ τῶν τεσσάρων κεράτων τοῦ θυσιαστηρίου τοῦ χρυσοῦ, *I heard one voice from the four horns of the golden altar.* The *golden altar before God* stands for Christ, the New Testament Priest prefigured by the altar of sacrifice, which stood before God in the tabernacle of the covenant (Exo. 27:2, 38:2). He renders our spiritual sacrifices acceptable to God (Heb. 13:10, 1 Pet. 2:5, Rev. 6:9).

The four horns of the altar represent the four Evangelists, who described the doctrine of Christ's conception, birth, baptism, conduct, miracles, suffering, death, resurrection, ascension, and whatever else He did and suffered for our sake. The voice of the four Evangelists has sounded throughout the whole world.

v. 14 λῦσον τοὺς τέσσαρας ἀγγέλους, *loose the four angels.* Loose, that is, announce that they are about to be loosed.

(1) Some understand *the four angels* to be "four barbarian peoples who come from distant shores and invade the territory of the empire, namely, the Tatars, the Mamluks, the Turks, and the Parthians, who tend to go out against the enemy on horseback rather than on foot. The power of their horses is rumored not only to be in their mouths, but also in their tails, for their javelins, coated in poison, are usually hurled backwards, striking the enemy that is in pursuit of them."

(2) It is better to say that they represent evil spirits, who came from all corners of the world to incite the kings and peoples around the Euphrates to make war against the Christians. Thus far they have been bound, that is, Christ has repressed them by His divine power so that they have not been able to cause as much bloodshed as they wish. The Euphrates River flowed through Babylon, which was the capital of tyrants and persecutors of the Church, whom God took out of the way. But after the saving doctrine about the golden altar—the person of Christ, with His office and benefits—was obscured both in the East and in the West through various heresies, and after the kingdom of Antichrist began in the East, these four evil angels, who were bound near the Euphrates, were again released by the just judgment and permission of God, and there arose in the East men who disturbed and devastated the Roman Empire and the Church—Arabs, Saracens and Turks, who were given divine permission, on account of the sins of men, to

incite cruel wars and copious bloodshed, and thus to usher in the second woe upon the Church.

The name of the river, "Euphrates," where those angels are said to have been bound and later released, leads us to this conclusion. For it has its origin in Armenia, passes through Syria and Mesopotamia, and drains into the Persian Gulf. The Saracens attacked those very regions. The city of Mecca is also situated near the Persian Gulf, where the tomb of Muhammad is located, to which the Turks make daily pilgrimages with a great convergence of men.

v. 15 οἱ ἡτοιμασμένοι εἰς τὴν ὥραν καὶ ἡμέραν καὶ μῆνα καὶ ἐνιαυτόν, *who had been prepared for this hour and day and month and year*. Those barbarians and cruel peoples had been prepared for these particular years, months and days, that is, for all times, to put Christians to death. Some take this determination of time to be 1,076 years, and they conclude from this that the persecution incited by the Saracens will last that long. We leave this conjecture for its own place.

v. 16 καὶ ὁ ἀριθμὸς τῶν στρατευμάτων τοῦ ἱππικοῦ, *and the number of the armies of the cavalry. The armies*, namely, those gathered together from the eastern peoples, for example, the Muhammadans, whose armies were being used by these four angels for killing.

Some take them to be the Goths and the Vandals, who brought with them a great army by which they destroyed everything. The Huns followed them, whose king, Attila, was said to be the scourge of the earth. But it is better understood concerning the Saracens and the Turks.

Δύο μυριάδες μυριάδων. *Two thousand thousand*, a definite and finite number is used for a large number.

v. 17 ἔχοντας θώρακας πυρίνους καὶ ὑακινθίνους καὶ θειώδεις, *having breastplates that were the color of fire and of hyacinth and of brimstone*. Concerning the tri-colored breastplates:

(1) Some think it signifies a threefold army made of up different peoples, such as those gathered from among the Saracens, the Turks, and the Tatars.

(2) It is better to say that the breastplates of fire and sulfur signify that these armies of flame, fire, and brimstone are going to burn and lay waste to

all things. Some interpret the brimstone as the lusts of those people. The color of the hyacinth breastplates represents the smoke that rises up from these fires.

καὶ ἐκ τῶν στομάτων αὐτῶν ἐκπορεύεται πῦρ καὶ καπνὸς καὶ θεῖον, *and out of their mouths proceed fire and smoke and brimstone.* The *fire, smoke and brimstone* represent instruments of slaughter, as understood from the following verse. All their plans and thoughts were turned to fires, destruction, and slaughter. They breathe out nothing but slaughter and fire. Not only that, but the Koran, which proceeded from the mouth of Muhammad, spits out nothing but war and bloodshed; blasphemies against Christ; corruptions of the heavenly doctrine, prefigured here by smoke; and lust, prefigured here by brimstone.

v. 18 Ὑπὸ τῶν τριῶν τούτων, *under these three,* namely, from the fire, smoke, and brimstone. The explanation is immediately added.

τὸ τρίτον τῶν ἀνθρώπων, *a third of men.* Muhammad's doctrine spread far and wide, and nearly a third of mankind was killed by it in a spiritual sense, that is, they were made subject to the second death. Not only that, but countless men were also killed in war by him and by those who have followed him.

v. 19 ἡ γὰρ ἐξουσία τῶν ἵππων ἐν τῷ στόματι αὐτῶν ἐστιν καὶ ἐν ταῖς οὐραῖς αὐτῶν, *for the authority of the horses is in their mouth and in their tails.*

Some manuscripts, including the one that Luther used, do not read τῶν ἵππων, *of the horses,* nor καὶ ἐν ταῖς οὐραῖς αὐτῶν, *and in their tails.*

(1) Some interpret this to mean that they used at the same time manifest power and serpent-like craftiness.

(2) It is better to interpret it this way: Whatever they command is immediately carried out. If a Turk orders one of his subjects to cast himself headlong from a mountain, the command is immediately obeyed.

(3) It can also be said that their power is in their mouth, because the Turks boast about the special divine revelations that were given to Muhammad, and about the spectacular victories that have been reported over the

army of Christians. For both reasons they pretend that the truth of their religion is confirmed.

αἱ γὰρ οὐραὶ αὐτῶν ὅμοιαι ὄφεσιν, *for their tails are like serpents*. The *tails* represent the priests and false teachers among the Turks (Isa. 9:15). They are like serpents on account of their venomous doctrine, and because they are instruments of the infernal serpent (Gen. 3:1, Rev. 12:9).

ἔχουσαι κεφαλὰς, *having heads*. (1) Some suggest this means they were crafty, cunning, and wise. (2) It is better to take it as the high-ranking officials among the Turks, such as the Sultans, Pashas, Begs, etc., in whom they trusted as their defenders and through whom they carried out great harm, even the devastation of regions, temples, schools, etc.

v. 20 Καὶ οἱ λοιποὶ τῶν ἀνθρώπων, *and the rest of men, etc.* Those who were left and were still unharmed by the plagues named thus far refused to be corrected by the example of those who had been killed by these plagues. They did not turn from their evil deeds to God nor abandon their idolatry, but carried on securely in their detestable sins.

τῶν ἔργων τῶν χειρῶν, *the works of their hands*, signify idols, as the context shows. Idolaters are said to be serving demons (Lev. 17:7, Deu. 32:17, Psa. 106:37, 1 Cor. 10:20).

It is also said that idols can neither see nor hear (Psa. 115:4, 135:16; Isa. 44:9).

Andreas Willetus (*De Eccles.*, p. 186): "The Holy Spirit is speaking here about the worship of images made of gold and silver that would take place after the opening of the seventh seal and the sounding of the sixth trumpet, which, according to the course of this prophesy, would continue for a long time after the worship of the idolatrous Gentiles had ceased, so that the Papal Church is necessarily understood here, since there is no other nation of the world that worships images in these parts of the world."

Chapter 10

Before the sounding of the seventh trumpet, John sees an angel in chapter 10, verse 11, who brings comfort in the face of those Antichrists and enemies of the Church. He is described:

I. With respect to his person , v. 1;
II. With respect to his conduct and speech, vv. 2-7;
III. With respect to the help he provides to the Church, both through John, v. 8 to the end of this chapter; and through the other two witnesses, in the next chapter.

v. 1 Καὶ εἶδον ἄλλον ἄγγελον, *and I saw another angel.*

(1) Bishops Aretas and Andreas Caesariensis understand this to be a created angel. Viegas follows them, as do Ribera and Cornelius. Viegas adds that this angel represented Christ. But he is said to be standing upon the sea and the earth.

(2) Lambert suggests that it signifies certain excellent words of the teachers of the Church. But the description of this angel does not fit with such things.

(3) Lyranus interprets it concerning Emperor Justin. Aureolus understands it to be Justinian, the grandson of Emperor Justin, who ordered the Code of Law to be written down.

(4) Many apply it to the Roman Pontiff, who spends his time thrusting his traditions onto the Church. He is called "mighty," because he has fortified his kingdom so that not even the most powerful kings are able to restrain him. He "comes down from heaven," because he pretends to be the Vicar of Christ (the first bishops were holy men). He is "cloaked in a cloud," because he covers up his hypocrisy with outward sanctimony. The "rainbow" signifies papal favors, the splendor of his ceremonies. His face is "like the sun," because he boasts that he acts in the stead of Christ. His feet are "like pillars

of fire," because his tyranny has lasted a long time. The "open book" signifies the papal doctrine.

It is better interpreted as Christ. It has been taken this way, from our own camp, by Hoehe, Kramer, and Flacius; by the papist Luis del Alcazar; and by many of the Calvinists. He is called an "angel" (Gen. 48:16; Rev. 8:3, 20:1, etc.) because of His office (Hos. 12:5, Mal. 3:1). The same angel appeared to Daniel in Daniel 12:7.

1. He aims to console the Church with this vision.

2. The description is set forth in such a way that it applies only to Christ.

3. This angel says in Rev. 11:3, "I will give power to the witnesses."

He is ἰσχυρὸν, *mighty*, because strength is ascribed to the lion (Rev. 5:5). He is called in Hebrew *gibbor* (Isa. 9:6). He is called *strong* because of His divine power, which belongs to Him essentially according to His divine nature, and personally according to His human nature, in which He surpasses all created angels.

καταβαίνοντα ἐκ τοῦ οὐρανοῦ, *coming down from heaven*, (1) by taking on human flesh (John 6:33, Psa. 72:6, Isa. 64:1); (2) by preaching the Word; (3) by the help that He supplies (Exo. 3:8, Isa. 41:4); and finally, (4) by inflicting punishment (Gen. 11:5, 19:24). The emphasis is on the third reason listed here.

περιβεβλημένον νεφέλην, *cloaked in a cloud*. The *cloud* is understood (1) by some to be the human nature of Christ, which He put on; (2) by others to be the preaching of the Gospel, in which He has, in a way, wrapped Himself up, since He pours down the rain shower of heavenly doctrine upon men. (3) Others think this is a symbol of divine majesty. (4) In the Old Testament, He appeared in a cloud quite often; He will come on the clouds; He comes to refresh His elect and make them fruitful. The first suggestion above seems preferable to the others.

Augustine, *Tract. 34 in John*: "He is covered with the cloud of flesh, not in order to obscure the light of the Sun, but in order to temper its brilliance." (Cf. Isa. 19:1.) Many of the fathers interpret the cloud as the flesh of Christ.

ἶρις ἐπὶ τῆς κεφαλῆς, *a rainbow on His head.* (1) The *rainbow* is a sign of divine grace and of our reconciliation with God (Gen. 9:8). We are preserved from the flood of divine wrath through Christ. (2) The rainbow is also a sign of serenity. Christ has brought the serenity of divine favor and peace in His descent from heaven. (3) It is likewise a sign of majesty (Sirach 43:12), and thus it appears on His head like a crown (Eze. 1:28). (4) It represents the manifold benefits of Christ. Whenever there is a rainbow, it appears in the thick rain clouds. Christ richly showers upon us the gifts of the Holy Spirit (Titus 3:7).

καὶ τὸ πρόσωπον αὐτοῦ ὡς ὁ ἥλιος, *and His face was like the sun.* (Cf. Rev. 1:16, Mat. 17:2.) He Himself is the "light of the world" (John 8:12). He shines upon us the beams of righteousness, He enlightens our hearts, etc. His body in heaven is clothed with infinite brightness. This signifies, therefore:

(1) The majesty of Christ. The sun is the highest and the most splendid light.

(2) The variety of His works. The sun shines it beams upon the whole world. The sun enlivens, dispels the clouds, banishes the cold and calms the winds.

Alcazar most ineptly applies this to "the splendor of the Roman Church, since she is the head of the mystical body of Christ."

οἱ πόδες αὐτοῦ ὡς στῦλοι πυρός, *His feet were like pillars of fire.*

(1) The right foot stands for Christ's mercy, the left for justice. (2) Some apply this to the steadfastness of the divine providence by which Christ sustains all things. (3) Others apply it to the faithful ministers of the Church. (4) It is better to say that it represents Christ's strength and power, by which He conquers the enemies of His Church. The feet prop up the whole body like columns do in a home. Heb. 1:3, "He upholds all things, etc."

Fire stands for (1) wrath against His enemies, whom He consumes; (2) the fire of grace in the Word of the Gospel, in the sending of the Holy Spirit.

v. 2 καὶ εἶχεν ἐν τῇ χειρὶ αὐτοῦ βιβλαρίδιον ἀνεῳγμένον, *and He had in His hand a little book that was open.* In chapter 5, He received a closed book from the hand of the One sitting on the throne. In chapter 6, He opened it. Here He holds it open in His hand.

(1) Some take it to be the Book of the Law and the Prophets, that is, the Scriptures. But the purpose here is to announce the future state of the Church. Nor can the Scriptures properly be called a βιβλαρίδιον, *a little book*.

(2) Others take it to be Christ Himself. They explain the seven seals as the seven mysteries of our redemption. But Christ is said to have received this little book.

(3) Aretas interprets it to be the secret of divine wisdom that has been made known to us.

(4) It represents those things that Christ has revealed to John concerning the last times, which John has described in his Revelation.

It is said to be open, because Christ has revealed those future, hidden things to John.

καὶ ἔθηκε τὸν πόδα αὐτοῦ τὸν δεξιὸν ἐπὶ τῆν θάλασσαν, *and He placed His right foot upon the sea*, etc. (1) Some think this signifies that this prophecy pertains to all men, whether they live on a continent or on the islands. (2) It is better to say that it denotes the universal dominion of Christ and the spread of the Gospel into all the lands of the world. He gathers the Church to Himself from all parts of the world. "To place one's foot somewhere" is to claim possession and dominion for oneself. Christ places His foot upon the earth and the sea, by virtue of His session at the illocal and omnipresent right hand of God.

He places His right foot, which is stronger, upon the sea, because when greater storms of persecution arise against the Church, Christ exerts greater power and strength.

v. 3 καὶ ἔκραξεν φωνῇ μεγάλῃ ὥσπερ λέων μυκᾶται, *and He cried with a loud voice as when a lion roars*. Some say that μυκᾶται is the lowing sound that cattle make, whereas ὠρύεσθαι is used for the roaring of lions. But that difference is not always observed.

This crying out signifies (1) the efficacy of the divine Word, that it is to be preached fearlessly and with great directness to instill terror in the enemy and the Antichrist; (2) the desire for our salvation in Christ. When a lion stalks his prey, he usually roars.

ἐλάλησαν αἱ ἑπτὰ βρονταί, *the seven thunders spoke.* (1) Some say that the seven thunders are a symbol of the horrible tortures that the damned will feel in hell after the final judgment, or of the terrible judgments of God.

(2) It is better to interpret them as the faithful and zealous teachers of the Gospel (Mark 3:17), who will fight against the Antichrist with the thunder of the Word. The voice of Christ will urge them to this battle.

v. 4 σφράγισον, *seal*, that is, hide it, by no means reveal it, but keep it hidden, for we seal what we want to remain secret and hidden. (Cf. Dan. 12:4, 9.)

v. 5 ἦρε τὴν χεῖρα αὐτοῦ εἰς τὸν οὐρανόν, *he raised his hand to heaven.* This was a gesture used in taking oaths (Gen. 14:22, Num. 14:30, Eze. 20:5).

v. 6 ἐν τῷ ζῶντι εἰς τοὺς αἰῶνας τῶν αἰώνων, *by Him who lives forever and ever*, by the true and eternal God, who is Life itself, who lives from eternity to eternity, and who gives life to all living creatures.

Christ confirms with an oath those things that He predicts concerning the end of the age, because He knew there would be mockers who would not believe it (2 Pet. 3:3), even as there were such men before the flood and in Sodom.

ὃς ἔκτισεν, *who created.* (Cf. Acts 4:24.) Therefore one is to swear by God alone.

ὅτι χρόνος οὐκ ἔσται ἔτι, *that there will be no more time.* When the trumpet of the seventh angel sounds, the persecutions caused by the enemies of the Church will cease, since the Last Day is going to put an end to them.

He confirms by oath that this world will perish, and then the ungodly will be sent to eternal punishment, while the godly will be honored with heavenly glory.

v. 7 τὸ μυστήριον τοῦ θεοῦ, *the mystery of God* is the perfect blessedness of the elect, which has been made known only to them; it lies hidden from the world.

ὡς εὐηγγέλισε, *as He preached the Gospel*. At that time, the sayings of the prophets will be fulfilled, concerning the destruction of all the Church's enemies, the coming of Christ for judgment, the eternal reign of Christ, and the perpetual Sabbath of the godly (Isa. 66:23; Eze. 38:2; Dan. 2:44, 7:26–27).

v. 8 πάλιν λαλοῦσα, *speaking again*, because John had already heard it (v. 4). **λάβε τὸ βιβλαρίδιον**, *take the little book*, because Christ has revealed to John the contents of this book (Rev. 1:1).

v. 9 κατάφαγε αὐτό, *devour it*. Books are metaphorically said to be "devoured" when they are avidly read, and when the things written in them are inwardly digested and stored in the entrails of the heart, inscribed on the tablets of the memory (Eze. 3:1).

πικρανεῖ σου τὴν κοιλίαν, ἀλλ' ἐν τῷ στόματί σου ἔσται γλυκὺ ὡς μέλι, *it will make your belly bitter, but in your mouth it will be sweet like honey*. This little book was sweet like honey in John's mouth; that is, the knowledge of those mysteries concerning future things delighted him (Psa. 119:103, Jer. 15:16). But he was thrust into great sadness due to the calamities he foresaw for the Church.

The enjoyment with the mouth is a symbol of the enjoyment that the godly experience from the revelation of divine mysteries, even before they fully experience them. The pain of the belly is a symbol of the pain that they experience from considering the persecution that is described in the next prophecy and that Antichrist will bring against the Church at the end of the age.

The preaching of the Word gives birth to torments: the world's hatred, persecution, exile, and martyrdom for the ministers of the Church.

For the inner man, the Word of the Gospel is sweet. But for the outer man, it is bitter on account of the mortification of the flesh.

v. 11 δεῖ σε πάλιν προφητεῦσαι ἐπὶ λαοῖς, *it is necessary for you to prophesy again to the peoples*, that is, *against the peoples*, as if he were using the Hebrew על. You must prophesy about the things that will happen to the peoples who speak different languages.

Chapter 11

The angel's help is described in the form of two witnesses. There are two parts:
I. The office of those witnesses;
II. Their fate in this office.

v. 1 Καὶ ἐδόθη μοι κάλαμος, *and I was given a reed*. John was given a reed which he was supposed to use for measuring.

Καὶ ὁ Ἄγγελος εἰστήκει, *and the angel stood*. These words are omitted in the Vulgate and in Luther's translation. But they are necessarily either added to the text, as some manuscripts include it, or they must be understood.

μέτρησον τὸν ναὸν τοῦ θεοῦ, *measure the temple of God*. The measuring reed is the Holy Scripture (Psa. 23:4, 45:7), according to which, as the only norm of faith and divine worship, one is to make judgments concerning the true Church, which is the "temple of God" (1 Cor. 3:17, 2 Cor. 6:16).

τὸ θυσιαστήριον, *the altar*, refers to the altar of sacrifice which is usually referred to simply as "the altar." It was located in the court of the priests.

Some take τοὺς προσκυνοῦντας, *those who worship*, to be the priests, but it is better to take in general about all the godly, who are spiritual priests before God.

This measuring signifies that, no matter how much both Antichrists, the Eastern and the Western, march onward in horrible fashion through corruptions of doctrine and bloodshed, nevertheless God will preserve for Himself the temple and the altar and those who worship in it, namely, the Church, which is the assembly of those who know, honor, and worship Him rightly on the basis of the Word. But it will be a "little flock" (Luke 12:32) that is able to be measured and numbered easily. This is a symbol, therefore, of the small number of believers, as spiritual priests. Some think this means that the Church, which was to be horribly devastated by Antichrist, would be rebuilt.

v. 2 καὶ τὴν αὐλὴν τὴν ἔξωθεν τοῦ ναοῦ, ἔκβαλε ἔξω, *and leave out the court that is outside the temple.* Exclude it from the dimensions so that you do not measure it. The explanation follows immediately.

The αὐλὴ ἡ ἔξωθεν is the outer court where the people would congregate. Luther read τὴν ἔσωθεν, which he rendered, "*Den innern Chor,*" the inner court. In one respect it was an outer court, and in another respect it was an inner court.

From the Word of God, which is the only norm according to which we are to make judgments about the true Church and her true members, it is clear that, although the Antichrist sits in the temple of God (2 The. 2:4), and even in the inner court, nevertheless he and his followers are not the true Church, and the Antichristian priests are not true members of the Church, much less do they have the authority to impose their traditions and superstitions on the Church.

The priests in the inner court are false, Antichristian and idolatrous priests.

ὅτι ἐδόθη τοῖς ἔθνεσι, καὶ τὴν πόλιν τὴν ἁγίαν πατήσουσι, *for it has been given to the Gentiles, and they will trample the holy city,* because the Antichristian teachers have introduced many pagan rites in the Church, and they are worse than pagans with respect to their life.

The holy city is Jerusalem (Mat. 4:5), which was a type of the true Church. The ministers of the Antichrist will trample it, that is, they will persecute and oppress the true confessors of the Gospel, and they will go about imposing their false doctrine on them.

μῆνας τεσσεράκοντα δύο, *for 42 months.* Those 42 angelic months contain 1,260 "days," that is, years (Rev. 11:3, 12:6, 13:5). The holy city is said to be trampled by the Gentiles for the same number of days as are attributed to the woman in the desert. Some claim that a definite period of time is being used for an indefinite or hidden period of time. But even if a fixed time is meant, we cannot know precisely from what point we are to begin the computation.

v. 3 Καὶ δώσω τοῖς δυσὶν μάρτυσίν μου, *and I will give my two witnesses*, scil. τὴν ἐξουσίαν, *authority*. (1) Some understand these witnesses to be the books of the Old and New Testaments.

(2) Others apply it to John Huss and Jerome of Prague, who came back to life in their successors.

(3) It is better taken in a general way to refer to the faithful teachers and confessors of the Church (Isa. 55:4; Luke 24:48; Acts 1:8, 10:39; Rev. 1:5, 2:13, 3:14) who oppose the Antichrist and expose his false doctrine and tyranny, who succeed one another in a continual series. God raised up some of them in the midst of the Antichrist's tyranny and persecution so that they might deliver a public testimony to the truth.

Two witnesses are introduced; they will be few in comparison with the multitude of the Antichristian assembly. In the meantime, it means that their testimony will be sufficiently steadfast, for they will rely on the Scriptures of the Old and New Testaments. They will preach the Law and the Gospel faithfully, and about them one will be able to say, "by the mouth of two or three witnesses, etc." (Deu. 19:15, John 8:17).

προφητεύσουσιν ἡμέρας χιλίας διακοσίας ἑξήκοντα, *they will prophesy for 1,260 days*. This, again, results in 42 angelic months, that is, 1,260 years.

Some interpret this to be the public proclamation of the divine Word and the orthodox decrees of the synods that began to prophesy—that is, to preach and teach—under Constantine.

περιβεβλημένοι σάκκους, *clothed in sackcloth*, that is, garments of mourning. This means (1) that they will prophesy at the time of the Antichristian persecution, a time that will be quite mournful and sad; (2) that they will preach repentance; (3) that they will be in a state of mourning on account of the Church, which will be miserably oppressed by the Antichristian tyranny.

v. 4 οὗτοί εἰσιν αἱ δύο ἐλαῖαι, *these are the two olive trees*. The faithful teachers of the Church, and in general all the godly, are compared to *olive trees*, (1) because of their *fertility* in doing good works, since the olive tree is very fertile; (2) because of their *firmness*. The wood of the olive tree is compromised neither by storm nor by rot nor by age; (3) because of the *richness of grace and love of the saints*; (4) *olive leaves* do not fall, just as the beauty of the good works of the saints does not fade away; (5) the *olive tree* is a symbol of the peace and mercy for which the saints strive; (6) *olives* are also, in this passage, a symbol of the comfort that the Holy Spirit works in the hearts of the godly through the preaching of the Gospel (Zec. 4:3). The Holy Spirit, who is the "oil of gladness" (Psa. 45:6), and the true "anointing" (1 John 2:20), works effective consolation in the hearts of men through the preaching of the Gospel which these two witnesses will carry out. He restores the weary souls, heals the wounded (Isa. 61:1–2) and comforts the weak.

καὶ αἱ δύο λυχνίαι, *and the two lampstands*, etc. Lampstands are a symbol of the enlightenment that the same Holy Spirit produces through the preaching of Law and Gospel (Exo. 25:31).

These two witnesses, are compared to lampstands, because through their purity of doctrine and holiness of life they light the way for others. Both parts of the analogy look back to Zechariah 4, where the governor Zerubbabel and the priest Joshua are represented by two olive trees standing on both sides of a lampstand.

For just as, at that time, it seemed impossible in the eyes of the Israelite people that the temple of the Lord could again be erected by these two men in those difficult times, so it seems impossible in our eyes that the Church should be preserved by these two witnesses under the reign of Antichrist. But just as God said at that time that it would happen, not through the strength of armies, but through the Spirit, so God subdues the Antichrist, not by a physical army, but by the Spirit of the mouth of Christ (2 The. 2:8, Isa. 11:4).

v. 5 καὶ εἴ τις αὐτοὺς θέλει ἀδικῆσαι, *and if anyone wants to injure them*. They will attack the Antichrist with great strength of spirit, and if anyone wishes to oppose them, they will defend themselves, not with external strength, but with the fire that proceeds from their mouth, that is, with the word of God, which is "like fire" (Jer. 5:14, 23:29; Heb. 4:12). They will also be inflamed with the zeal of the Spirit in their preaching, so that the enemies of the Word feel a fire in their consciences that will torment them more severely than fire does the body. Their fiery prayers will also be granted, so that God consumes their persecutors with the fire of His wrath, just it was granted to Elijah that fire from heaven fell upon those who came to take him into custody (2 Kings 1:10, 12).

v. 6 οὗτοι ἔχουσιν ἐξουσίαν κλεῖσαι τὸν οὐρανόν, *these have the authority to shut heaven.* Just as Elijah shut heaven with his prayers so that it did not send down rain for three and a half years (1 Kings 17:1; Luke 4:25; James 5:17), so these two witnesses will shut heaven to impenitent sinners so that neither the dew of divine grace nor the salutary rain of the Holy Spirit descend upon them (Psa. 68:10, Zec. 14:17). They will, in like manner, pronounce all kinds of plagues on the impenitent in the name of Christ, which will most certainly oppress them.

καὶ ἐξουσίαν ἔχουσιν ἐπὶ τῶν ὑδάτων, στρέφειν αὐτὰ εἰς αἷμα, *and they have authority over the waters, to turn them into blood.* Just as Moses changed water into blood before the king of Egypt and struck the land of Egypt with all kinds of plagues (Exo. 7 ff.), so these two witnesses will pronounce plagues upon the ungodly who despise the Word, and especially on those who hold the Church captive with their traditions. The gifts and benefits of God will be turned into curses and punishments because of their ingratitude and abuse of those gifts. These two witnesses will announce that God is going to withhold seasonal and late rains so that the earth does not bear its fruit, and at the same time He will rain down war and bloodshed so that the waters are turned into blood. He will also inflict on them the other plagues He has threatened (Lev. 26, Deu. 28).

v. 7 Καὶ ὅταν τελέσωσι τὴν μαρτυρίαν αὐτῶν, τὸ θηρίον τὸ ἀναβαῖνον ἐκ τῆς ἀβύσσου ποιήσει πόλεμον, *and when they complete their testimony, the beast that comes up from the abyss will make war.* The testimony of these prophets is their preaching.

The beast coming up from the abyss is the Antichrist, whom they are attacking, whose supremacy is of the devil (Rev. 13:11, 17:8).

νικήσει αὐτοὺς, *he will overcome them.* He will vanquish and kill them with respect to their body and life, using external power.

v. 8 καὶ τὸ πτώματα αὐτῶν ἐπὶ ταῖς πλατείαις, *and their corpses on the streets, etc.* This is said spiritually, that is, figuratively, according to the spiritual sense.

The great city is Rome and wherever the power of the Church of Rome extends, since the head of the Roman Church resides in Rome.

It is called: (1) Sodom, because of physical and spiritual fornication, that is, idolatry, because of Sodom-like sins;

(2) Egypt, because of the tyranny that it exercises against the godly;

(3) Jerusalem, because it still to this day crucifies Christ in His members (Zec. 2:8, Acts 9:5). It follows the ungodliness of Jerusalem, which it manifested in crucifying Christ.

ὅπου, *where*, that is, under whose rule and dominion the Lord was crucified. Or it refers to Rome, as the place where Christ crucified was preached (Gal. 3:1).

This is said for the consolation of those prophets, so that they remember that it is an honorable thing for them to die for Christ in the same city where Christ was crucified for them.

Jerome, in *Epistle 17*, which he wrote to Marcella in the name of Paula and Eustochius, says this in treating this passage: "The names Egypt and Sodom do not refer to Jerusalem, but to that world that is the great city built by Cain, (1) because in this same chapter Jerusalem was called "the holy city"; (2) because in Holy Scripture, the world, not Jerusalem, is often referred to as Egypt and Sodom." (Cf. Eze. 16:55; Jude 5 and 6.)

v. 9 καὶ βλέψουσιν ἐκ τῶν λαῶν, *and from the peoples they will see*, etc. This means that the Antichrist, during his reign, will so cruelly pursue the confessors of the Word who oppose his tyranny that he will not be satisfied with their death, but will also put their unburied corpses on display to terrorize the others, even digging them up from their graves.

The *three and a half days* stand for a brief and short time, by way of synecdoche. The papists understand this to mean that "the kingdom of the Antichrist will last for only three and a half years."

v. 10 καὶ οἱ κατοικοῦντες ἐπὶ τῆς γῆς χαροῦσιν, *and those who dwell on the earth will rejoice*. The ungodly and earthly men (Rev. 8:13). The Antichristian tyrants and their followers will rejoice over them, that is, over their death, and will publicly boast of their slaughter.

ὅτι οὗτοι οἱ δύο προφῆται ἐβασάνισαν τοὺς κατοικοῦντας, *for these two prophets tormented those who dwell*, because they rebuked their idolatry, superstitions, and other sins, and announced God's judgments upon them.

v. 11 Καὶ μετὰ τὰς τρεῖς ἡμέρας καὶ ἥμισυ, *and after the three and a half days*, during which their unburied corpses lay in the streets, πνεῦμα ζωῆς ἐκ τοῦ θεοῦ εἰσῆλθεν ἐπ' αὐτούς, *the Spirit of life from God came upon them*. The papists take these things literally. But everything in this book is figurative.

The Spirit of life came upon them, that is, God would continually raise them up, for He would stir up other faithful and genuine teachers in their place. The joy and exultation of the Antichristian persecutors did not last long, for in the place of the witnesses who were executed, God substituted and stirred up others who, by preaching the Word, will attack the Antichrist and his kingdom and errors by the same strength of spirit and with the same boldness. Therefore these two witnesses will be raised up in their successors, whom God will "clothe with power from on high" (Luke 24:49), so that they may continue the battle against the Antichrist. This is what Herod said about Christ: "He is John the Baptist who has risen from the dead" (Mat. 14:2, Mark 6:14).

καὶ φόβος μέγας ἔπεσεν, *and great fear fell*. They were afraid that they would again be tortured by them (v. 6). They were discovering with fear and terror that not all the witnesses had been taken out of the way, but that new ones were continually being raised up.

v. 12 καὶ ἤκουσαν, *and they heard*. The two witnesses who had been killed by the Antichrist and raised again heard a φωνὴν μεγάλην, *a loud voice*.

Their ascension into heaven means: (1) that the souls of the faithful teachers and martyrs of Christ are made partakers of heavenly glory and joy, even though their bodies remain buried; (2) that God will protect these witnesses with the cloud of His omnipotence; (3) that even in the most severe persecutions, they will be raised up by this comfort of being taken up into glory.

καὶ ἐθεώρησαν αὐτοὺς οἱ ἐχθροὶ αὐτῶν, *and their enemies saw them*, they saw them ascend into heaven, that is, they were able to gather from their perseverance, patience, and the blessed way in which they died, that they were faithful servants of God, and that they were consequently received into heavenly glory.

v. 13 σεισμὸς μέγας, *a great earthquake*. This earthquake signifies the shaking of the Antichristian kingdom, for many empires that marched on Rome inflicted bloody massacres on it and laid waste to the city, etc.

ὀνόματα ἀνθρώπων, *names of men*, that is, men. (Cf. Acts 1:15, Rev. 3:4.) *Seven thousand*, all of them called by their names.

καὶ οἱ λοιποὶ ἔμφοβοι ἐγένοντο καὶ ἔδωκαν δόξαν, *and the rest became fearful and gave glory*. They acknowledged and confessed the righteous judgment of God, they feared God, and they separated themselves from the kingdom of the Antichrist.

v. 14 Ἡ οὐαὶ ἡ δευτέρα ἀπῆλθεν, *the second woe has passed*. With the first two woes, all kinds of physical punishments are announced for the ungodly. But the third woe announces the eternal punishment of hell. (Cf. Rev. 8:13, 9:12.)

The seventh trumpet and the third woe are then described, v. 15 to the end of chapter 11.

v. 15 φωναὶ μεγάλαι, *loud voices*, namely, of the angels and the spirits of the blessed, giving thanks to Christ the Victor.

ἐγένετο ἡ βασιλεία τοῦ κόσμου τοῦ κυρίου ἡμῶν, *the kingdom of the world has become the kingdom of our Lord*. The kingdoms of the world have been destroyed, the enemies wiped out. Now the heavenly Father alone reigns with Christ. The kingdoms of the world have come into their possession; they have yielded to Him, etc.

This is a reference to Daniel 2:44. "In the days of those kingdoms God will set up a kingdom." The sense, therefore, is this: The end of the world and Judgment Day are approaching (James 5:9), when the kingdoms of this world will be removed (1 Cor. 15:25). All the enemies of Christ will be placed under His feet. The kingdom of glory will begin, in which Christ will reign eternally with the Father (Dan. 7:14).

v. 16 Καὶ οἱ εἴκοσι καὶ τέσσαρες πρεσβύτεροι, *and the twenty-four elders, etc.* These are a type of the entire Church Triumphant (Rev. 4:4).

v. 17 ὁ ὤν, *who is,* immutable in divine essence, καὶ ὁ ἦν, *and who was,* from eternity, καὶ ὁ ἐρχόμενος, *and who is to come,* who remains eternally (Rev. 1:4).

εἴληφας τὴν δύναμίν σου τὴν μεγάλην, *You have taken Your great power.* You have exercised and demonstrated Your great power against the enemies of the Church, whom You have placed under Your Son's feet. (Cf. Psa. 110:1, 1 Cor. 15:26.)

καὶ ἐβασίλευσας, *and You have reigned.* You demonstrated Your royal power after You made all Your enemies a footstool for Your feet. You reign in the kingdom of glory for all eternity. You show that You are the King of kings, etc.

v. 18 καὶ τὰ ἔθνη ὠργίσθησαν, *and the nations were angry.* The nations persecuted the Church with terrible rage. Therefore Your wrath came upon them, and by it, You cast them down into hell (Deu. 32:22).

ἦλθεν ἡ ὀργή σου, *Your wrath has come,* the Day of Wrath has come. He has determined to pour it out against the ungodly.

καὶ ὁ καιρὸς τῶν νεκρῶν, *and the time of the dead,* has come. The time has come for the dead to be raised, "some to life, others to disgrace" (Dan. 12:2).

κριθῆναι, *to be judged,* a passive verb. Luther translated it actively, *zu richten.* The sense is the same. "The day is coming in which the world will be judged in justice" (Acts 17:31), and the reward of grace, namely, the crown of life and of glory, will be presented to the godly confessors.

καὶ διαφθεῖραι τοὺς διαφθείροντας, *and to destroy those who destroy.* The day is coming when they will be cast down into eternal destruction who corrupted and destroyed the inhabitants of the earth with their idolatry and false doctrine, with their ungodly and scandalous life, with bloodshed and fire, and who persevered in these terrible deeds without repentance.

v. 19 Καὶ ἠνοίγη ὁ ναὸς τοῦ θεοῦ ἐν τῷ οὐρανῷ, *and the temple of God in heaven was opened.* The opening of the temple of God in heaven signifies the most glorious revelation of glory and happiness that the blessed obtain in heaven (Col. 3:4, 1 John 3:2). It represents the entrance of the elect into heavenly glory, that they may serve God (Rev. 7:15). When it says in Rev. 21:22 that there is no temple in the heavenly Jerusalem, it should be understood concerning a material and earthly temple.

καὶ ὤφθη ἡ κιβωτὸς τῆς διαθήκης αὐτοῦ ἐν τῷ ναῷ, *and the ark of His covenant was seen in the temple.* Concerning the ark, (1) some think it means the hidden mysteries of the future things that are prefigured as being hidden in the ark. So the sense is that God has revealed to him His mysteries, which, until that point, were hidden from the Church.

(2) Primasius, Bede, and Rupert take it to refer to the human nature of Christ, which is shown to be visible and profitable to the elect. Both explanations can be combined. Christ Jesus, who was prefigured by the ark of the covenant in the Old Testament, will then be seen by all the elect in unspeakable joy; He will reveal all mysteries to them very clearly.

καὶ ἐγένοντο ἀστραπαὶ, *and there were lightnings, etc.* (1) In the Day of Judgment, God will send forth thunder and lightning against the Antichrist and his followers (Psa. 11:6). A fiery ray will flash against them from the tribunal of Christ (Dan. 7:10). In other words, the sentence of condemnation has been pronounced (Mat. 25:41).

(2) The Antichrist and all the ungodly will be cast down into hell by this sentence like lightning (Rev. 20:14).

Chapter 12

This chapter contains the beginning of the fourth vision, in which are described two groups that are contrasted with one another, the woman and the dragon, Michael and the dragon, v. 1 to the end of the chapter.

v. 1 Καὶ σημεῖον μέγα ὤφθη ἐν τῷ οὐρανῷ, *and a great sign was seen in heaven*. *A great sign*, that is, signifying great things.

γυνὴ περιβεβλημένη τὸν ἥλιον, *a woman clothed with the sun*. (1) Some take this woman to be "Mary ever-virgin, the mother of Christ the Savior." Piscator and Tossanus say that the words, ἐν γαστρὶ ἔχουσα, *having in her womb*, refer to "the time when Christ was to be born." But Methodius, together with Andreas Caesariensis, properly deny that "the Blessed Virgin is here symbolized, since the birth of Christ had already taken place, whereas John is dealing with future things."

(2) Therefore, it is better to say that this woman represents the true Church Militant on this earth, whose state is being described, not such as it was before the first coming of Christ—this opinion can be opposed with the same argument that was used to oppose the earlier one—but such as it is before Christ's second coming.

Blasius de Viegas on this passage: "The common exposition of the interpreters is that this woman is the Church. Therefore, those who interpret this vision concerning Blessed Mary are following, not the literal and historical sense, but the figurative and allegorical sense. Besides this, the whole vision is incompatible with the Virgin."

This woman appears as clothed with the *sun*. (1) By faith, she is clothed with Christ, the Sun of Righteousness (Mal. 4:2). For all true believers and living members of the Church put on Christ in Baptism by faith (Gal. 3:27), and then also by the holy conduct of their life (Rom. 13:14). This is the robe of righteousness in which believers are pleasing to God (Isa. 61:10).

(2) She will eventually be clothed with heavenly glory, in which she will shine like the sun (Mat. 13:43).

ἡ σελήνη ὑποκάτω τῶν ποδῶν αὐτῆς, *the moon under her feet*, because the Church tramples and holds in contempt the riches and pleasures of this world, for they are like the phases of the moon: variable and mutable.

καὶ ἐπὶ τῆς κεφαλῆς αὐτῆς στέφανος ἀστέρων δώδεκα, *and upon her head a crown of twelve stars*. The *crown* is a symbol of the glory that the Church has from Christ her Head, as well as the gifts of the Holy Spirit.

The twelve stars in the crown signify the twelve apostles, through whose doctrine the faithful are led to heavenly glory. The Church holds this doctrine as the crown of her heart; she is adorned with it as with a beautiful crown before God.

v. 2 καὶ ἐν γαστρὶ ἔχουσα, *and having in her belly*. Piscator and Tossanus claim that this is a symbol of the approaching time when Christ was to be born. Κράζει ὠδίνουσα, *she cries out in labor*, that is, she desired the coming of Christ by which she was to be set free. This represents that earnest desire with which the godly in the Old Testament awaited the birth of Christ. Καὶ βασανιζομένη τεκεῖν, *and in pain to give birth*, because the Church was oppressed before the birth of Christ.

But we have already admonished that John, in this passage, is not acting as a historian who describes the things that have taken place, but as a prophet who is foretelling future things (Rev. 1:1).

Therefore, it is better to say that this vision signifies the persecutions that the New Testament Church has sustained under pagan emperors and under the Antichrist. For she is known to give birth to her spiritual children, true believers, with great pain, and she is subject to great persecutions in this world (Gal. 4:19).

v. 3 καὶ ὤφθη ἄλλο σημεῖον ἐν τῷ οὐρανῷ, καὶ ἰδοὺ δράκων μέγας, *and another sign was seen in heaven, and behold, a great dragon*. The word "dragon" comes from the Greek word δέρκειν, "to see clearly." This etymology agrees best with the matter being discussed, namely, with the devil, who is intent to harm the godly at all times, in every way possible, and to strike them with his poisonous venom.

This dragon, therefore, is a symbol of the devil (v. 9). He is called "great," who later is called "the ancient serpent, Satan," (1) because of his power over the ungodly (Eph. 2:2). "He is at work in the sons of disobedience"; (2) because of the great size of his kingdom, to which all the ungodly belong.

πυρρὸς, *fiery red*. This color is a symbol of cruelty, because it is red like the spilled blood of the godly (John 8:44). He is a murderer; he incites bloody wars.

ἔχων κεφαλὰς ἑπτὰ, *having seven heads*. These heads are a symbol of the perfect craftiness and cunning in his methods (Eph. 6:11). In order to propagate his kingdom, he uses the work of cunning men who devise all kinds of heresies and cover them up with spectacular colors. He likewise uses the work of the most powerful men, who instigate persecutions against the Church.

κέρατα δέκα, *ten horns*. These are a symbol of the strength he wields. "*Gross Macht und viel List*"—"deep guile and great might, etc."

καὶ ἐπὶ τὰς κεφαλὰς αὐτοῦ διαδήματα ἑπτὰ, *and upon his heads, seven diadems*. The word "diadem" is from the Greek word διαδέω, "to bind, to encircle." It is the band that is especially used as a royal headband, a white circlet. (Cf. Cael. Rhodig., Book XXIV, *Lect. Antiq.*, ch. 6.) These diadems signify that the ungodly kings of this age submit to him who uses their work to incite persecutions against the Church.

v. 4 καὶ ἡ οὐρὰ αὐτοῦ σύρει τὸ τρίτον τῶν ἀστέρων, *and his tail drew a third of the stars*. The devil seduces some of those teachers of the Church who once shined as brightly as the stars with their doctrine and life (Rev. 1:20), so that they turn to earthly things, namely, riches, honor, and pleasure, forgetting their prior heavenly conduct. He also seduces many believers who were once zealous in confessing the doctrine and, through their holy conduct, were lamps giving light to the world. (Cf. Phi. 2:15.)

This means that the devil deceives many notable and famous people in this world with his flattery and treachery and turns their hearts away from heavenly things to earthly things.

Καὶ ὁ δράκων ἕστηκεν ἐνώπιον τῆς γυναικὸς τῆς μελλούσης τεκεῖν, *and the dragon stood before the woman who was about to give birth*, that is, he lay in wait to trap her, or rather, he rashly and impudently opposed her to her face.

ἵνα ὅταν τέκῃ τὸ τέκνον αὐτῆς καταφάγῃ, *so that when she gave birth, he might devour her child*, that is, that he might kill him and completely wipe him out. Those who say this refers to Mary explain it this way, "that Satan tried to kill Christ, first through Herod, then in temptations, and then through the Pharisees, priests and scribes." But it is better to take it as a reference to the members of Christ's mystical body, such that the devil seeks to kill and swallow up the true believers, who are the spiritual sons of God and of the Church. (Cf. 1 Pet. 5:8.)

v. 5 καὶ ἔτεκεν υἱὸν ἄρσεν, *and she bore a male son*. Those who apply this to Mary explain thus:"The Church before Christ was finally granted the object of her desire when Christ was born." But it is better to take it to refer to the members of Christ. The Church gives birth to Christ in the members of His mystical body. For Christ has a twofold body: first, a personal body, that is, the true human nature that He has personally joined with His divine nature. According to this personal body, that is, according to the human nature that was personally united with the Logos, He was born a single time of the Virgin Mary. Secondly, He has a spiritual or mystical body, whose members are all those who are truly godly, of whom He Himself is the Head. According to this spiritual body the Church still gives birth to Him on a daily basis. For whatever properly applies to the members is attributed to the Head on account of the spiritual and intimate union of the Head and the members. (Cf. Hos. 11:1; Mat. 2:15; Acts 9:4–5; Gal. 4:19; Col. 1:24.)

This woman gave birth under Emperor Constantine the Great in the very Synod that was celebrated in Nicaea in the year 325 after having previously endured many persecutions under the pagan emperors for nine full angelic months and twelve days, being pregnant from Christ, her Bridegroom. The son whom she bore is the public profession and affirmation of Christ Jesus throughout the whole Roman world. But the dragon, in his attempt to snuff out the one who was born, stirred up the Arians and other heretics. But this son was taken up into heaven, etc., as follows afterward.

ὃς μέλλει ποιμαίνειν πάντα τὰ ἔθνη ἐν ῥάβδῳ σιδηρᾷ, *who will shepherd all the nations with a rod of iron*. This majesty and power belong chiefly and properly to Christ, but in a certain way He communicates it to believers as members of His mystical body.

καὶ ἡρπάσθη τὸ τέκνον αὐτῆς πρὸς τὸν θεὸν, καὶ τὸν θρόνον αὐτοῦ, *and her child was caught up to God and His throne.* Christ, the Head of the Church and His mystical body, when His earthly ministry was completed, ascended into heaven and was placed at the right hand of His heavenly Father, and thus He was removed from the infernal dragon's fury that assailed Him during His days in the flesh. But the members of His mystical body, that is, those who truly believe, have also been resurrected together with Him and exalted to the heavens in Christ (Eph. 2:5).

v. 6 καὶ ἡ γυνὴ ἔφυγεν εἰς τὴν ἔρημον, ὅπου ἔχει ἐκεῖ τόπον ἡτοιμασμένον ἀπὸ τοῦ θεοῦ, *and the woman fled into the desert, where she has a place prepared by God.* Piscator explains this flight as the flight of Christians from the city of Jerusalem into the town of Pella. On account of the brutal persecutions, the members of the Church, the true confessors, will be forced to flee from one place to another (1 Cor. 4:11, Heb. 11:38). They will be compelled to hide from the tyrannical persecutors and to be fed in the desert.

ἵνα ἐκεῖ τρέφωσιν αὐτὴν ἡμέρας χιλίας διακοσίας ἑξήκοντα, *that they may feed her there for 1,260 days.* In this way, then, that male child obtained God as his defender and was caught up into heaven by Him, and mother Church found lodging in some quiet places. But above all, this signifies that during Antichrist's reign, the true Church will be carried off into hiding and will have no external glory, but will be preserved as in the desert somewhere. For God powerfully preserved her and protected her under the shadow of His wings, not only at the time of the persecutions of the pagan emperors, but also at the time of those persecutions incited against the Church by the Antichrist. He fed her by the word of the two witnesses described above, since the true confessors were forced to hide together with them in the forests and deserts. The number "1,260 days" stands for the same number of years that the tyranny of the Antichrist will endure.

v. 7 Καὶ ἐγένετο πόλεμος ἐν τῷ οὐρανῷ, ὁ Μιχαὴλ καὶ οἱ ἄγγελοι αὐτοῦ τοῦ πολεμῆσαι, *and there was war in heaven, Michael and his angels were making war, etc.*

(1) Lyranus takes Michael to be Emperor Heraclius, who made war against Khosrau on behalf of the Christians.

(2) Others take him to refer to Constantine the Great, while they take the dragon to refer to Maxentius, Maximus, and Licinius.

(3) Blasius de Viegas, Ribera, and Cornelius de Lapide think it refers to the supreme angel among those who stood fast on the truth. Daniel mentions Michael the archangel in Dan. 10:13. (Cf. Jude 9.) But after the devil was cast out of heavenly glory and happiness once for all because of his apostasy, he no longer enters heaven.

(4) It is better to take him as Christ, (i) for the name "Michael" applies to Him above all others. "Who is like God," that is, equal to God. He is of one essence and power with the Father. (ii) In Dan. 12:1, He is likewise called "Michael." (iii) The hymn of praise in v. 10 expressly deals with Christ. "Now is salvation accomplished, and the kingdom of our God, and the authority of His Christ." (iv) Michael is emphatically said to have fought together with His angels, who were created by Him and appointed to serve Him (Col. 1:16). This name sends us back to the twelfth chapter of Daniel, where it is predicted that, in the last days, Michael will fight for His people. It is the prevailing office of an angel to defend the Church. Since the dragon is attacking the woman, that is, the Church and her true members, with great might, Christ undertakes her defense and fights against the dragon. (v) From the Hebrews: "Michael, in Dan. 12:1, is called the High Priest of heaven, offering the prayers and souls of the righteous to God" (Manahem 13:1). (See Masius, *In Josuam*, p. 95.)

Drusius (*Ad Jos.*, p. 43) denies that Michael can be interpreted as Christ. "For," he says, "Michael and his angels fight for the Lamb, who is Christ." We reply that, in v. 11, which Drusius presses, those who have "overcome" are not Michael and his angels, but the Christian brethren, namely, those whom the dragon accused before the face of God. They are the ones who overcame by the blood of the Lamb. With the word "angels," we understand, not only the blessed spirits in heaven (Mat. 16:27, 24:31), but also all the believers of the Church, just as the "angels of the dragon" are not only evil spirits, but also the persecutors, heretics, and similar scales of the dragon. This explanation is confirmed from 2 Cor. 10:5.

The fighting of Michael and the dragon we interpret to be the vanquishing of heathenism through the preaching of the Gospel.

Ambrosius Ansbertus on this passage: "Michael, which means, 'Who is like God?,' represents Christ. A battle has been fought in heaven. That is, on account of heaven, for the sake of the salvation of all the elect, Michael fought with the dragon. That is, Christ, by preaching, suffering, and dying, fought for the salvation of the human race. The angels of Michael, namely, the apostles of Christ, fought with the dragon, namely, by preaching, working miracles, and ultimately dying for the name of Christ."

Luis de Alcazar likewise interprets Michael as Christ, and His angels as the apostles and preachers who cast out the dragon, that is, the devil and his worship, from the heathen. He interprets the dragon and his angels as Nero, Simon Magus, and others through whom the infernal dragon sought to assail the Church.

v. 8 καὶ οὐκ ἴσχυσαν, *and they*—that is, the dragon and his angels—*did not prevail*. For how could the devil prevail against Christ, who is "the power of God" (1 Cor. 1:24)? "The prince of this world is coming, etc." (John 14:30). Here, then, is fulfilled what Christ predicted (Mat. 16:18).

οὐδὲ τόπος εὑρέθη αὐτῶν ἔτι ἐν τῷ οὐρανῷ, *nor was their place found any longer in heaven*. They were expelled from heaven, put to flight and sent into exile (Psa. 37:36, Dan. 2:35). But this took place in a vision and is expressed in the form of a parable, as in 1 Kings 22:21 and Job 1:6.

v. 9 καὶ ἐβλήθη ὁ δράκων ὁ μέγας, ὁ ὄφις ὁ ἀρχαῖος, *and the great dragon was cast out, the ancient serpent*. (Cf. Rev. 20:2.) He is called a serpent in Gen. 3:1. He is a serpent on account of his craftiness, and because he seduced our first parents through a serpent. He is called ancient, because already long ago, immediately after the world was made, he deceived the first human beings, and he has been practicing his cruelty and deceptions for a long time.

This casting out signifies the efficacy of the glorious and victorious resurrection and ascension of Christ, by which He conquered the devil and hell. It also signifies the preaching of the Gospel, through which the devil is, in a sense, expelled from heaven and crushed under our feet (Luke 10:18, Rom. 16:20).

Διάβολος, *devil*, comes from the Greek word διαβάλλειν, *to dash to pieces*, because he perverts and dashes the Scriptures to pieces (Mat. 4:6). He also causes ruin by blaspheming, because he blasphemously accuses God before men, men before God, and men before one another (Gen. 3:5, Job 1:9).

Σατανᾶς, *Satan, adversary*, because he is the sworn enemy of God and men (Zec. 3:1).

ὁ πλανῶν τὴν οἰκουμένην ὅλην, *who deceives the whole world*, those who do not allow themselves to be ruled by the Spirit of God, but have the spirit of the world as their ruler (1 Cor. 2:12).

ἐβλήθη εἰς τὴν γῆν, *he was cast down to the earth*. To the lower regions of the earth. This is a reference to the curse that God inflicted on the serpent after the transgression of our first parents. "You will crawl on your belly."

καὶ οἱ ἄγγελοι αὐτοῦ μετ' αὐτοῦ ἐβλήθησαν, *and his angels were cast down with him*. This casting down of the dragon and his angels from heaven signifies that, after Christ conquered the devil by His death and resurrection and removed his power (Heb. 2:14), and, in His ascension, plundered the principalities and powers (Col. 2:4, 15) and sat down at the right hand of His heavenly Father, He saw to it that this victory was published throughout the entire world, and thus, by the preaching of the Gospel, He saw to it that this reported victory over the devil was announced in the whole world. In this way, the devil was expelled from the hearts of men and crushed under His feet (Rom. 16:20). "I saw Satan as lightning, etc." (Luke 10:18). Next, this victory and casting out of Satan took place at the time of Constantine, when the most severe persecutions under the pagan emperors ceased and the Church was granted respite. But chiefly this battle and subsequent victory over the infernal dragon has our times in view, when, through the preaching of the Gospel, the kingdom of the Antichrist has been opposed and the doctrine of demons expelled from the Church (1 Tim. 4:1). And finally, that casting out will take place most perfectly on the Day of Judgment, when the dragon, together with his angels, will be thrown into the infernal lake (Rev. 20:14).

v. 10 καὶ ἤκουσα φωνὴν μεγάλην, *and I heard a loud voice*. This is the victory ode of the godly on account of Michael's victory over the dragon, for in this battle Michael is set forth as the Church's unconquered hero and avenger.

ὁ κατήγορος τῶν ἀδελφῶν ἡμῶν, *the accuser of our brothers.* This phrase is omitted from Luther's German translation.

v. 11 καὶ αὐτοὶ ἐνίκησαν αὐτὸν διὰ τὸ αἷμα τοῦ ἀρνίου, *and they*—that is, the believers—*overcame him on account of the blood of the Lamb,* because they firmly believe that Christ, for their sakes, conquered the devil and his infernal powers through His death and the shedding of His blood; and in true faith, they set His victory against the devil's accusations (Rom. 8:33).

καὶ διὰ τὸν λόγον τῆς μαρτυρίας αὐτῶν, *and on account of the word of their testimony,* because they remained constant in confessing the Gospel, which is the testimony about Christ.

καὶ οὐκ ἠγάπησαν τὴν ψυχὴν αὐτῶν ἄχρι θανάτου, *and they did not love their life until death.* They did not love their life in such a way that they abandoned the truth of the Gospel in order to preserve it, but remained constant in confessing Christ until death.

v. 12 διὰ τοῦτο εὐφραίνεσθε οἱ οὐρανοί, καὶ οἱ ἐν αὐτοῖς σκηνοῦντες, *therefore, rejoice, O heavens, and those who dwell therein.* The heavens represent all the elect believers of God, whose "names are written in the heavens" (Luke 10:20), and whose "conduct is in heaven" (Phi. 3:20).

Οὐαὶ τοῖς κατοικοῦσι τὴν γῆν, *woe to those who inhabit the earth.* (Cf. Rev. 3:10, 13:14.) These are the ungodly, who cling in their hearts to earthly things, "who set their mind on earthly things" (Phi. 3:19), who "love the world and the things that are in the world" (1 John 2:15), even though all things in the world—honor, riches, pleasure and power—are as unsteady as the sea.

The inhabitants of the earth are contrasted with the inhabitants of heaven, where the godly have their πολίτευμα, their *citizenship*. The inhabitants of the earth aspire toward earthly things and suspire after earthly things until they finally expire. For those who inhabit the earth, their face may well look upward, but their soul is fixed on the earthly things for which they pine away.

ὅτι κατέβη ὁ διάβολος πρὸς ὑμᾶς, *for the devil has gone down to you.* The time of judgment is approaching, when he will be cast headlong into the infernal lake so that he cannot freely exert his tyranny on this earth.

v. 13 Καὶ ὅτε εἶδεν ὁ δράκων…ἐδίωξεν τὴν γυναῖκα, *and when the dragon saw… he pursued the woman.* He would stir up terrible persecutions against the Church of Christ, because the devil never stops laying traps for believers and persecuting the Church, until his kingdom is completely destroyed and he is cast with all the damned into the infernal lake.

Thus in this section, the state of the Church on earth before the final coming of Christ is being described.

v. 14 καὶ ἐδόθησαν τῇ γυναικὶ δύο πτέρυγες, *and there were given to the woman two wings.* This is a metaphor that stands for an astonishing and unexpected liberation. It signifies: (1) the happy and speedy course of the Gospel. For even if the Church is banished from one place and sent into exile, yet it finds a home in another place; (2) divine protection, that, in the midst of the most severe persecutions incited by the devil, God takes His beloved people and shelters them under the shadow of His wings (Deu. 32:11; Psa. 27:5; Psa. 91:4), and at times, He frees them from danger and tribulation through miraculous means.

Two wings of a great eagle, that is, like the wings of some great eagle.

These are not the wings of a pigeon, but of an eagle, because the confessors of Christ do not run away out of some baseless fear, but must continue serving God in the Church for a while longer out of reverent obedience. The great eagle is brave, because the Church flees, not in timidity, but in bravery, to follow God's will better in the place and time that is most pleasing to Him.

ἵνα πέτηται εἰς τὴν ἔρημον, *that she may fly into the desert.* The desert represents a remote and hidden place.

ὅπου τρέφεται ἐκεῖ καιρὸν καὶ καιροὺς καὶ ἥμισυ καιροῦ, ἀπὸ προσώπου τοῦ ὄφεως, *where she may be nourished for a time and times and half a time from before the face of the serpent.* The *time, times and half a time* signify three and a half years. (Cf. Dan. 7:25, 17:7; Rev. 11:2–3.) If calculated in months, it amounts to 42 months. If calculated in days, it amounts to 1,260 days, counting 30 days per month. It signifies, by way of synecdoche, a time defined by God, but unknown to us.

v. 15 καὶ ἔβαλεν ὁ ὄφις ὀπίσω τῆς γυναικὸς ἐκ τοῦ στόματος αὐτοῦ ὕδωρ ὡς ποταμόν, ἵνα αὐτὴν ποταμοφόρητον ποιήσῃ, *and the* *serpent spewed water after the woman from his mouth like a river, that he might cause her to be carried away by the river.* He *spewed water after the woman,* that is, he gathered a vast army, that it might be able to wipe out and ruin the Church, while stirring up the powerful men of this age against her with deception and lies.

The river has three meanings: (1) The temptation that takes place through flattery and great promises of temporal goods and pleasures of this age. By this water of pleasures, many are seduced and cast headlong into ruin. (2) Persecution (Psa. 65:8, 124:4–5). (3) The heresies that men will imbibe like water (Job 15:17).

That he might cause her to be carried away by the river, that is, that the river of persecution might carry her away. The Greek construction is quite lovely.

After the persecutions ceased and the Church was given peace, the devil tried another manner of attack in the year 361. He *spewed a great river after the woman,* namely, the cruel tyrant Julian the Apostate. But *the earth swallowed up this river,* that is, that tyrant was wounded in the Persian war and buried in a tomb. *Therefore the dragon went off to make war with her seed,* that is, with the rest of the saints, through heresies and persecutors. The woman is kept *in the desert,* that is, in a small assembly made up of few people, *for a time, times, and half a time,* that is, in angelic days, 1,260 years. If one begins counting from the time of Julian, then the end will come in the year 1622.

v. 16 καὶ ἐβοήθησεν ἡ γῆ τῇ γυναικὶ καὶ ἤνοιξεν ἡ γῆ τὸ στόμα αὐτῆς, *and the earth helped the woman, and the earth opened its mouth,* etc. The earth helps believers in the face of dangerous temptations, because when they see the example of those who live in carnal pleasures and then suffer a miserable result, they are made to fear. The earth helps believers in the face of persecutions and heresies as they are laid to rest in her by the singular benefit of God, just as the raging torrent is swallowed up by the earth; and as, by the just judgment of God, the tyrants and persecutors are suddenly swept away and deposited in the earth. God quite often acts by His miraculous providence so that the enemy armies that seek to destroy the Church are miraculously wiped out.

v. 17 καὶ ὠργίσθη ὁ δράκων ἐπὶ τῇ γυναικὶ, *and the dragon was furious with the woman,* because neither by temptations with flattery nor by persecutions and heresies could he prevail against her and her true members.

καὶ ἀπῆλθε ποιῆσαι πόλεμον μετὰ τῶν λοιπῶν τοῦ σπέρματος αὐτῆς, *and he went away to make war against the rest of her seed,* that is, with the believers of the early Church who were born of the preaching of the Gospel, and with the small, surviving assembly of believers.

τῶν τηρούντων τὰς ἐντολὰς τοῦ θεοῦ καὶ ἐχόντων μαρτυρίαν τοῦ Ἰησοῦ Χριστοῦ, *who keep the commandments of God and have the witness of Jesus Christ,* who steadfastly keep the word of the Gospel, which is the testimony about Christ (Rev. 6:9).

v. 18 Καὶ ἐστάθην ἐπὶ τὴν ἄμμον τῆς θαλάσσης, *and [the dragon] stood upon the sand of the sea,* namely, so that he might bring out of it the beast by whom he would persecute the Church, as discussed in the next chapter. Luther translates in the first person and has this sentence referring to John, since the words καὶ εἶδον, *and I saw,* follow, which is also why these words are included at the beginning of the next chapter in his translation.

Chapter 13

This chapter contains a detailed explanation of the persecutions that were previously described in general terms, namely, who the chief angels and instruments of the dragon will be. They are depicted as two beasts, so there are two parts to this chapter:
   I. The description of the first beast, where he comes from, in what form he appears, in what his authority consists;
   II. The description of the second beast, which comes up out of the earth. He has two horns like the Lamb, exercises all the authority of the first beast before him, and causes those who dwell on the earth to worship the first beast, whose mortal wounds have been healed. He performs great miracles.

v. 1 Καὶ εἶδον ἐκ τῆς θαλάσσης θηρίον ἀναβαῖνον, *and I saw a beast coming up out of the sea.*

This beast symbolizes the old Roman Empire under the heathen emperors, who stirred up terrible persecutions against the Christians and in this way showed themselves to be savage beasts.

Lyranus takes this beast to be the son of Khosrau, the king of Persia. Salmeron (Last Volume, *Comm. in N.T.*, f. 365) takes it to be Muhammad. But these explanations do not agree with the text, as the entire context makes clear.

The fact that John saw this beast coming up out of the sea stands for the fact that the Roman Empire rose out of the confluence of many peoples (Rev. 17:15) and reached its peak.

ἔχον κεφαλὰς κεφαλὰς, *having seven heads.* Some take these seven heads to be the seven chief cities or capitals of the Roman Empire: (1) Rome in Italy; (2) Constantinople in Thrace; (3) Antioch in Asia; (4) Alexandria in Egypt; (5) Jerusalem in Syria; (6) Carthage in Africa; (7) Toledo in Spain. All of these cities turned away from the true faith to the ungodly doctrines of both Antichrists—the Muhammadan and the Papistic.

It should be noted that the same number of heads and horns is attributed to the dragon in Rev. 12:3, which is why it is later said of this beast that the dragon "gave it his power, throne and authority." Cf. Rev. 17:9, where it says that these seven heads are "the seven mountains" on which the city of Rome was founded, which was the capital of the Roman Empire, "and seven kings," who will be treated more fully in chapter 17.

καὶ κέρατα δέκα, *and ten horns.* These ten horns, on which diadems are placed, represent the ten chief kingdoms or royal provinces that once made up the Roman Empire, namely, (1) Syria, (2) Egypt, (3) Asia, (4) Greece, (5) Italy, (6) Gaul, (7) Spain, (8) Africa, (9) Germany, (10) England and its neighboring northern kingdoms.

καὶ ἐπὶ τῶν κεράτων αὐτοῦ δέκα διαδήματα, *and on his horns were ten diadems,* because these ten provinces, which were still included in the Roman Empire at the height of its existence, were ten distinct kingdoms, each of which had its own crown and government.

καὶ ἐπὶ τὰς κεφαλὰς αὐτοῦ ὀνόματα βλασφημίας, *and upon his heads were names of blasphemy.* This signifies (1) the blasphemous idolatry of the heathen, to which the first Roman emperors were devoted; (2) the use of the divine name, or at least of divine authority, which was common among the heathen emperors of Rome, and even peculiar to them. Diocletian dared to claim the name of God for himself. The horrendous blasphemy of Julian is notorious: "You have won at last, O Galilean!"

v. 2 καὶ τὸ θηρίον ὃ εἶδον ἦν ὅμοιον παρδάλει, *and the beast that I saw was like a leopard, etc.* (Cf. Dan. 7:4 ff.) The first monarchy, the Babylonian one, was prefigured as a lion; the second, the Persian, as a bear; the third, the Greek, as a leopard. So when it says that this beast was like a leopard, with feet like a bear's feet and a mouth like a lion's mouth, it means that the Roman monarchy shares something in common with all three.

The leopard is a symbol: (1) of speed in attacking kingdoms and provinces (Jer. 5:6, Hab. 1:8); (2) of cruelty, because the Roman emperors were intensely eager to shed blood.

The feet of a bear are a symbol: (1) of strength and power, for they planted their feet firmly in the kingdoms which they conquered; (2) of cunning; (3) of cruelty.

The mouth of a lion is a symbol: (1) of insatiable greed; (2) of pride; (3) of blasphemy; (4) of the horrendous edicts that were promulgated against the Christians.

καὶ ἔδωκεν αὐτῷ ὁ δράκων τὴν δύναμιν αὐτοῦ καὶ τὸν θρόνον αὐτοῦ καὶ ἐξουσίαν μεγάλην, *and the dragon gave him his power and his throne and great authority*. Even though the Roman Empire, like other kingdoms, was also ordained by God under heathen emperors (Rom. 13:1), nevertheless, since the infernal dragon, "the prince of this world" (John 14:30, Eph. 6:12), influenced the heathen emperors to abuse their power by persecuting Christians, therefore it is said that the dragon gave the heathen emperors his great authority, that is, the abuse of power, and also his throne, which he erected in Rome through idolatry and other very serious sins. They increased their power by destroying peoples, to which they were instigated by the devil.

v. 3 καὶ εἶδον μίαν ἐκ τῶν κεφαλῶν αὐτοῦ ὡς ἐσφαγμένην εἰς θάνατον, καὶ ἡ πληγὴ τοῦ θανάτου αὐτοῦ ἐθεραπεύθη, *and I saw one of his heads as if it had been slain to death, and its mortal wound was healed.*

(1) Some understand this to be Nero, who killed himself, and with whom the line of the early emperors passed away. It seemed, therefore, that in him and with him the Roman Empire would perish, since many provinces defected from it and many civil wars arose. But through Vespasian, Nero's successor, it was built up again, and the city of Rome, which was burned and devastated at Nero's decree, was enlarged with new buildings.

(2) When the Roman Empire was later ripped apart by foreigners like the Huns, the Vandals, and the Goths, it was again furnished with auxiliary troops by Charlemagne.

(3) Some take it to be the city of Rome, which, although it was conquered and plundered many times—by Alaric, king of the Goths, in the year 420; by Genseric, king of the Vandals, in the year 455; by Odoacer, king of the Heruli; by the Lombards, etc.—nevertheless it was healed again by the Roman Pontiffs.

Καὶ ἐθαυμάσθη ὅλη ἡ γῆ ὀπίσω τοῦ θηρίου, *and the whole earth was amazed at the beast.* The vast majority of men were devoted to heathen idolatry at that time, so they were amazed at the glory and greatness of the Roman Empire at its height, especially since, after the wound was inflicted, it was healed again.

v. 4 καὶ προσεκύνησαν τὸν δράκοντα, *and they worshiped the dragon.* Inasmuch as the Gentiles worshiped idols, they worshiped the demons (Psa. 96:5, 1 Cor. 10:20). They worshiped the beast, inasmuch as they obeyed the emperors' edict concerning idol worship. Indeed, they even held the emperors to be gods and rendered them divine honor. They received the emperors by apotheosis into the ranks of the gods.

τίς ὅμοιος τῷ θηρίῳ, *who is like the beast?* They thought the Roman Empire was invincible. And when they were admonished to disregard the commandments of the Roman emperors and be converted to Christianity, they would respond, "Who can resist so much majesty and power?"

v. 5 Καὶ ἐδόθη αὐτῷ στόμα λαλοῦν μεγάλα καὶ βλασφημίας, *and a mouth was given to him to speak great things and blasphemies.* He was given authority by the dragon, according to the permission and just judgment of God. The *great things and blasphemies* stand for the proud boasting about the authority of the empire and about its perpetual victories. Proud edicts were made by those kings, blasphemies against God Himself, and against His holy word (Dan. 11:36).

καὶ ἐδόθη αὐτῷ ἐξουσία ποιῆσαι μῆνας τεσσεράκοντα δύο, *and authority was given to him to act for 42 months,* that is, 1,260 years (Rev. 11:2). This number corresponds to the number of years that the holy city was trampled and the two witnesses prophesied (Rev. 11:2) and that the woman was kept in solitude from the face of the dragon (Rev. 12:6). Therefore, it means that the Antichristian tyranny would last as long as the ancient Roman Empire endured.

v. 6 καὶ ἤνοιξε τὸ στόμα αὐτοῦ εἰς βλασφημίαν πρὸς τὸν θεόν, *and he opened his mouth for blasphemy toward God, etc.* The tabernacle of God stands for the Church, of which the Old Testament tabernacle of the covenant was a type (Exo. 26:1), which is the "house of God" (1 Tim. 3:15), in which He is pleased to dwell. *Those who dwell in heaven* represent the true and living members of the Church Militant on earth, whose conduct is in heaven

(Phi. 3:20), among whom God dwells as in His temple. (Cf. John 14:23; 1 Cor. 3:16, 6:19; 2 Cor. 6:16.)

v. 7 καὶ ἐδόθη αὐτῷ πόλεμον ποιῆσαι μετὰ τῶν ἁγίων καὶ νικῆσαι αὐτούς, *and it was given to him to make war with the saints and to conquer them*, that is, externally and bodily, for the persecutors of the Church could not harm the salvation of the confessors, nor the word of God, nor were they able to deprive them of the grace of God and of salvation.

καὶ ἐδόθη αὐτῷ ἐξουσία ἐπὶ πᾶσαν φυλὴν καὶ γλῶσσαν καὶ ἔθνος, *and authority was given to him over every tribe and language and nation*, for the Roman Empire had brought practically all of Europe, Asia, and Africa under its authority, which is why it was able to stir up persecutions against the Christians with so much success.

v. 8 καὶ προσκυνήσουσιν αὐτῷ οἱ κατοικοῦντες ἐπὶ τῆς γῆς, *and the inhabitants on the earth worshiped him*, those who have their minds set on earthly and carnal things, who have not been born again through the Spirit of God, who care nothing for heavenly things (Jer. 17:13).

Ὧν οὐ γέγραπται τὰ ὀνόματα ἐν τῇ βίβλῳ τῆς ζωῆς, *whose names are not written in the Book of Life*, who are not among those whom God elected to eternal life in Christ, the Lamb of God. (Cf. Eph. 1:4; Phi. 4:3; Dan. 12:1; John 13:18.)

ἐσφαγμένου ἀπὸ καταβολῆς κόσμου, *slain from the beginning of the world*. (1) Primasius explains it as "the slain Lamb, who is from the beginning of the world." But the Greek does not allow this. For it does not say, ἀρνίον ἐσφαγμένον τὸ ἀπὸ καταβολῆς κόσμου.

Socinus (Part 2, *De Christo*; *De Servat.*, ch. 26., Part 4., ch. 13) and Schmaltz (*Contra Frantz.*, p. 116) assert that this is an example of hyperbaton or hypallage, a transposition of word order, and thus that phrase, *from the beginning of the world*, should not be seen as referring to the following words about being slain, but to the inscription in the Book of Life. He proves this from the parallel passage, Rev. 17:8. Aretas, Emanuel Sa, Beza, Junius, and Piscator agree with this.

We reply: (1) Primasius, Ambrosius Ansbertus, Haymo, Rupert, and Lyranus recognize that "the Lamb is said to have been slain from the beginning of the world." Tossanus proves this explanation and demonstrates three ways in which the Lamb was slain from the beginning of the world. (2) Even if, with great difficulty, this is taken as a hyperbaton, it remains, then, that Christ is the Lamb from eternity in whose book the inscription was made. But Christ is only said to be the Lamb with regard to the sacrifice made by slaughter. (3) There is no compelling need to change the natural word order. (4) The passage in Rev. 17:8 is not entirely, but only partially, parallel to this passage, namely, with respect to the continuing inscription of those who would believe in the Book of Life. It is dissimilar: (1) with regard to the different placement of the phrase, which, in Rev. 13, is ascribed to the meritorious and motivating cause of predestination, whereas in Rev. 17, it is ascribed to predestination itself. (2) The passage in Rev. 13 more expressly denotes the cause of the inscription in the Book of Life, namely, the slaughter, that is, the whole obedience of Christ.

How, then, and in what sense is Christ said to be *the Lamb slain from the beginning of the world?* We reply: (1) With regard to the decree, for already from the beginning of the world—indeed, from all eternity—God made the decree concerning the redemption of the human race through the suffering and death of Christ, that in the fullness of time He should be offered in sacrifice as the spotless Lamb for the sins of the world (1 Pet. 1:19–20). Haymo on this passage: "Certainly He was slain in predestination, for before all the ages God the Father decreed in the Son and in the Holy Spirit that at the end of the ages He would come and be slain, so that by His death He might atone for our death."

(2) With regard to the proclamation, for already from the beginning of the world the slaughter of this Lamb had been preached, namely, when it was preached in the protevangel that the seed of the woman would crush the serpent's head (Gen. 3:15).

(3) With regard to the types, when God clothed our first parents with tunics made from the skins of slaughtered sheep (Gen. 3:21). The sacrifice of this Lamb was also prefigured by all the Old Testament sacrifices, but especially by the paschal lamb (Heb. 10:1, Exo. 12:6, 1 Cor. 5:7).

(4) With regard to efficacy, for by virtue and by the efficacy of the reconciliation made by Christ, all the Old Testament believers were justified

before God and saved, and thus this slaughter was beneficial even before it took place; it had its efficacy already from the first beginning of the world.

Some (Abele and others) add that this Lamb was slain, not in Himself, but in His members. But, (1) the phrase "from the beginning of the world" usually refers to eternity (Mat. 13:35); (2) the fact that Christ is slain in His members cannot be the cause for anyone being written in the Book of Life; the cause is that He Himself suffered.

v. 9 Εἴ τις ἔχει οὖς, *if anyone has ears*, let him hear that which has already been set forth concerning this beast, and also what will be set forth. (Cf. Luke 8:8; Rev. 2:7, 11, 17, 29; 3:6, 13, 22.)

v. 10 εἴ τις αἰχμαλωσίαν συνάγει, *if anyone gathers captivity*. This phrase is connected to a passage of consolation, by which the Church is strengthened against the severe persecutions she is about to suffer. *Whoever leads into captivity, into captivity*, that is, infernal captivity, *he will be led*. The sense is that God will not always tolerate these persecutions at the hand of the heathen emperors, but will repay them with due penalties, so that those who led others captive and killed them with the sword, will themselves be cast headlong into eternal captivity and death (Isa. 33:1, 2 The. 1:6). Consequently, these words indicate the penalty of retaliation that God will carry out against the persecutors of the faithful. Indeed, even in this life the capital of the Roman Empire will be laid waste and some of its inhabitants will be led away captive, while others will fall by the sword.

Ὧδέ ἐστιν ἡ ὑπομονὴ καὶ ἡ πίστις τῶν ἁγίων, *here is the patience and the faith of the saints*. While the saints are being persecuted for the sake of their confession of the Gospel, their patience and faith are both assaulted and exercised. (Cf. 1 Pet. 1:7, Rev. 14:12.)

v. 11 Καὶ εἶδον ἄλλο θηρίον, *and I saw another beast*. This second beast represents the papal kingdom which followed the first beast, that is, the ancient Roman Empire (2 The. 2:7–8). After the strength of the Roman Empire was broken, the papal reign began.

ἀναβαῖνον ἐκ τῆς γῆς, *coming up out of the earth*, that is, out of the abyss which is under the earth, namely, hell (Rev. 11:7). Or rather, he is said to come up from the earth, because the papal reign had tenuous beginnings and then spread by earthly means; namely, through greed, pride, cunning and force.

εἶχε κέρατα δύο ὅμοια ἀρνίῳ, *he had two horns like the Lamb*. Some take these two horns to be the two Antichrists, or the twofold army of the Antichrist who receives the authority of the first beast. The first Antichrist spread throughout Asia and Africa and throughout the churches of that region and laid waste to much of Europe. They call this Eastern Antichrist "Magog" or "uncovered." This is Muhammad. The second Antichrist is "Gog," or "covered." He sits in the midst of the temple of God, wants to be known as the "Vicar of Christ," although he himself denies Christ. This is the pope. The two horns symbolize the twofold authority which the pope arrogates to himself, namely, ecclesiastical and civil authority.

The first beast had names of blasphemy on his seven heads, because it is a simple matter to discern and to shun heathen idolatry, which is openly blasphemous. But this second beast has "two horns like the Lamb." He pretends to be the Lamb, because the pope boasts that he is the Vicar of Christ; he attempts to confirm his dogmas with the sayings of the Old and New Testaments; he arrogates to himself the supreme authority in ecclesiastical and political matters in the name of Christ; he pretends to promote the kingdom of Christ through hypocrisy.

ἐλάλει ὡς δράκων, *he speaks like the dragon*. He taught the "doctrines of demons" (1 Tim. 4:1). He seduced many with promises of honor and riches, just as the serpent long ago seduced our first parents (Gen. 3:2). Haymo on this passage: "Just as the devil long ago spoke to the woman through the serpent with evil persuasion, and through her deceived the man, so also these wicked people seduce whomever they can with their depraved doctrine and separate them from faith in Christ."

v. 12 καὶ τὴν ἐξουσίαν τοῦ πρώτου θηρίου πᾶσαν ποιεῖ ἐνώπιον αὐτοῦ, *and he exercises all the authority of the first beast in his presence*, because the Roman Pontiffs took possession of the seat of the Roman Empire and claimed all of its authority for themselves. They expelled the Roman emperors from the city of Rome and took possession of their throne, and then, just as the Roman emperors boasted that all the kingdoms of the world belonged to them and that they were the lords of the whole earth, so also the Roman Pontiffs boast about having the same authority.

καὶ ποιεῖ τὴν γῆν, *and makes the earth*, etc. The Roman Pontiffs reintroduced heathen idolatry into the Church through the religious invocation of the saints. They merely changed the names. Indeed, they also permit the name of God and divine honors to be attributed to themselves, just as the Roman emperors once did.

v. 13 καὶ ποιεῖ σημεῖα μεγάλα, *and he performs great signs*, etc. This beast performs counterfeit signs and wonders, not by divine power, but by the effective working of the devil (Mat. 24:14; 2 The. 2:9). Some take this to refer to the magic arts.

ἵνα καὶ πῦρ ποιῇ καταβαίνειν ἐκ τοῦ οὐρανοῦ, *so that he also causes fire to descend from heaven*. The Complutensian edition reads: καὶ πῦρ, ἵνα ἐκ τοῦ οὐρανοῦ καταβαίνῃ, *and fire, so that it descends from heaven*.

(1) Ansbertus on this passage: "The beast with two horns will cause fire to descend from heaven onto the earth, because the preachers of Antichrist, in falsely imitating the Church, pretend that they are giving the Holy Spirit to their followers by the laying on of hands."

(2) Primasius: "So that he makes fire descend from heaven, that is, from the Church to those on earth, since, either from a variety of nations or from the cunning of a deceptive enemy, he makes his ministers speak in many new languages, so that they proudly take this as a sign that they have obtained the gift of the Holy Spirit."

(3) *He will make fire descend from heaven*, that is, he does miraculous and astounding things, for the general is understood from the specific. John has in view the saying among the Hebrews which was received at that time, which the Jews still recite today: "If anyone causes fire to descend from heaven," for, "if anyone wishes to prove that he is a man of God or to prove the Law of Moses by means of a miracle from heaven, let him be anathema."

(4) The most compatible interpretation is that John has in view the story of Elijah, who caused fire to come down from heaven upon those who came to take him captive (2 Kings 1:10, 12). It means, therefore, that the Roman Pontiffs would boast that they do miracles in the Roman Church

that are as great as those performed by the prophets and apostles. He is especially indicating the fiery thunderbolt of excommunication, which the Pontiff threatens against all those who wish to oppose him.

ἐνώπιον τῶν ἀνθρώπων, *in the sight of men*, binding the eyes of men, or, as Aretas says, "stealing the eyes of those who see." Bellarmine, Book III, *De Pont. Rom.*, ch. 15: "deluding the sight of men."

v. 14 καὶ πλανᾷ τοὺς κατοικοῦντας ἐπὶ τῆς γῆς, *and he leads astray the inhabitants of the earth.* The Pope persuades his followers to acknowledge him as the supreme lord in the whole Roman Empire, indeed, in the whole world, who is not only able to command kings and princes, but also the Roman Emperor himself. But he is also an ape of the Roman Empire; he has cardinals instead of electors and canonical law instead of civil law.

ποιῆσαι εἰκόνα τῷ θηρίῳ, *to make an image to the beast,* (1) to celebrate the Roman emperors and, on their behalf, to honor those princes who had no jurisdiction over the city and Roman territory. (2) The image of the beast can be understood in this way, that the Pope has fashioned the ecclesiastical tyranny of the Roman See according to the image of the political monarchy. (3) It is an enallage, using a single image in place of many, as Alcazar acknowledges. The Holy Spirit lumps together all the splendid pomp of the papal images and statues, that is, the papal idolomania, and calls it "the image of the beast". Moreover, He is alluding to the story of Daniel, where the king made an edict that, under the penalty of death, the 60-cubit-tall golden image was to be worshiped (Dan. 3:6).

v. 15 Καὶ ἐδόθη αὐτῷ δοῦναι πνεῦμα τῇ εἰκόνι τοῦ θηρίου, *and he was given to give spirit to the image of the beast.* Some take this to refer to the constitution of the papal monarchy, so that the pope can set up his monarchy and, with his decrees, give men a higher or lower status, as he pleases. Some take it in this way: To put spirit in the image, that is, to bring it to life. For unless he confirms the Roman Emperor-elect, he is considered to be dead, that is, nothing.

καὶ ποιήσῃ, ὅσοι ἂν μὴ προσκυνήσωσι, *and he causes those who do not worship, etc.*, that is, he seeks to kill all those who do not wish to acknowledge the Pope as the head of the Church and the supreme monarch in the whole Roman Empire, or indeed, in the whole world.

v. 16 χάραγμα ἐπὶ τῆς χειρός, *a mark on the hand*. The *mark on the right hand* is the oath with which the clergy are bound to the pope. The mark on the forehead indicates the subjection with which the laity are bound to the pope. He requires from everyone that they confess the papal faith and promise to obey his laws. Some apply this to the sign of the cross, which is made in conjunction with the anointing with oil in the Sacrament of Confirmation on the foreheads of those who honor the Papacy.

v. 17 ἵνα μή τις δύνηται ἀγοράσαι, *that no one may buy*, etc. Anyone who wants to do business in those places where the Pope reigns must profess the Roman religion. For these three phrases—the mark, the name of the beast, and the number of his name—all signify one and the same thing, namely, the profession of the papistic religion.

v. 18 Ὧδε ἡ σοφία ἐστίν, *here is wisdom*. A great mystery lies in the number of the name of the beast, and great wisdom is required in order to investigate it, which is why the next words follow.

ὁ ἔχων τὸν νοῦν, ψηφισάτω τὸν ἀριθμὸν τοῦ θηρίου, ἀριθμὸς γὰρ ἀνθρώπου ἐστί, *he who has the mind, let him calculate the number of the beast, for it is a man's number*. Man's number, (1) a number which can be discovered and calculated by man. Thus "man's measurement" (Rev. 21:17) is a measurement that is used among men. Therefore, man's number is plain, easy, and used by men. Thus in Isa. 8:1, Lyranus interprets "man's writing" as "writing that is easy and plain."

(2) It is said to be man's number, lest anyone should conclude that the years here are to be numbered in the same way as in Daniel 9:29, where the years until the coming of Christ were to be numbered in groups of seven, which is subtle and quite difficult, nor is it obvious to anyone. Counting is a human practice and requires the intellect. "A number," therefore, is used for "to count," which is why it is not used with the definite article ὁ ἀριθμός, but it is said indefinitely, "for it is man's number." Thus Richard de S. Victore, Aretas, Alcazar and Ribera understand it.

It is better to conclude that it refers to the object. *It is a man's number*, that is, it signifies a man, namely, the Roman Pope, who has been prefigured up until now as a kind of beast.

καὶ ὁ ἀριθμὸς αὐτοῦ χ ξ ς, *and his number is 666.*

Long ago there were those who thought the middle letter ξ should be written as the Greek letter ρ, so that it reads χρς, an abbreviation for the name of Christ. They concluded that the Antichrist would deceive Christians and Jews with this sign, so that they would mistake him for Christ. But if that were the case, the number would not be 666, but 706, because the Greek letter ρ does not equal 60, but 100.

(2) The first Greek letter, χ, equals 600; the second letter, ξ, equals 60; and the third letter, ς, equals 6. (Although in some manuscripts, the letter ς is written with stigma, which equals 90, thus producing the number 750. The fact that this is found in many Greek manuscripts is due to the carelessness of the copyists.)

(3) This number 666 is contained in the Hebrew word רומיית, *Roman*, and in the two Greek words, ἐκκλησία Ἰταλικά, *Italian church*.

(4) Irenaeus (Book V, p. 335) applies it to the word Λατεῖνος, *Latin*. Eusebius follows him (Book V, *Hist. Eccles.*, ch. 8), as does Aretas (*In Apocalypsin*), because the Greeks use letters for their numbers. But John wrote Revelation in the Greek language.

The Pope has the seat of his kingdom in Latium, since Italy was once called Latium. He commands the Sacraments to be administered and the Divine Service to be celebrated in the Latin language, even in those places where the people do not know Latin. He prefers the Latin edition of the Bible to the original text, and he disseminates his bulls and decrees in Latin.

(5) Blessed Luther takes it as the number of years that the Pope's earthly kingdom will endure. But some start counting from the time when the Pope arrogated to himself the tyrannical power from the emperors themselves, namely, from John XII, who took office in AD 956 and began to demand an oath from the emperors (*ca. Tibi Domino, Dist. 63*). Others start counting from the time when the Roman Antichrist began to exert his power, namely, from the year AD 666. Others start counting from the time when this prophecy was revealed to John, ending in the year when the Antichrist began to rule as lord in the Church.

Chapter 14

There are three parts:
I. The strengthening of the elect in the midst of the Antichristian persecutions;
II. An admonition of the faithful teachers of the Church against the Antichrist;
III. A description of the Last Judgment.

v. 1 Καὶ εἶδον, καὶ ἰδοὺ ἀρνίον ἑστὸς ἐπὶ τὸ ὄρος Σιών, *and I saw, and behold, the Lamb standing upon Mount Zion*. The Lamb is an image of Christ (Rev. 5:6). In this passage, He is seen on Mount Zion, that is, the Church, which is prefigured in the Old Testament by Mount Zion, on which the city of David was built. (Cf. Psa. 2:6, Zec. 9:9; Heb. 12:22.) For lest anyone should imagine that no true believers would remain in the midst of that universal seduction of the Antichrist, Christ shows Himself visibly on Mount Zion as an indication that He will preserve the Church for Himself in the midst of the Antichrist's persecutions and seductions, and He will be present for her with His gracious presence.

καὶ μετ' αὐτοῦ ἑκατὸν τεσσεράκοντα τέσσαρες χιλιάδες, *and with Him 144,000*. This number signifies the great multitude of believers (Rev. 7:4.)

ἔχουσαι τὸ ὄνομα τοῦ πατρὸς αὐτοῦ γεγραμμένον ἐπὶ τῶν μετώπων αὐτῶν, *having the name of His Father written on their foreheads*. Aretas and Andreas Caesariensis read, ἔχουσαι τὸ ὄνομα αὐτοῦ καὶ τὸ ὄνομα τοῦ πατρὸς αὐτοῦ, *having His name (i.e., the Lamb's name) and the name of His Father*. It also reads this way in the Complutensian edition and the Parisian edition compiled by Robert Stephanus in the year 1550. I suggest that this reading, noted in the margin, is preferable to the other that we have in our codices, because it is through, and on account of, Christ that God is a Father to us.

Just as the Antichrist imprints his mark on the foreheads of those who cling to him (Rev. 13:16), so God has sealed those whom He has elected to eternal life. Therefore, this mark—the name of the Lamb's Father—is contrasted with the mark that the Antichrist has placed on the forehead of those who are associated with his kingdom. It means that, no matter how much the Antichrist rages, nevertheless the foundation of God stands firm, having this seal: "God knows His own" (2 Tim. 2:19), and indeed, it is just as certain as if He had impressed a seal on their foreheads (Rev. 7:3). For this reason, believers truly carry around the name of the heavenly Father on their foreheads, so that they are "not ashamed of the Gospel" (Rom. 1:16), but confess it with an intrepid spirit.

v. 2 καὶ ἤκουσα φωνὴν ἐκ τοῦ οὐρανοῦ, *and I heard a voice from heaven.* The many waters signify the multitude of God's elect singing praises (Rev. 1:15, 19:6).

καὶ ὡς φωνὴν βροντῆς μεγάλης, *and like the sound of loud thunder.* Thunder represents: (1) the amazing strength of the Holy Spirit, the power with which they are clothed from on high (Luke 24:49); (2) the fearless spirit and penetrating voice of the elect as they glorify God (Mark 3:17).

καὶ φωνὴν ἤκουσα κιθαρῳδῶν, *and I heard the sound of harpists.* This represents the sweetness of divine praise in the mouth of the elect. It is a reference to David, who praised God with the harp (1 Sam. 16:23; Psa. 43:4; Psa. 71:22).

v. 3 καὶ ᾄδουσιν ὡς ᾠδὴν καινὴν, *and they sang as a new song.* While the ungodly are busy blaspheming God and worshiping the beast, the elect are singing (Rev. 13:9).

The new song signifies a unique and extraordinary song about the great benefits that Christ gave to the elect in the New Testament, when He renewed them by His Spirit.

ἐνώπιον τοῦ θρόνου καὶ τεσσάρων ζῴων καὶ τῶν πρεσβυτέρων, *before the throne,* namely, of the Lamb, *and the four animals and the elders,* that is, the 24 elders. (Cf. Rev. 4:5, 5:9.)

καὶ οὐδεὶς ἐδύνατο μαθεῖν τὴν ᾠδὴν, *and no one could learn the song, etc.* No one could learn that song, because only the godly praise God rightly (Psa. 33:1), and without faith, God cannot rightly be invoked or worshiped (Rom. 10:14, 1 Cor. 12:3).

οἱ ἠγορασμένοι ἀπὸ τῆς γῆς, *who were purchased from the earth*. They were purchased by Christ from the earth, that is, from the human race, which is earthly, corrupt, "sold under sin" (Rom. 7:14). They were purchased at a great price (1 Cor. 6:20, 7:23), that they should no longer cling to earthly things with improper love, but should dwell in heaven with their spirits. These are they who also applied to themselves with true faith this redemption made by Christ.

This means that they are true and genuine disciples of the Gospel, who are eager to learn this song, since they were purchased from the earth.

v. 4 οὗτοί εἰσιν οἳ μετὰ γυναικῶν οὐκ ἐμολύνθησαν, *these are they who were not defiled with women*. The papists apply this to celibacy. But using this reasoning, it would follow that marriage is contamination, pollution, even Antichristian. This verse refers to those who did not pollute themselves through spiritual adultery and fornication, that is, through idolatry, heresies, and false forms of worship. Instead, they preserved the purity of doctrine and kept it uncontaminated.

παρθένοι γάρ εἰσιν, *for they are virgins*. This signifies the virginity of faith of which the apostle speaks in 2 Cor. 11:2, and the holiness of life, for which those who are truly godly are earnestly zealous (1 Pet. 1:15).

οὗτοι οἱ ἀκολουθοῦντες τῷ ἀρνίῳ ὅπου ἂν ὑπάγῃ, *these are the ones who follow the Lamb wherever He goes*. For they are His Bride, inasmuch as the soul is betrothed to Him by faith. (1) They cling to Christ by true faith. (2) They obey His precepts. (3) They follow His example and walk in His footsteps. (4) They have communion with Christ in cross and glory. (Cf. Mat. 16:24, 19:28; John 14:3, 17:24; 1 Pet. 2:21.) They do not retreat when the Lamb leads them through thorns to heavenly glory (1 The. 4:17).

οὗτοι ἠγοράσθησαν ἀπὸ τῶν ἀνθρώπων ἀπαρχὴ τῷ θεῷ καὶ τῷ ἀρνίῳ, *these were purchased from among men, firstfruits to God and to the Lamb*. God chose them from eternity in Christ to be firstfruits, and in the fullness of time He brought them forth by the word of truth, according to His will, "that they might be the firstfruits of His creation" (James 1:18). They have been sanctified for God, just as in the Old Testament the firstfruits were consecrated to Him. Christ, as the only New Testament Priest, takes pleasure in them, just as the offering of firstfruits in the Old Testament was pleasing to God.

v. 5 καὶ ἐν τῷ στόματι αὐτῶν οὐχ εὑρέθη δόλος, *and in their mouth was found no deceit.* In this way they also follow the Lamb (Isa. 53:9, 1 Pet. 2:22). ἄμωμοι γάρ εἰσιν, *for they are spotless, etc.* They "washed their robes and made them white in the blood of the Lamb" (Rev. 7:14). They eagerly pursue a blameless life (1 Cor. 5:8, Eph. 1:4, Phi. 2:15, 2 Pet. 3:14). That which they believe with the heart they also confess with the mouth, and what they profess with the mouth they also demonstrate with works. They are not hypocrites, boasting about their own perfect righteousness, but they recognize their weaknesses and imperfections and fortify themselves with this consolation, that one day before the throne of God in eternal life, they will be perfect and cleansed from every sin (Eph. 5:27).

v. 6 Καὶ εἶδον ἄλλον ἄγγελον, *and I saw another angel.* Since God not only raised up any number of faithful teachers in the midst of the Antichrist's tyranny who assessed the Antichristian abominations and exhorted men to repent, but also manifested the Antichrist at the established time and attacked his kingdom with great might, therefore three angels are introduced in order, the first of whom is here being described.

πετόμενον ἐν μεσουρανήματι, *flying in the midst of heaven.* This signifies the swift course of the Gospel, which must be preached among various peoples shortly after the Antichrist is revealed, and that the Gospel will be proclaimed publicly and fearlessly against the Antichrist. From this, it is obvious that Blessed Luther is represented by this angel, for God used him especially as His instrument for revealing the Antichrist and attacking his kingdom.

ἔχοντα Εὐαγγέλιον αἰώνιον, *having the eternal Gospel.* He did not preach human traditions, but the pure doctrine of the Gospel.

It is called "the eternal Gospel": (1) because it was decreed in the eternal counsel of God, which is manifested to the world in the preaching of the Gospel; (2) thus it was promised already at the very beginning of the world; (3) it contains the doctrine about the eternal Son of God and the eternal salvation of the elect; (4) it will endure until the end of the world, and no power or lies of the Antichrist will be able to prevail against it; (5) it offers spiritual and eternal benefits.

εὐαγγελίσαι τοὺς κατοικοῦντας ἐπὶ τοὺς καθημένους ἐπὶ τῆς γῆς, *to preach to the inhabitants of the earth*, lest anyone should be able to feign ignorance as an excuse.

v. 7 φοβήθητε τὸν θεὸν, *fear God*, not the Antichrist and human traditions. δότε αὐτῷ δόξαν, *give Him glory*. Acknowledge that He alone is your Savior, and that you cannot be saved by the merits of your works.

ὅτι ἦλθεν ἡ ὥρα τῆς κρίσεως αὐτοῦ, *for the hour of His judgment has come*, when a reckoning will be rendered to each one concerning his faith and life.

καὶ προσκυνήσατε, *and worship*, not mute idols nor dead saints, but the living God, the Creator of all (Acts 4:24).

v. 8 Καὶ ἄλλος ἄγγελος ἠκολούθησε...ἔπεσε Βαβυλὼν, *and another angel followed... "Fallen is Babylon."* (Cf. Isa. 21:8; Jer. 51:8; Rev. 18:2.)

Babylon stands for the kingdom of Antichrist, whose capital is Rome, that great city, just as Babylon was once the capital of the Assyrian Kingdom. "Babylon" means "confusion." It means, therefore, that Rome is the filthy sewer from which all heresies and confusions arise. The Israelites were detained in the Babylonian captivity. The Antichrist holds Christians captive through human traditions.

ὅτι ἐκ τοῦ οἴνου τοῦ θυμοῦ τῆς πορνείας αὐτῆς πεπότικε πάντα ἔθνη, *for all nations have drunk from the wine of the wrath of her fornication*. From the burning wine of fornication, that is, from the poisonous or virulent wine. For the word θυμός corresponds to the Hebrew חמה, which sometimes means "poison" (Psa. 58:5). But the meaning of the word θυμοῦ can also be used. It is called "the wine of wrath," because God permits such seduction and blindness out of His righteous indignation, in order that contempt for the Gospel may be punished (2 The. 2:10).

Luther does not read the word θυμοῦ.

She made the nations drink of the wine, etc. That is, she led all nations astray into superstition and idolatry by her lies and corruptions. This preaching of the angel is likewise fulfilled today, for after Luther plundered the Papacy, his faithful coworkers publicized this divine work and preached it in the whole world.

v. 9 Καὶ τρίτος ἄγγελος ἠκολούθησεν αὐτοῖς, *and a third angel followed them.* This angel represents the faithful teachers who warn the Church to beware of the Antichrist's seduction. More and more, over and over, they uncover the Antichristian abominations and urge men under the threat of eternal damnation to turn away from them.

εἴ τις τὸ θηρίον προσκυνεῖ καὶ τὴν εἰκόνα αὐτοῦ, *if anyone worships the beast,* that is, the Roman Pontiff, *and his image.* The image of the beast represents the papal kingdom (Rev. 13:16). καὶ λαμβάνει χάραγμα ἐπὶ τοῦ μετώπου αὐτοῦ ἢ ἐπὶ τὴν χεῖρα αὐτοῦ, *and bears a mark on his forehead or upon his hand,* who, against his own conscience, professes to be among the followers of the Roman Pontiff and binds himself to him by oath (Rev. 13:16).

v. 10 καὶ αὐτὸς πίεται ἐκ τοῦ οἴνου τοῦ θυμοῦ τοῦ θεοῦ, *he himself will also drink of the wine of the wrath of God.* (Cf. Psa. 75:9; Isa. 51:17; Jer. 25:15.)

βασανισθήσεται ἐν πυρὶ καὶ θείῳ, *he will be tormented with fire and brimstone,* in the infernal lake. ἐνώπιον τῶν ἁγίων ἀγγέλων, *in the sight of the holy angels,* so that the angels will see it. καὶ ἐνώπιον τοῦ ἀρνίου, *and in the sight of the Lamb,* as Judge.

v. 11 καὶ ὁ καπνὸς τοῦ βασανισμοῦ αὐτῶν, *and the smoke of their torment,* that is, of the fire with which they are tormented. ἀναβαίνει εἰς αἰῶνας αἰώνων, *it goes up forever and ever,* because this fire will be unquenchable. (Cf. Isa. 66:24; Mark 9:44, 46, 48.)

καὶ οὐκ ἔχουσιν ἀνάπαυσιν, *and they have no rest.* The punishments of hell will not only be eternal, but also continuous and without interruption.

v. 12 Ὧδε ὑπομονὴ τῶν ἁγίων ἐστίν, *here is patience of the saints.* It is required that the saints and the godly who suffer persecution by the Pontiff await with a temperate spirit the time when God will destroy the kingdom of the Pope and throw his followers into the infernal lake. But this has special reference to the angels, that is, those faithful teachers of the Church who oppose the Antichrist. They discharge their office accompanied by severe persecutions. Therefore they will need patience. (Cf. Heb. 10:35.)

Ὧδε οἱ τηροῦντες τὰς ἐντολὰς τοῦ θεοῦ καὶ τὴν πίστιν Ἰησοῦ, *here are those who keep the commandments of God and the faith of Jesus*. It is required that they keep the commandments of God and faith, that is, the sound doctrine concerning Christ, and that they not give any place to the seductions of the Antichrist. For it is better to be subjected to persecution for a time than to be tortured with the beast in the infernal flames for eternity.

v. 13 Καὶ ἤκουσα φωνῆς ἐκ τοῦ οὐρανοῦ, *and I heard a voice from heaven*. Since the Antichrist will put to death many preachers of the Gospel and faithful confessors (Rev. 13:15), a consolation is added which not only the holy martyrs, who sealed the truth of the evangelical doctrine with their blood, but also others who suffer persecution, should embrace, namely, that death will not harm them, but will rather benefit them, since "they die in the Lord," that is, on account of the confession of His name, with true faith in Christ, with the true invocation of God (Rom. 16:12, 1 Cor. 7:39). Nor is their salvation postponed until long after their death, but immediately after they die they are made partakers of it.

Beza understands those who died in the Lord as the martyrs alone, so that it corresponds to the Hebrew ביהוה, "for the sake of God," which Bellarmine eagerly embraces. In response, we grant that the martyrs are chiefly represented here, but we deny that they alone are represented. The particle ב denotes either the means or the object, or something that holds a kind of object in itself. It would be absurd to take it as a means in this passage. Therefore, it denotes the object, as one can see far better when compared with these phrases: Romans 16:12, "those who are in the Lord and labor in the Lord;" 1 Cor. 7:22, "who has been called in the Lord a servant;" v. 39, "to marry in the Lord." It designates the status in which those who died were, namely, clinging to the Lord.

ἀπάρτι, *from now*, immediately following death. Suidas translates, "plainly, altogether, fully," so that it is the same thing as ἀπηρτισμένως, perfectly, with the full number, so that nothing is lacking, nothing is left over.

Piscator concludes that this adverb should not be put together with the word μακάριοι, *blessed*, but with the participle ἀποθνῄσκοντες, *who die*, so that it signifies the suffering that is to begin shortly thereafter. Lampadius explains it in practically the same way, Part 3, *Mellificii*, p. 408: "The blessed *who die from now on*, that is, who die after the revelation of the Gospel, who die in the Lord." We reply: This is a peculiar and artificial explanation of the word ἀπάρτι. Ambrose, Bede, and Haymo explain it as "from the time of death." Beza proves the same explanation, *In Annotat. Majoribus ad N.T.*, adding this rationale: "It is necessary to combine this particle with the word μακάριοι, *blessed*, for otherwise, those who died in prior ages would not be included in this sentence." For this reason, he also opposes the explanation of Lampadius.

ναί, λέγει τὸ πνεῦμα, ἵνα ἀναπαύσωνται ἐκ τῶν κόπων αὐτῶν, *yes, says the Spirit, that they may rest from their labors, etc.*, from all the trouble, from every adversity, from all the toil they endured in this life.

τὰ δὲ ἔργα αὐτῶν ἀκολουθεῖ μετ' αὐτῶν, *and their works follow after them*. Their works, that is, the recompense for their works, which is given by grace. In His great kindness and out of the generosity of His grace, God will repay with eternal rewards the good works of the godly, especially their steadfastness in confession.

v. 14 Καὶ εἶδον, καὶ ἰδοὺ νεφέλη λευκή, *and I saw, and behold, a white cloud*. The next two visions depict the terrible judgment of God against the ungodly, who are now ripe for punishment, that is, those who did not want to receive any admonition or correction.

The white cloud is a symbol: (1) of holiness and purity; (2) of righteousness and justice; (3) of royal majesty, for kings of old used to wear a white garment; (4) perfect happiness. Christ ascended into heaven in a cloud (Acts 1:11); He will return for judgment on a cloud (Mat. 24:30, 26:64; Luke 21:27).

ὅμοιος υἱῷ ἀνθρώπου, *like a Son of Man*. This represents Christ Jesus, the Son of God and of Mary (Psa. 8:5, Dan. 7:13, Rev. 1:13), who has been made "Judge of the living and the dead" (Acts 17:31), "to whom the Father has given authority to execute judgment, because He is the Son of Man" (John 5:27).

ἔχων ἐπὶ τῆς κεφαλῆς στέφανον χρυσοῦν, *having on His head a golden crown*. A golden crown is a sign (1) of dominion in heaven and earth (Mat. 28:19). The heavenly Father "has crowned Him with glory and honor" (Psa. 8:6, Heb. 2:7). For kings wear crowns, and the administration of the Last Judgment belongs to the royal office of Christ. It is also a sign (2) of the victory that Christ will carry away on the Day of Judgment from the Antichrist and from all the enemies of His Church.

καὶ ἐν τῇ χειρὶ αὐτοῦ δρέπανον ὀξύ, *and in His hand a sharp sickle*. The sharp sickle stands for His divine power and might, according to which He will punish the ungodly in the judgment and will suppress them as easily as when the reaper harvests the mature crops with his sickle. He cuts them down to the ground when they are ripe for punishment and when they have filled up the measure of their sins.

v. 15 καὶ ἄλλος ἄγγελος ἐξῆλθεν ἐκ τοῦ ναοῦ, *and another angel came out of the temple*, which John saw in heaven (v. 17).

κράζων ἐν μεγάλῃ φωνῇ τῷ καθημένῳ ἐπὶ τῆς νεφέλης, *crying out with a loud voice to the One sitting on the cloud*. A created angel cries out to Him who sits on the cloud, that is, to Christ the Judge, not as if he wanted to command Him, but in order to set forth the desire of the angels and the blessed—their desire for the time of judgment to arrive against the ungodly (Rev. 6:10, 12:17), just as when a servant says to his master, the head of the family, that it is time to harvest the field.

This angel also represents the faithful teachers of the Church, who cry out with groaning to Christ, not with carnal, but with divine fervor, that He would hasten His arrival for judgment and send His harvesting angels to gather the weeds from His kingdom (Mat. 13:41–42).

πέμψον τὸ δρέπανόν σου, *send forth Your sickle*. O Lord, gird Yourself, we pray, to administer the Final Judgment.

ὅτι ἦλθε σοι ἡ ὥρα τοῦ θερίσαι, *for the hour has come for You to reap*, that is, the consummation of the age (Mat. 13:39). All things are ripe for judgment.

ὅτι ἐξηράνθη ὁ θερισμὸς τῆς γῆς, *for the harvest of the earth is ripe*. The ungodly are ripe for punishment. Therefore, it is time to gather the wheat into Your barn and to collect the weeds in bundles and throw them into the fire (Mat. 13:30).

Philip Nicolai explains this as the conversion of the Gentiles, based on John 4:35.

v. 16 ἐπὶ τὴν γῆν, *upon the earth*, that is, into the grain field that is on the earth, namely, against the ungodly, who were ripe for judgment.

καὶ ἐθερίσθη ἡ γῆ, *and the earth was harvested*. The ungodly were cut down like weeds with the sickle of wrath and divine judgment and thrown into the fire.

v. 17 Καὶ ἄλλος ἄγγελος *and another angel*, etc. The same thing is expressed with the metaphor of the grape harvest as was previously described with the metaphor of the grain harvest.

v. 18 καὶ ἄλλος ἄγγελος ἐξῆλθεν ἐκ τοῦ θυσιαστηρίου, *and another angel came out from the altar*, namely, the one that was seen in heaven in v. 17.

ἔχων ἐξουσίαν ἐπὶ τοῦ πυρός, *having power over the fire*, that he may send the ungodly into the infernal flames after the Last Judgment.

τρύγησον τοὺς βότρυας τῆς ἀμπέλου τῆς γῆς, *gather the clusters of the vine of the earth*. Execute the Final Judgment, for the clusters, that is, the ungodly, are ripe for punishment.

v. 19 ἔβαλεν εἰς τὴν ληνὸν τοῦ θυμοῦ τοῦ θεοῦ τὴν μεγάλην, *cast them into the great winepress of the wrath of God*. The word *lacus* or "lake" in this verse does not mean a standing body of water enclosed with shores, but the basin of a winepress where grapes are squeezed.

It signifies hell, where the devils and all the ungodly are to be crushed as in a winepress.

v. 20 καὶ ἐπατήθη ἡ ληνὸς ἔξω τῆς πόλεως, *and the winepress was trampled outside of the city*, that is, the City of God, outside heaven, where God manifests His glory to the elect, for a great chasm exists between them and the damned (Luke 16:26). And *outside*, that is, outside of the heavenly Jerusalem, are the ungodly (Rev. 22:15).

καὶ ἐξῆλθεν αἷμα ἐκ τῆς ληνοῦ, *and blood went out from the winepress.* This signifies: (1) the great multitude of the damned; (2) the just and eternal punishment of the ungodly; (3) the terrible suffering of hell. How terrible and abominable it would be if someone were to see a knight riding around for 1,600 stadia, that is, 26 miles, in blood that reaches up to the bridle of his horse! And yet the punishment of the ungodly will be far more terrible and abominable, for they will be an abomination to all flesh (Isa. 66:24).

The ungodly shed the blood of others, and therefore their own blood will be shed in great abundance.

Chapter 15

This chapter contains the beginning of the fifth vision and the preparation of the seven angels. There are two parts.
  I. A description of the songs of the godly, vv. 1–4;
  II. The dispatching of the seven angels to pour out their bowls, v. 5 to the end of the chapter.

v. 1 Καὶ εἶδον ἄλλο σημεῖον, *and I saw another sign.* The seven angels represent the ministers of the Church, who are called by God and sent out in great numbers to announce, through the Word, the final punishments that await the Antichrist and all the ungodly.

v. 2 ὡς θάλασσαν ὑαλίνην μεμιγμένην πυρί, *like a sea of glass mingled with fire.*

(1) Some think this sea is a symbol of the world or of the human race. It is made of glass because of its fragility. The fire mixed in with it denotes either the persecutions with which the world attacks the godly and tries to devour them by fire (Luke 12:49), or the wrath of God by which the world will be consumed.

(2) But it is better to say that it represents Baptism, which is not simply water, but has the fire of the Holy Spirit mixed in with it (Mat. 3:11). By this Sacrament, men are regenerated into sons of God.

καὶ τοὺς νικῶντας ἐκ τοῦ θηρίου, *and those who are victorious over the beast*, who defeated the beast by true faith and the steadfast confession of the name of Christ (Heb. 11:33).

καὶ ἐκ τῆς εἰκόνος αὐτοῦ, *and over his image*, so that they neither worshiped the beast, nor his image, nor did they receive the mark or the number of his name, that is, they refused to cling to the Antichrist.

ἑστῶτας ἐπὶ τὴν θάλασσαν τὴν ὑαλίνην, *standing upon the sea of glass.* They remember their Baptism, in which they promised that they would acknowledge, worship, and call upon God alone as the true God.

ἔχοντας κιθάρας τοῦ θεοῦ, *having harps of God*, (1) which God had given them; (2) which they were employing for divine praises; (3) with which they were singing praises to God for the victory that had been gained against the Antichrist (Rev. 5:8, 14:2).

v. 3 ᾄδουσι τὴν ᾠδὴν Μωσέως, *they sing the song of Moses*. When God drowned Pharaoh and his whole army in the Red Sea, Moses and the children of Israel sang a special Eucharistic Song (Exo. 15:1). So, too, the believing and elect give thanks to God with a special song, praising Him for freeing them from the kingdom and slavery of the Antichrist.

καὶ τὴν ᾠδὴν τοῦ ἀρνίου, *and the song of the Lamb*, for Christ granted them this victory over the Antichrist; Christ taught them this song; it had been composed in praise of Christ. At the same time, however, it signifies that the true confessors of the Gospel hold in due esteem the Scriptures of the prophets, of whom Moses was chief, and of the apostles, who are the apostles of the Lamb (Rev. 21:14). They also founded the truth of their doctrine on these Scriptures, while the Antichrist and his followers hold them in contempt and prefer their own traditions to the Scriptures.

μεγάλα καὶ θαυμαστὰ τὰ ἔργα σου, *great and wonderful are Your works*. (Cf. Psa. 111:2, 139:14, 145:17.) "Who would not fear You?" (Jer. 10:7).

v. 4 ὅτι μόνος ὅσιος, *for You alone are holy*, essentially, originally, perfectly. Indeed, You are Holiness itself (Isa. 6:3).

ὅτι πάντα τὰ ἔθνη ἥξουσι καὶ προσκυνήσουσιν, *for all nations will come and worship*. (Cf. Isa. 66:23.) You have executed Your judgments against the Antichrist and his followers.

v. 5 ἠνοίγη ὁ ναὸς τῆς σκηνῆς τοῦ μαρτυρίου, *the temple of the tabernacle of the testimony was opened*. It is called the *temple of the tabernacle* because the temple that John saw was similar to Solomon's Temple, which was built in place of the tabernacle and designated for divine worship.

The tabernacle and the temple prefigured the glory of the heavenly Jerusalem, in which God manifests His glory and majesty to the angels and the elect, just as He dwelt with His gracious presence in the Mosaic tabernacle and in Solomon's Temple. The opening of this temple in heaven signifies that the faithful teachers of the Church who preach against the Antichrist have their calling from God, and that the temple of God had been shut, as it were, under the Papacy.

v. 6 καὶ ἐξῆλθον οἱ ἑπτὰ ἄγγελοι, *and the seven angels came out* (Rev. 14:17). ἐνδεδυμένοι λίνον καθαρὸν, *wearing pure linen*. The two witnesses in Rev. 11:3 were "clothed in sackcloth," for they would be made sorrowful at the time of the Antichrist's dominion. But these seven angels were clothed with linen robes, pure and bright, like victors. These robes are also (1) a symbol of purity, holiness, and glory; (2) a symbol of the doctrine in which they go forth, free of all corruption.

περιεζωσμένοι περὶ τὰ στήθη ζώνας χρυσᾶς, *girded around their chests with golden bands*. The band around the chest is a symbol of zeal for their office, that they were prepared to spread the pure doctrine and to fulfill God's will (cf. Luke 12:15) as the angels do (Psa. 103:20).

Golden bands stand for the illustrious gifts of the Holy Spirit with which they are equipped.

v. 7 καὶ ἐκ τῶν τεσσάρων ζῴων, *and of the four animals*. The fact that the seven bowls are given to the seven angels by one of the four animals signifies: (1) that God is putting off His indignation and judgments for a time, reserving them as in a bowl until the time comes to pour them out (Rom. 2:5); (2) that the sound teachers received the deposit of the pure doctrine from their predecessors.

v. 8 καὶ ἐγεμίσθη ὁ ναὸς καπνοῦ, *and the temple was filled with smoke*. Smoke signifies that the majesty and glory of God blind our eyes, just as smoke does, and that we cannot gaze upon it in this life because of our weakness (Exo. 19:18; Isa. 6:4; Cf. Exo. 40:34; 1 Kings 8:10).

It also signifies that God is powerfully present with His Church and Ministry until the Antichrist is thoroughly destroyed, and that the judgments of God are inscrutable to us until God Himself reveals them.

Chapter 16

There are, appropriately, seven parts to this chapter, one for each of the seven angels who have the seven bowls of divine wrath.
    I.   Where does the first angel pour out his bowl? (v. 2);
    II. Where the second? (v. 3);
    III. Where the third? (vv. 4–7);
    IV. Where the fourth? (vv. 8–9);
    V. Where the fifth? (vv. 10–11);
    VI. Where the sixth? (vv. 12–16);
    VII. Where does the seventh angel pour out his bowl? (v. 17 to the end of the chapter.)

v. 1 Καὶ ἤκουσα μεγάλης φωνῆς ἐκ τοῦ ναοῦ, *and I heard a loud voice from the temple*, that is, from heaven (Rev. 14:17). λεγούσης τοῖς ἑπτὰ ἀγγέλοις, *saying to the seven angels*, to the teachers of the Church.

ὑπάγετε καὶ ἐκχέατε τὰς φιάλας τοῦ θυμοῦ τοῦ θεοῦ, *go and pour out the bowls of the wrath of God*, that is, full of the plagues that come from divine wrath.

v. 2 ἐπὶ τὴν γῆν, *upon the earth*. When it says that one bowl is poured out upon the earth, another upon the sea, and a third upon the streams, etc., it means that God will stir up the elements and all creation against the ungodly for punishment.

The first angel pours out his bowl upon the earth, that is, he directs his rebuking office against the human traditions and earthly doctrine of the Antichrist.

καὶ ἐγένετο ἕλκος κακὸν καὶ πονηρὸν, *and a bad and evil sore came*. This plague corresponds to the sixth Egyptian plague (Exo. 9:10). It represents the inner anguish of conscience in those who are made partakers of the papal idolatry, for human doctrines and traditions cannot soothe the conscience.

Some interpret this as the Gallic disease, which is common among the priests of Italy who indulge in fornication.

v. 3 εἰς τὴν θάλασσαν, *into the sea*. The second angel addresses the luxurious and ungodly life of the Antichrist, who has his seat in Rome, on the shore of the sea.

Some take the sea to be men of every race in the world. But it directly and properly deals with the Antichrist.

καὶ ἐγένετο αἷμα ὡς νεκροῦ, *and it became blood, as of a dead man*. This plague corresponds to the first Egyptian plague (Exo. 7:17) and signifies that the followers of the Antichrist, by their luxurious and ungodly life, are alienated from the life which is from God (Eph. 4:18), that they are dead in sins (1 Tim. 5:6) and heap blood upon themselves (Psa. 51:16), and that, to those who wallow in the muddy sea of sins, the Word of God becomes the smell of death (2 Cor. 2:16).

Some interpret this as the deadly corruption of the Word, producing terrors of conscience and driving those who drink it, that is, who put their faith in the corrupted word, to despair.

v. 4 εἰς τοὺς ποταμοὺς καὶ τὰς πηγὰς τῶν ὑδάτων, *into the rivers and the springs of water*. The third angel addresses the external and political power that the Pope arrogates to himself over the peoples and kingdoms that adhere to him.

καὶ ἐγένετο αἷμα, *and it turned to blood*. This plague corresponds to the tenth Egyptian plague (Exo. 12:29). It refers to grisly wars and bloodshed, that the peoples, represented by the sea, and the kings and rulers, symbolized by the rivers, will wage one grisly war after another, even though they all adhere to the Antichrist. Their author and instigator is the Roman Pontiff.

v. 5 Καὶ ἤκουσα τοῦ ἀγγέλου τῶν ὑδάτων, *and I heard the angel of the waters*. This angel of the waters is the third angel who poured out his bowl on the rivers and springs.

ὅτι ταῦτα ἔκρινας, *because You have judged these things*. You have executed Your judgment against the ungodly followers of the Antichrist.

ὅτι αἷμα ἁγίων, *because they profusely shed the blood of the saints*, the holy confessors of the Gospel, καὶ προφητῶν, *and of the prophets*, the faithful teachers of the Church.

αἷμα αὐτοῖς ἔδωκας πιεῖν, *You gave them to drink blood.* They earned this punishment for themselves by their cruelty. Just as the Egyptians' water was turned to blood and their firstborn were killed (Exo. 7:21, 12:29) because they had ordered the little Israelite boys to be thrown into the river (Exo. 1:22), so the Antichristian cruelty, by which they copiously shed the blood of the godly confessors of Christ, is punished by the just judgment of God with wars and death.

v. 7 Καὶ ἤκουσα ἄλλου τοῦ θυσιαστηρίου λέγοντος·, *and I heard another*, namely, another angel, *from the altar*, namely, the altar in heaven (Rev. 14:18).

ἀληθιναὶ καὶ δίκαιαι αἱ κρίσεις σου, *true and righteous are Your judgments*, by which You punish those who obstinately despise the Gospel.

v. 8 ἐπὶ τὸν ἥλιον, *upon the sun*. The fourth angel addresses the pride and worldly pomp of the Antichrist, which is symbolized by the splendor of the sun.

καὶ ἐδόθη αὐτῷ καυματίσαι τοὺς ἀνθρώπους ἐν πυρί, *and it was given to him to burn men with fire.* This signifies the anguish and anxiety of conscience, because men doubt the grace of God, and thus they feel a notable raging in their heart, as if they were set in a burning flame. This punishment is inflicted on them because of their contempt for the doctrine of the Gospel.

Some say this has to do with the unusual heat, dryness, and sterility that follows a failure of crops and famine. But it is better interpreted as the inner burning of anxiety and a despairing conscience.

v. 9 καὶ ἐκαυματίσθησαν οἱ ἄνθρωποι καῦμα μέγα, *and men were burned with a fierce heat.* The Pontiff causes this heat in the hearts of men by tormenting the conscience in various ways.

καὶ ἐβλασφήμησαν τὸ ὄνομα τοῦ θεοῦ, *and they blasphemed the name of God.* In the end, despair is born of perpetual doubt.

δοῦναι αὐτῷ δόξαν, *to give Him glory*. The glory of righteousness and mercy is given to God through true repentance.

v. 10 ἐπὶ τὸν θρόνον τοῦ θηρίου, *upon the throne of the beast*. The fifth angel attacks the very seat of the Antichrist and demonstrates the falsehood of his boast, namely, that he is the Vicar of Christ and the Successor of Peter.

καὶ ἐγένετο ἡ βασιλεία αὐτοῦ ἐσκοτωμένη, *and his kingdom became darkened*. Darkness is a symbol of the contempt that spreads into the kingdom of the Pope. For when the brilliant light of the Gospel was brought forth from the papal darkness through Blessed Luther and his coworkers, the authority and glory of the papal See was diminished and obscured, and contempt was poured out upon his throne when it was demonstrated from the word of God that he is not the Vicar of Christ, but the Antichrist.

καὶ ἐμασῶντο τὰς γλώσσας αὐτῶν ἐκ τοῦ πόνου, *and they were gnawing their tongues from the pain*. On account of the damage inflicted on the papal See and the revelation of the papal errors, they were so enraged that they gnashed their teeth and gnawed their tongues from the pain.

v. 11 καὶ ἐβλασφήμησαν τὸν θεὸν τοῦ οὐρανοῦ, *and they blasphemed the God of heaven*, from pain of the heart and from anguish of conscience.

v. 12 ἐπὶ τὸν ποταμὸν τὸν μέγαν τὸν Εὐφράτην, *upon the great river Euphrates*. Just as Babylon accumulated great wealth by having the Euphrates river flowing nearby, so the Roman Antichrist had his monetary snares, largely resulting from indulgences, cloaks, taxes, papal bulls, etc. The sixth angel addressed these sources of acquiring wealth.

The Euphrates is a symbol of the wealth by which the figurative Babylon (that is, Rome) is fortified, just as, long ago, the eastern Babylon was fortified by the Euphrates.

καὶ ἐξηράνθη τὸ ὕδωρ αὐτοῦ, *and its water was dried up*, etc. When Cyrus attacked Babylon, he diverted the Euphrates and the rivers near the city elsewhere, in order to prepare for himself a path into the city (Jer. 51:32). So this passage predicts that God will prepare a way for the kings coming from the east so that they will be able to destroy the kingdom of the Antichrist, which is the figurative Babylon.

The kings from the east, namely, the ones who are coming, are understood by some to be hostile kings, like Darius, king of the Medes, and Cyrus, king of the Persians, were to the Babylonians. But it is better to take it in a general way to refer to the godly kings and rulers who receive the light of the Gospel once the Antichristian errors are refuted. For the rising of the sun is a symbol of something good and favorable (Rev. 7:1).

The doctrine of the Gospel is the doctrine about Christ, who is the "dawn from on high" (Luke 1:78).

v. 13 Καὶ εἶδον ἐκ τοῦ στόματος τοῦ δράκοντος, *and I saw from the mouth of the dragon, etc.* The dragon stands for the devil. The beast stands for the Antichristian kingdom, that is, the Roman See, where, together with the Pope, the Cardinals, Bishops and prelates of the Antichristian kingdom are in control. The false prophet stands for the head of the Antichristian kingdom, namely, the Roman Pontiff.

For just as the voice of a prophet is attributed preeminently to Christ (Deu. 18:15; Acts 3:22), so also the title of false prophet is attributed preeminently to the Antichrist, according to Augustine, Book XX, *De Civitate Dei*, ch. 14.

Some apply this to the precursor of the Antichrist and to his chief minister, just as John the Baptist, who is called a prophet of the Most High by his father Zacharias (Luke 1:76), was the forerunner of Christ.

The πνεύματα ἀκάθαρτα, *unclean spirits*, represent the men who are driven and influenced by unclean spirits, namely, the false teachers who are sent off to spread the papal errors.

Ὅμοια βατράχοις, *like frogs*, because they croak loudly at the true teachers of the Church and annoy the godly with their noise. But at the same time, with their calumnies they inflame the pontifical princes against the confessors of the Gospel. This is a reference to the second Egyptian plague, the plague of frogs (Exo. 8:1).

v. 14 εἰσὶν γὰρ πνεύματα δαιμόνων, *for they are spirits of demons*, because they preach the doctrine of demons (1 Tim. 4:1).

ποιοῦντα σημεῖα, *performing signs.* (Cf. Mat. 24:24; 2 The. 2:9.)

ἃ ἐκπορεύεται ἐπὶ τοὺς βασιλεῖς τῆς γῆς, *which go out upon the kings of the earth.* The impudent Sophists incite kings and princes against the confessors of the Gospel with their daily pleas to accost them with war.

τῆς ἡμέρας ἐκείνης τῆς μεγάλης, *of that great day.* The croaking of the Sophist frogs and the wars of those notable men, the followers of the Antichrist, will last until the Day of Judgment, when Christ will completely destroy the Antichrist with the brightness of His coming (2 The. 2:8).

v. 15 Ἰδοὺ ἔρχομαι ὡς κλέπτης, *behold, I come as a thief.* (Cf. Rev. 3:3.) Because men are secure and imagine the kingdom of the Antichrist to be indestructible, John introduces Christ Himself as a speaker. "Behold, I am coming suddenly for judgment. Therefore, let everyone guard himself against security, from ungodliness and from apostasy to the Antichrist."

μακάριος ὁ γρηγορῶν, *blessed is he who keeps watch,* who guards himself against carnal security, καὶ τηρῶν τὰ ἱμάτια αὐτοῦ, *and who keeps his garments,* that lovely garment of the imputed righteousness of Christ which is put on by true faith, and the pure garment of holy living. (Cf. Mat. 22:11; 2 Cor. 5:2; Gal. 3:27; Rev. 3:4, 18; Rev. 19:8.)

v. 16 Καὶ συνήγαγεν αὐτοὺς εἰς τὸν τόπον τὸν καλούμενον Ἑβραϊστὶ Ἁρμαγεδδών, *and He,* namely, God, *gathered them together in the place which is called in Hebrew, Armageddon.*

(1) Aretas reads it as ἐρμαγεδὼν, as many Hebrew words were very poorly rendered by the Greeks in the New Testament.

(2) Some think it should be read *garon haroma,* which means, "the destruction of the lofty one, Rome." Dr. Silberschlag agrees with their conclusion (*De Antichr.,* p. 24) so that the sense is: "All those who oppose the kingdom of Christ and cling to the Antichrist will assemble in the place where that ancient and lofty city of Rome once was, and now is rebuilt and restored. They will suffer the same destruction and the same plague that ancient Rome suffered in the very place where that ancient city lies. The servants of the Antichrist will rally there primarily because the Antichrist will have his seat fixed there." But the word גָּרוֹן, *garon,* does not mean "destruction." It means "throat," so called from the intersections, or from the attraction of spirit, from *garar,* "he drew, he cut, he dragged."

(3) Drusius says that this word is a composite of חרמא, "destruction" (the city where the Jews killed every last one of the Canaanites was called Hormah, Num. 21:3), and גְּרְהוֹן, *gerhon*, or the shortened form גֵּרוֹן, *gerron*, which means "their army," so that the place obtains its name from the outcome, namely, the destruction of the armies.

(4) Some say that the word is a composite from two Hebrew words, הַר מְגִדּוֹ, *har Megiddo*, the Megiddo or Megiddon mountain, the place that received its name from the mourning that took place because of the defeat King Josiah suffered at the hand of Pharaoh Neco of Egypt (2 Kings 23:29; 2 Chr. 35:22; Zec. 12:11). It signifies the lamentable outcome of that battle for those kings, so that the sense is that God will gather the idolatrous kings who serve the Antichrist and fight against the Church in a place where they will suffer a notable defeat, just as Josiah did on mount Megiddo.

(5) Some interpret it as *harma*, that is, "a hill," and *Gedon*, that is, "a multitude of people," so that the sense is that those kings who fight against the Church will be gathered in a place where the bodies of the dead are tossed in a heap.

(6) Blessed Luther explains it as "damned soldiers, a cursed army, wretched warriors." The third explanation above seems the simplest. It means that the army of the Antichrist will be thoroughly destroyed, so that, for this reason, the Antichrist will not be able to prevail against the true Church either with sophistic frogs or with a militant army.

v. 17 ἐπὶ τὸν ἀέρα, *into the air*. The seventh angel will address the followers of the Antichrist because, by their magic arts, they made a pact with the Devil, who is the "prince of the air" (Eph. 6:12), and keep familiar company with him.

ἀπὸ τοῦ θρόνου, *from the throne*, namely, of God (Rev. 21:6).

Γέγονε, *it is done*. The decisive sentence has been carried out against the beast. The kingdom of the Antichrist will be destroyed, never to be rebuilt. The temporal plagues are at an end. The final judgment and the eternal plagues will follow for the Antichrist and for his followers.

v. 18 καὶ ἐγένοντο φωναὶ καὶ βρονταί, *and there were noises and thunderings*. This signifies the final destruction and ruin of the Antichristian kingdom, that God will fight against it from above, with thunder and flashes of lightning, and from below, with earthquakes, so that, for this reason, the whole system of the world will be overthrown, together with the kingdom of the Antichrist, by this thundering and by this earthquake, for Christ will wipe out the Antichrist at His coming (2 The. 2:8). Noises, thunder, lightning, earthquakes, etc., are signs of the divine wrath by which Antichrist's kingdom will be destroyed.

v. 19 καὶ ἐγένετο ἡ πόλις ἡ μεγάλη εἰς τρία μέρη, *and the great city was divided into three parts*. The *great city* is a reference to Rome, symbolized by Babylon (Rev. 14:8–9; ch. 17 and 18). The city is so shaken and dissipated by the earthquake that it completely falls, together with all who dwell in it, from the upper class down to the lower class of men. Some apply this to the dissensions in the ecclesiastical, political, and domestic estates that will precede the final ruin of Antichrist.

καὶ αἱ πόλεις τῶν ἐθνῶν ἔπεσαν, *and the cities of the Gentiles fell*, namely, the cities of the peoples who cling to the Antichrist and who acknowledge him as their head.

δοῦναι αὐτῇ τὸ ποτήριον τοῦ οἴνου τοῦ θυμοῦ τῆς ὀργῆς αὐτοῦ, *to give her the cup of the wine of the wrath of His anger* (Isa. 51:22, 28; Jer. 25:15). God will bring upon the city of Rome its well-deserved punishments.

v. 20 καὶ πᾶσα νῆσος ἔφυγε, *and every island fled, etc*. All things were shaken so much that they came crashing down upon the ground, so that neither islands nor mountains were seen any longer.

v. 21 καὶ χάλαζα μεγάλη, *and a great hail*. This hail denotes the severe weight of divine wrath that presses down upon the ungodly so hard that they erupt in blasphemies. This is a reference to the Egyptian plagues in which hail was mixed with fire (Exo. 9:22).

Chapter 17

This chapter contains the beginning of the sixth vision and thus the explanation of the essential parts of the main chapters. There are two parts:
I. The description of the harlot of Babylon;
II. The explanation of that description, given to John by the angel (v. 7 to the end of the chapter).

v. 1 Καὶ ἦλθεν εἷς ἐκ τῶν ἑπτὰ ἀγγέλων, *and one of the seven angels came* (Rev. 15:1). τὸ κρίμα, *the judgment*, that is, κατάκριμα, *the condemnation.* "I will show you the condemnation of the harlot," that is, "the condemned harlot," a Hebraism. For in Hebrew, when two nouns are joined in a state of regimen, the second takes on the nature of an adjective. It is also possible to understand condemnation as a metonymy for the temporal and eternal punishments that will eventually be mentioned (Rev. 18:2). But the picture of this harlot is set forth to John in v. 3 as something that he is to consider.

The πόρνην μεγάλην, *great harlot*, stands for the Antichristian, Roman, and papal Church that was a pure virgin at the time of the Apostles (2 Cor. 11:2), but afterwards, it was later adulterated and made a harlot through spiritual fornication, that is, idolatry, false doctrine and superstition (Isa. 1:21; Nah. 3:4).

τῆς καθημένης ἐπὶ ὑδάτων πολλῶν, *who sits on many waters*, who rules over many peoples (v. 15). Indeed, she arrogates to herself dominion over all peoples and churches.

v. 2 μεθ' ἧς ἐπόρνευσαν οἱ βασιλεῖς τῆς γῆς, *with whom the kings of the earth committed adultery*. Many great rulers have embraced her idolatry, false worship forms and errors (Judges 2:17; Jer. 3:1; Nah. 3:8).

καὶ ἐμεθύσθησαν ἐκ τοῦ οἴνου τῆς πορνείας αὐτῆς, *and became drunk from the wine of her fornication* (Rev. 14:8). She deceived many peoples with her doctrine. She dressed in purple and seduced them to commit spiritual fornication, just as harlots often set love potions before their lovers.

Therefore, this cannot be referring to pagan Rome, for Rome allowed her peoples free autonomy to follow their religions and superstitions. Indeed, she received her religion from them. Leo, *Sermon 1, De Petro & Paulo*: "This city, ignoring the Author of its progress, since it ruled over practically all nations, was slave to the errors of all nations and seemed to adopt a grand religion for itself, because it spurned no falsehood."

v. 3 καὶ ἀπήνεγκέ με εἰς ἔρημον ἐν πνεύματι, *and he carried me away into the desert in spirit*. In the desert, he views those things that cause the Church of Christ to be deserted.

Καὶ εἶδον γυναῖκα, *and I saw a woman*, the great harlot, καθημένην ἐπὶ θηρίον κόκκινον, *seated on a scarlet beast* (Dan. 7:7; Rev. 13:1). This beast represents the ancient Roman Empire, which the Roman Pontiffs seized for themselves and subjugated to themselves. It is called a scarlet beast because of the blood of the godly which the pagan emperors shed, and in this way they made themselves similar to the red dragon (Rev. 12:3).

γέμον ὀνομάτων βλασφημίας, *full of names of blasphemy*, because in the Roman Empire, when it was still pagan, a terrible and blasphemous idolatry reigned. On the other hand, the name and doctrine of Christ were castigated with terrible blasphemies.

ἔχων κεφαλὰς ἑπτὰ καὶ κέρατα δέκα, *having seven heads and ten horns* (v. 9 and 12). The explanation follows.

v. 4 καὶ ἡ γυνὴ ἦν περιβεβλημένη πορφύρᾳ καὶ κοκκίνῳ καὶ κεχρυσωμένη χρυσίῳ καὶ λίθῳ τιμίῳ καὶ μαργαρίταις, *and the woman was dressed in purple and scarlet, and gilded with gold and with precious stones and pearls*. This external splendor and pomp symbolizes the Roman Church, since experience bears witness that, in the wardrobe of the Pontiff, the Cardinals, the Bishops, and the Abbots, especially in the Mass, all things glitter with gold and pearls. The Cardinals in particular march along dressed in purple.

ἔχουσα χρυσοῦν ποτήριον ἐν τῇ χειρὶ αὐτῆς, *having a golden cup in her hand*. The cup in which the figurative harlot gives her lovers her love potion is golden, because the Pontiff promises honor, riches, glory, and power to those who receive and defend the papal dogmas. He pretends to seek nothing more than the salvation of men. He uses the Sophists to disguise his dogmas with attractive arguments. But this golden cup is full of the abomination of false doctrine, idolatry, superstitions, and errors, all of which is spiritual fornication.

v. 5 καὶ ἐπὶ τὸ μέτωπον αὐτῆς ὄνομα γεγραμμένον, Μυστήριον, *and upon her forehead a name is written, "Mystery."* This signifies that there is a great mystery hidden in this description of the great harlot. The mystery is that she stands for Babylon the Great, figuratively speaking. Not the ancient Babylon that was the capital city of the kingdom of Assyria, but Antichristian Rome, just as the explanation set forth in v. 10 demonstrates. Furthermore, she is…

ἡ μήτηρ τῶν πορνῶν καὶ τῶν βδελυγμάτων τῆς γῆς, *the mother of harlots and of the abominations of the earth,* because both spiritual and bodily fornication, along with other serious sins, reign supreme in Rome and are propagated from that city into the whole world.

Not only is she the mother of πορνῶν, *harlots,* as several Greek manuscripts have it, but also of πόρνων, *male prostitutes,* as the Complutensian and Royal editions have it. That is, she is considered the mother of the Catamites or Ganymedes.

v. 6 καὶ εἶδον τὴν γυναῖκα μεθύουσαν ἐκ τοῦ αἵματος τῶν ἁγίων, *and I saw the woman drunk from the blood of the saints.*

(1) The Remi, *In Annot.* on this passage, sect. 6, take this to be "the whole body of persecutors of the Church, that is, all the persecutors there have ever been since the beginning of the world." But (i) the angel says to John in v. 1, "I will show you the condemnation of that great harlot," speaking of a time in the future. (ii) Afterwards he says in v. 2 that the woman is drunk with the blood of the martyrs of Jesus Christ. Therefore, he is talking about that persecution that follows the manifestation of Christ. (iii) He says in v. 18, "And the woman that I saw is that great city that has dominion over the kings of the earth." Therefore, that harlot is a certain city and government, not an indefinite multitude. (iv) John testifies in ch. 1:1 that those things were revealed to him that must soon take place, that is, in the future. Therefore, this verse cannot be referring to ancient persecutions of the Church.

(2) Therefore, this verse is referring to Rome, drunk on the blood of the martyrs which it has copiously shed and "drunk," as it were, like a shameless woman who has engorged herself with wine and becomes drunk and flushed in the face.

Jerome, Book II, *Adv. Jovinian.*, addresses Rome in this way: "With a change of mind you can avoid that curse that was threatened against you by Christ in Revelation." He says, *In Praefat. ad Paulinian.*: "While I lived in Babylon," that is, Rome, "and was an inhabitant of the purple harlot."

v. 8 θηρίον ὃ εἶδες ἦν καὶ οὐκ ἔστι, *the beast that you saw was and is not.* (1) *The beast that you saw*, or "that you see," *was*, namely, was in the hands of Roman men, *and is not*, that is, is no longer in the hands of a Roman man, but in the hands of a foreigner, namely, Trajan, who was from the nation of Spain.

(2) It is better to take it in the following way: The original Roman Empire at first had great authority and prosperity; it was endowed with great power. But afterwards it suffered a notable decline and was no longer fortified with the same authority and power it once had.

καὶ μέλλει ἀναβαίνειν ἐκ τῆς ἀβύσσου, *and will ascend out of the abyss.* Luther translates: "will come again." But in Greek it says μέλλει ἀναβαίνειν, "will ascend." A beast will ascend from the abyss, namely, when the Roman Antichrist seizes that empire, it will again be lifted up; it will experience growth. The abyss stands for hell, from whence the Antichrist originates.

καὶ εἰς ἀπώλειαν ὑπάγει, *and goes to perdition*, because the Antichrist and his followers will be condemned, if they do not repent (Rev. 19:20).

ὧν τὰ ὀνόματα οὐ γέγραπται, *whose names are not written, etc.*, who are not numbered among the elect.

βλέποντες τὸ θηρίον, ὅ, τι ἦν, καὶ οὐκ ἔστι, καίπερ ἐστί, *seeing the beast that was, and is not, and yet is.* Seeing the original Roman Empire, which had formerly collapsed, but afterwards was restored by the Antichrist. Καί πέρ ἐστι, *nevertheless is.* The Roman Pontiff does not want to admit that he is a monarch and emperor, and yet, in truth, that is what he is, no matter how much he goes by the title of "Peter's successor." He has seized the principal regions belonging to the Roman Empire, including the city of Rome itself.

v. 9 ὧδε ὁ νοῦς ὁ ἔχων σοφίαν, *here is the mind that has wisdom.* Because in this explanation, the location and the character of the beast is not expressly stated, and yet, at the same time, it is outlined with certain indications, in such a way that its name can easily be discovered with the attendant fulfillment and experience.

Αἱ ἑπτὰ κεφαλαὶ ὄρη εἰσίν ἑπτὰ, *the seven heads are seven mountains,* the seven hills of the city of Rome: (1) Palatine Hill, (2) Capitoline Hill, (3) Aventine Hill, (4) Esquiline Hill, (5) Caelian Hill, (6) Viminal Hill, (7) Quirinal Hill.

Propertius, Book III, *Eleg.* 10. *De Roma:* "The high city of seven hills that presides over the whole world."

Lessius takes this beast to be the devil, who reigns in the world, whose seven heads are the ungodly kings of the seven ages of the world. But (1) from the circumstances it is apparent that the beast is describing the Roman state. (2) A certain political estate is often designated by Daniel and John with the title of "beast." The devil is called, "the dragon who gave authority to the beast." (3) In the same sense the woman is said to be sitting on a beast. But the woman, that is, the city of Rome, does not rule over the devil. (Cf. Dounamum, p. 58.)

v. 10 καὶ βασιλεῖς ἑπτά εἰσιν, *and they are seven kings.* The seven kings stand for the seven forms of government employed in the Roman Empire until the coming of the Antichrist. For there were (1) kings, (2) consuls, (3) decemviri, (4) military tribunes, (5) dictators, (6) Caesars, (7) Goths and Vandals, who occupied Rome several times. Others number in the seventh place the Roman Pontiffs who seized the empire for themselves and changed it into another form of government.

οἱ πέντε ἔπεσαν, *five have fallen.* (1) The first five forms of government had already come to an end by the time of John. Five kings or heads of state passed away before the time of John. The sixth, which was the emperor, existed at that time. The seventh, which is the government of the Roman Bishops or Patriarchs, had not yet come. (For although there were Roman Bishops ever since the time of the apostles, the heads of the Roman state did not depart before the seat of the Empire was transferred from Rome.)

And when he comes, he says, he must remain for a short time, that is, from the time the seat of the Empire was transferred to Constantinople until the fall of the Roman Empire in the West, from that time until the reign of the Pope was instituted by Phocas, it could be said of this beast that "he was, is not, and yet is."

(2) Those who interpret the seventh king as the Goths and Vandals explain it this way: Five have fallen, that is, the first five forms of government came to an end before John's time. One is, that is, the sixth form of government was still active. Another had not yet come, that is, the seventh form of the Empire under the Goths and Vandals, was not yet present. And when it comes, it must remain for a short time, because the Goths and Vandals were expelled from Rome again after a short time.

(3) Some explain it in the following way: Five of those kings, that is, the Emperors, fell, that is, they died, namely, Servius Sulpitius Galba; Marcus Salvius Otho; Aulus Vitellius; Titus Flavius Vespasianus; Titus Titi, the son of Vespasianus. There was one, the sixth, at the time of John, namely, Flavius Domitianus. John wrote these things during his last days, as Irenaeus testifies, Book V. Another, the seventh, was not yet, and when he came, he would remain for a short time. This is Nerva, who lasted one year, four months and nine days. The eighth, who is added to these seven, is Ulpius Trajanus.

But the first explanation should be preferred to the others, inasmuch as it agrees best with the text and with the matter itself.

v. 11 καὶ τὸ θηρίον ὃ ἦν καὶ οὐκ ἔστι καὶ αὐτὸς ὄγδοός ἐστι, *and the beast that was and is not is also himself the eighth*. The Roman Pontiff, who earlier was called the seventh, is now called the eighth, because he not only recovered the original dignity and glory of the Roman Empire after the Goths, Vandals, and other barbarian peoples were expelled from Italy, but he also increased them and thus instituted a new form of government, as it were.

καὶ ἐκ τῶν ἑπτά ἐστι, *and he is of the seven*. He will draw the Roman Empire to himself, and he will rule in Rome, where the seven forms of government were employed.

καὶ εἰς ἀπώλειαν ὑπάγει, *and he is going to perdition*. The kingdom of the Antichrist will also have its end at the appointed time.

It should be noted in this passage that the Pontiffs themselves admit that "the Antichrist is one of the heads of the beast." Bellarmine admits, Book III, *De Rom. Pont.*, ch. 15: "The Antichrist is designated as the seventh king, who is the seventh head of the beast." Mich. Christoph., Part 2, *De Antichr.*, p. 37: "The Catholics admit and prove most convincingly that the Antichrist is signified by the last head of the beast. From that fact it necessarily follows that a certain state is signified by the seven-headed beast, whose final head is Antichrist. Nevertheless, the claim made by some should not on that account be rejected, namely, that the Antichrist is called the beast by synecdoche. For in this they are following John, who, both in several other passages refers to the Antichrist with the title of 'beast,' and especially in chapter 17, where, after he has numbered the heads of the beast, he specifically says in v. 11 that the last, which is Antichrist, is the beast, and afterwards he attributes that title to him three times, vv. 12, 13, 17." Suarez, Book V, ch. 6, par. 6 & 7: "The common exposition is that this beast is the Antichrist. But this exposition does not exclude the conclusion of those who claim that the beast is the Roman Empire, for the first statement is not understood comprehensively; it refers to the chief head of that beast."

v. 12 Καὶ τὰ δέκα κέρατα ἃ εἶδες δέκα βασιλεῖς εἰσιν, *and the ten horns that you saw are ten kings*. There were ten kingdoms that were subject to the ancient Roman Empire: (1) Syria, (2) Egypt, (3) Asia, (4) Greece, (5) Africa, (6) Spain, (7) Gaul, (8) Italy, (9) Germany, (10) Poland and the neighboring northern kingdoms. Some list the kings in this way: (1) The king of Gaul, (2) of Spain, (3) of Portugal, (4) of Neapolis, (5) of England, (5) of Denmark, (6) of Sweden, (7) of Poland, (9) of Hungary, (10) of Bohemia.

οἵτινες βασιλείαν οὔπω ἔλαβον, *who have not yet received a kingdom*, because at the time when John wrote these things, the Roman Empire was not yet divided, and the kings listed above were not yet under the authority of the Roman Empire.

ἀλλὰ ἐξουσίαν ὡς βασιλεῖς μίαν ὥραν λαμβάνουσιν μετὰ τοῦ θηρίου, *but they receive authority as kings for one hour with the beast*. When the Roman Empire diminishes, each of these ten provinces will have its own king and will shine, in principle, together with the royal Roman Empire, or with the two-horned beast (Rev. 13:11) because of what follows.

μετὰ τοῦ θηρίου, *with the beast.* The Vulgate has, "after the beast." But the Pontiffs themselves do not interpret this preposition temporally; they interpret it with regard to subjection. "After the beast," says Ribera on this passage, "that is, following the beast and obedient to him." Viegas on this passage: "They receive a kingdom with the beast, that is, at the time of Antichrist, or after the beast, namely, they follow him and obey him as family members." Lessius, *De Antichr.*, p. 116: "After the beast," is interpreted, "under the devil."

v. 13 οὗτοι μίαν γνώμην ἔχουσι, καὶ τὴν δύναμιν καὶ τὴν ἐξουσίαν τῷ θηρίῳ διαδιδώσουσιν, *they have one mind, and they will distribute power and authority to the beast.* The sense is that they will all hold to the Roman Antichrist at one time and will give their power to him, as if they received their royal power and dignity from him.

v. 14 οὗτοι μετὰ τοῦ ἀρνίου πολεμήσουσιν, *they will fight with the Lamb.* They will fight with Christ and His Church in order to eradicate and destroy it (Rev. 5:6, 14:1).

καὶ τὸ ἀρνίον νικήσει αὐτούς, ὅτι κύριος κυρίων ἐστὶ, *and the Lamb will overcome them, for He is Lord of lords* (1 Tim. 6:15, Rev. 19:16). His power is invincible.

καὶ οἱ μετ' αὐτοῦ κλητοὶ καὶ ἐκλεκτοὶ καὶ πιστοί, *and those who are with Him are called and chosen and faithful.* Those who fight under the banner of Christ will overcome with Him by His power.

v. 15 τὰ ὕδατα ἃ εἶδες, *the waters that you saw,* in v. 1, λαοὶ, *peoples,* etc. (Cf. Isa. 8:7; Jer. 47:2.) These are individual kingdoms and provinces in which there are different groups of people and common forms of speech.

v. 16 καὶ τὰ δέκα κέρατα ἃ εἶδες, *and the ten horns that you saw,* v. 3, μισήσουσιν τὴν πόρνην, *will hate the harlot.* Those ten kings will no longer hold the Roman Pontiff in such high esteem, but will follow him with hidden hatred.

ἐπὶ τὸ θηρίον, *upon the beast.* The Complutensian edition reads κατὰ τὸ θηρίον, *against to the beast.* Bellarmine seems to follow this understanding, Book III, *De Rom. Pont.*, ch. 13. But this reading is refuted by Rev. 18: 4 & 6, where this destruction is carried out, not on the Antichrist and his accomplices, but rather on the people of God.

καὶ ἠρημωμένην ποιήσουσιν αὐτὴν, *and they will make her desolate.* They will no longer come to Rome as often and with such an abundance of men in order to offer their services to the harlot.

καὶ γυμνὴν, *and naked.* The money that they used to send to Rome, they will reserve for themselves, and they will undertake to uncover the ignominy of her nakedness, that is, her errors, in their kingdoms.

καὶ τὰς σάρκας αὐτῆς φάγονται, *and they will eat her flesh.* (Cf. Job 19:22, Psa. 27:2.) What the Pope drew to himself with flattery and fraud, they will tear away from him. They will afflict and persecute him.

καὶ αὐτὴν κατακαύσουσιν ἐν πυρί, *and they will burn her,* that is, the city, *with fire.* They will burn up the seat of the Antichrist with fire.

v. 17 ὁ γὰρ θεὸς ἔδωκαν εἰς τὰς καρδίας, *for God put it into their hearts, etc.* Until the words of God are fulfilled, that is, the prophecies set forth thus far. God will stir up some brave heroes from those ten kingdoms who will again snatch away from the Roman Antichrist what he had taken away from the Roman Empire, and they will restore it to the Empire. Nevertheless, it can be gathered from Rev. 18:9 that some will remain joined to the beast, and thus, by synecdoche, those who are represented by them. The kings of the earth who committed fornication with the harlot of Babylon will mourn over her ruin. Likewise from Rev. 16:15, where the kings of the earth are gathered for the battle which is to be taken up on behalf of the beast and the false prophet.

v. 18 ἡ πόλις ἡ μεγάλη, *the great city,* namely, Rome and the Antichrist who will exercise his dominion in Rome (Rev. 16:19), for at the time of John that city had dominion over the kings of the earth, and the Roman Pontiff today arrogates to himself the same power.

172

Chapter 18

This chapter contains the same things as chapter 14, namely, a prediction of the punishments threatened against the city of Rome. There are three parts:
    I. The angel's warning about the ruin of Babylon, vv. 1–3;
    II. An exhortation for the godly to depart from Babylon, where a complaint is inserted about the spiritual commerce of the Antichrist, along with consolation for the godly, vv. 4–20;
    III. The ruin threatened against the Antichrist is depicted with a millstone being cast into the sea, v. 21 to the end of the chapter.

v. 1 εἶδον ἄγγελον, *I saw an angel*. This angel represents some notable teacher of the Church whose divine mission is indicated by his descent from heaven.

Some take this angel to be Christ. (1) He descends from heaven. (2) All authority is given to him. (3) He is the Light of the world. But John, in Revelation, calls Christ many times "Lamb," "Son of Man," "Alpha & Omega," "Tree of Life," whereas he uses the word "angels" to refer to the teachers of the Church. Christ proclaimed the ruin of Babylon not immediately, but mediately. Therefore, the angel is better understood as Luther, who was divinely called and sent.

ἔχοντα ἐξουσίαν μεγάλην, *having great authority*. "For the Gospel is the power of God for salvation" (Rom. 1:16), and "the Word of God is living and effective" (Heb. 4:12).

καὶ ἡ γῆ ἐφωτίσθη ἐκ τῆς δόξης αὐτοῦ, *and the earth was illumined with his glory*. For the Gospel is a very bright light by which men are enlightened for eternal life in the true knowledge of God (1 Cor. 4:6). But this authority and splendor especially indicate that this notable teacher of the Church would be notable for his fearless spirit and great authority, so that he dares to take a stand.

v. 2 ἔπεσε, ἔπεσε Βαβυλὼν ἡ μεγάλη, *fallen, fallen is Babylon the great*, that great city, that is, Antichristian Rome.

ἐγένετο κατοικητήριον δαιμόνων, καὶ φυλακὴ παντὸς πνεύματος ἀκαθάρτου, *she has become a dwelling place of demons, and a prison for every unclean spirit*.

φυλακὴ, *a prison* is more than an οἰκτήριον, *a dwelling place*. For the sense is that he has fortified his palace with defenses and guards, and has surrounded it with attendants and bodyguards. But it will be completely laid waste and devastated, because demons and birds of prey live in deserted and desolate places. These unclean animals also represent the frogs that are the spirits of demons, whose ancient habitation was once the city of Rome (Rev. 16:13–14).

v. 3 ὅτι ἐκ τοῦ οἴνου τοῦ θυμοῦ τῆς πορνείας αὐτῆς πέπωκε πάντα τὰ ἔθνη, *for all nations have drunk from the wine of the wrath of her fornication*. By the righteous indignation and permission of God, she forced her idolatry on many peoples.

καὶ οἱ βασιλεῖς τῆς γῆς μετ' αὐτῆς ἐπόρνευσαν καὶ οἱ ἔμποροι τῆς γῆς ἐκ τῆς δυνάμεως τοῦ στρήνους αὐτῆς ἐπλούτησαν, *and the kings of the earth committed fornication with her and the merchants of the earth became rich from the power of her luxury*. These merchants signify the Cardinals, Archbishops, Bishops, and papal prelates who became rich through papal merchandise, for they sold indulgences, Masses, works of supererogation, papal dispensations and other similar goods at a high price.

From the power of her luxury, that is, from violent luxury or lasciviousness. When the Hebrews join two nouns in a definite state of construction, the second takes the place of an adjective.

v. 4 ἐξέλθετε ἐξ αὐτῆς, *come out of her*. Christ, who is the Word of the Father, sends down this word as if from heaven by which He exhorts His Christian people to separate themselves from the Antichristian Babylon.

v. 5 Ἠκολούθησαν αὐτῆς αἱ ἁμαρτίαι ἄχρι τοῦ οὐρανοῦ, *her sins have followed up to heaven*. Her sins followed one after another, so much so that they rose up like a huge mountain that reaches heaven, that is, they have come into the sight of God (Gen. 18:20).

καὶ ἐμνημόνευσεν ὁ θεὸς τὰ ἀδικήματα αὐτῆς, *and God remembered her iniquities.* Just as God is said to forget sins when He remits them and does not punish a man on account of them, so He is said to remember sins when He punishes a man on account of them.

v. 6 ἀπόδοτε αὐτῇ, *render to her.* This command is given to those who were about to destroy and wipe out Rome. *Render to her the evil that she inflicted on you.* Wipe out the Roman Babylon.

καὶ διπλώσατε τὰ διπλᾶ, *repay her double.* Bring upon her more injury than she brought upon you.

v. 7 ὅσα ἐδόξασεν ἑαυτήν, *in the measure that she glorified herself.* She lived in luxury like an impudent and shameless harlot. Τοσοῦτον δότε αὐτῇ βασανισμὸν, *in the same measure give her torment.* You should mete out to her with the same measure (Luke 6:38).

κάθημαι βασίλισσα, *I sit as queen.* In the seat of Peter, I am the Vicar of Christ and the Successor of Peter. I hold the highest authority in the whole Church and in the political realm. I reign over kings and princes.

καὶ χήρα οὐκ εἰμὶ, *and I am not a widow.* I have not failed until now, nor shall there fail to be a successor in the apostolic seat of Peter.

καὶ πένθος οὐ μὴ ἴδω, *and I will never see mourning.* I shall always prevail over my enemies. Victory and happiness will ever stay by my side.

v. 8 διὰ τοῦτο, *for this reason,* on account of this luxury and those haughty boastings, ἐν μιᾷ ἡμέρᾳ ἥξουσιν, *in one day they will come.* Plagues will come upon her unexpectedly.

καὶ ἐν πυρὶ κατακαυθήσεται, *and she will be burned with fire,* namely, by the ten horns—the ten kings who will hate her and separate themselves from her (Rev. 17:16).

ὁ κρίνων αὐτήν, *who judges her.* The strength of the Antichrist could not be suppressed by the arm of man, but God is strong enough to vanquish her.

v. 9 Καὶ κλαύσονται αὐτὴν, *and they will mourn her.* This is referring to those who clung to the harlot even until her destruction.

v. 10 ἀπὸ μακρόθεν ἑστηκότες, *standing at a distance.* They desert her and withdraw from her (v. 17). A similar phrase is found in Psa. 38:12. The merchants no longer want anything to do with her, although up to this point they practically lay in her lap.

οὐαὶ οὐαί, ἡ πόλις ἡ μεγάλη, *woe, woe to you, O great city.* You have been miserably devastated and ruined.

Ἐν μιᾷ ὥρᾳ ἦλθεν ἡ κρίσις σου, *in one hour your judgment has come.* You have been overthrown with sudden ruin; your destruction was unexpected. Soon and unexpectedly your punishment has come upon you.

v. 11 Καὶ οἱ ἔμποροι τῆς γῆς κλαίουσι, *and the merchants of the earth mourn.* These merchants stand for the bishops, prelates, priests and monks who sell cloaks, furnishings, and other merchandise, for under the papacy, heaven—and even God Himself!—is for sale. (Cf. 2 Pet. 2:3.)

κλαίουσι ἐπ' αὐτῇ, *they cry over her,* while others cry because of her. Luther: *"bey sich selbst."*

v. 12 καὶ σηρικοῦ, *and of silk.* Blessed Luther omitted this in his German translation, because he had translated βύσσου as *"Seiden,"* silk.

καὶ πᾶν ξύλον θύϊνον, *and every kind of sweet wood.* This is said to be a species of cedar, giving off a sweet aroma, a flawless species, which is why it was once used in the construction of temples.

καὶ μαρμάρου, *and of marble.* Blessed Luther likewise omitted this in his German translation.

v. 13 καὶ κινάμωμον, *and cinnamon.* Luther translates *"Cinnamet,"* which is the bark of the cinnamon tree.

Θυμιάματα, *fragrant oils.* Luther translates *"Thymian."*

Μύρον, *myrrh,* a precious resin.

κτήνη σωμάτων, *cattle of bodies.* Some take these bodies to be common men, servants, slaves. They take ψυχὰς, *souls,* as a reference to free men who are kidnapped and sold as slaves.

Some interpret these ψυχὰς simply as souls, and the σώματα as bodies, because the Pontiff persuades men that he is able to free their souls from purgatory, and he demands payment for their graves.

v. 14 καὶ ἡ ὀπώρα τῆς ἐπιθυμίας τῆς ψυχῆς, *and the fruit of the longing of your soul*, that is, that for which your soul longs.

πάντα τὰ λιπαρὰ καὶ τὰ λαμπρὰ, *all the things that are rich and splendid.* Anything in the world that was splendid and valuable was conveyed to the Pontiff in Rome. Or the Pope, Cardinals and Bishops certainly could have arranged for themselves to have it, because the treasures of the whole world were conveyed to Rome. For since the Pope boasted that he could free men's souls from purgatory through Masses, indulgences, works of supererogation, etc., the riches of the whole world were eagerly sent to him in great abundance, and for gold and silver they received paper and lead, that is, papal bulls.

v. 16 κεχρυσωμένη ἐν χρυσῷ καὶ λίθῳ τιμίῳ, *gilded in gold and precious stones.* Some manuscripts read κεχρυσωμένοι, but this is erroneous. The Babylonian harlot was described in the same way in the preceding chapter (Rev. 17:4) because Antichristian Rome is depicted in both chapters.

v. 17 ὅτι μιᾷ ὥρᾳ ἠρημώθη ὁ τοσοῦτος πλοῦτος, *for in a single hour such great riches came to nothing.* Some read it as an exclamation, others as a question: *How did such great riches come to nothing in a single hour?*

Καὶ πᾶς κυβερνήτης, *and every shipmaster, etc.* These again represent the papal clergy, especially the legates *a latere*, who wander about through desert and sea in order to expand the kingdom of the Pope and increase his success. For they have transported indulgences, golden roses, "Lambs of God," and similar merchandise across the seas and sold them for a high price.

v. 18 τίς ὁμοία τῇ πόλει τῇ μεγάλῃ, *who is like the great city?*, namely, the city that has now fallen headlong into ruin.

v. 19 ἔβαλον χοῦν, *they threw dust, etc.*, as a sign of mourning and sadness. (Cf. Joshua 7:6, Job 2:12.)

μιᾷ ὥρᾳ ἠρημώθη, *in one hour it was made desolate.* The great river Euphrates, that is, their abundant income, was dried up (Rev. 16:12).

v. 20 Εὐφραίνου ἐπ' αὐτὴν οὐρανὲ, *rejoice over her, O heaven!*, that is, you godly and holy ones whose "conduct is in heaven" (Phi. 3:20). (Cf. Isa. 44:23, 49:13; Jer. 51:48.)

καὶ οἱ ἅγιοι ἀπόστολοι καὶ οἱ προφῆται, *and the holy apostles and prophets*, you who prophesied in your writings about this destruction of Babylon.

ἔκρινεν ὁ θεὸς τὸ κρίμα ὑμῶν, *God has judged your judgment*. He has avenged the tyranny and cruelty that she inflicted on you.

v. 21 Καὶ εἶρεν εἷς ἄγγελος ἰσχυρὸς λίθον, *and one strong angel took a stone* (Jer. 51:64). This signifies (1) that the ruin of Babylon will happen suddenly; (2) irreparable damage, because a millstone falls with great force and cannot be drawn back again out of the sea.

v. 22 καὶ φωνὴ κιθαρῳδῶν, *and the voice of harpists* (Isa. 24:28; Jer. 7:34, 25:10; Eze. 26:13). Nothing within the city limits that serves either to sustain life or to add pleasure to it, which is also somewhat necessary, will be found any longer in Antichristian Rome after its destruction.

v. 23 καὶ φῶς λύχνου οὐ μὴ φανῇ, *and the light of a lamp will no longer shine*. These words are omitted in Luther's German translation. But the sense is that there is nothing in the city's future except for darkness, that is, mourning and sadness.

καὶ φωνὴ νυμφίου, *and the voice of a bridegroom* (Jer. 7:34, 16:9, 25:10, 33:11; Baruch 2:23). All gladness will cease, along with all hope of restoring things to a better state.

ὅτι οἱ ἔμποροί σου ἦσαν οἱ μεγιστᾶνες τῆς γῆς, *for your merchants were the great men of the earth*, the papal prelates, who are called "merchants" in v. 11. They seized the first places of leadership and the political dominion for themselves and became greater than those who were princes by birth with regard to riches, luxury, pomp and power.

ὅτι ἐν τῇ φαρμακείᾳ σου ἐπλανήθησαν πάντα τὰ ἔθνη, *for all nations were led astray by your sorcery*. You bewitched them with the wine of your fornication, Rev. 17:2, 18:3.

v. 24 καὶ ἐν αὐτῇ αἷμα προφητῶν, *and in her the blood of the prophets*, etc., who were killed on the earth because of their confession of the true doctrine. Since the Roman Antichrist stirred up many persecutions and cruel wars against the confessors of the Gospel and caused many thousands of people to be slaughtered through the Spanish Inquisition, therefore God will vindicate the shedding of these innocent men's blood and will utterly destroy the kingdom of the Antichrist.

Chapter 19

This chapter describes the execution of judgment on the Last Day in three parts:
  I. ψαλμῳδία, *psalmody,* the celebration of the elect because of the just judgment of God;
  II. ὁμιλία, *homily,* the dialogue of the angel with John concerning this judgment;
  III. δικαιοκρισία, *righteous judgment,* a description of the coming of Christ for judgment and the destruction of the world.

v. 1 Καὶ μετὰ ταῦτα ἤκουσα ὡς φωνὴν ὄχλου πολλοῦ, *and after these things I heard what was like a sound of a great multitude.*

This great multitude represents not only the angels, but also all the saints in heaven (Rev. 7:9). The greatest multitude is of the angels (Dan. 7:10, Heb. 12:10). Many souls have also been received into heaven.

Ἡ σωτηρία καὶ ἡ δόξα, καὶ ἡ τιμὴ, καὶ ἡ δύναμις Κυρίῳ τῷ Θεῷ ἡμῶν, *salvation and glory and honor and power to the Lord our God.* To God be praise, honor and glory because of the salvation furnished to the elect and because of the powerful deliverance by which He brought them out from under the tyranny of the Antichrist. For since, in the preceding chapter, the heavens, that is, the inhabitants of heaven, were invited to rejoice at the destruction of the Antichrist, they now joyfully praise God.

v. 2 Ὅτι ἀληθιναὶ καὶ δίκαιαι αἱ κρίσεις αὐτοῦ, *for true and just are His judgments* (Rev. 15:3; 16:3).

τὴν πόρνην τὴν μεγάλην, *the great harlot,* the Roman Antichrist. ἐν τῇ πορνείᾳ αὐτῆς, *by her fornication,* by her spiritual fornication, that is, idolatry and false doctrine.

Καὶ ἐξεδίκησε τὸ αἷμα, *and He has avenged the blood.* She suffers the due penalties for the innocent blood she shed.

v. 3 Καὶ ὁ καπνὸς αὐτῆς, *and her smoke*. That city (Rome) will be utterly destroyed and laid waste for all eternity, and it will never be rebuilt. But this has in view especially the eternal torments to which the followers of the Antichrist will be subjected who did not repent (Rev. 14:11, 19:20).

v. 4 Καὶ ἔπεσαν οἱ πρεσβύτεροι, *and the elders fell down, etc.* These elders stand for all those who are truly believing and elect.

καὶ τὰ τέσσαρα ζῷα, *and the four animals*. These symbolize all the faithful teachers of the Church.

Ἀμήν, *amen*. Truly this is so; the judgments of God are true and just.

v. 5 Καὶ φωνὴ, *and a voice*, namely, of an angel. But some interpret this to be the voice of Christ, since He is said to have come from the throne.

v. 6 Καὶ ἤκουσα ὡς φωνὴν ὄχλου πολλοῦ... Ὅτι ἐβασίλευσε Κύριος, *and I heard what was like the sound of a great multitude...for the Lord has begun to reign*. The kingdoms of the world have been destroyed, and the kingdom of glory will now begin (Rev. 14:2). The sound of a great multitude signifies the joyful celebration of all the blessed in heaven.

v. 7 Ὅτι ἦλθεν ὁ γάμος τοῦ Ἀρνίου, *for the wedding of the Lamb has come*. The joyful Day of Judgment is at hand, when the spiritual Bride of Christ—the true Church and every faithful soul—is led into the blessedness of the heavenly nuptials.

Καὶ ἡ γυνὴ αὐτοῦ ἡτοίμασεν ἑαυτήν, *and His Wife has prepared herself*. The Church is called the Bride of Christ in this life, because, through the Holy Spirit, she is betrothed to Christ (Hosea 2:19); He has given her the guarantee of the Spirit. In the future, she is called His Wife, because at that time she comes into possession of the heavenly goods (2 Cor. 11:2, Rev. 21:1, 1 The. 4:17).

v. 8 Καὶ ἐδόθη αὐτῇ ἵνα περιβάληται βύσσινον καθαρόν καὶ λαμπρὸν, *and she was given to wear fine linen, clean and bright*. It was given to her, namely, by Christ the Bridegroom, from whom all the righteousness and holiness of the Church descends (Eph. 5:26, Rev. 3:18).

The linen stands for the wedding garment, namely, the perfect righteousness of Christ (Isa. 61:10), because by faith she wears Christ and is dressed in His righteousness, even as the following explanation demonstrates.

τὸ βύσσινον τὰ δικαιώματα ἐστί τῶν ἁγίων, *the linen is the righteousnesses of the saints.*

"The righteousnesses." (1) The righteousness that has been given and imputed to believers by faith (Gal. 3:27), which produces the fruit of good works; (2) the indwelling and actual righteousness that has been initiated in this life and will be perfected on the Day of Judgment.

v. 9 Καὶ λέγει μοι, *and he,* namely, the angel who was speaking with me, *says to me,* Γράψον, *write.* Blessed Luther omitted this in his German translation.

Μακάριοι οἱ εἰς τὸν δεῖπνον τοῦ γάμου τοῦ Ἀρνίου κεκλημένοι, *blessed are they who have been called to the wedding feast of the Lamb,* who obey that call and put on the wedding garment by faith (Mat. 22:11).

Οὗτοι οἱ λόγοι ἀληθινοὶ εἰσι τοῦ Θεοῦ, *these words of God are true.* They will most certainly be fulfilled at their proper time.

v. 10 Καὶ ἔπεσον ἔμπροσθεν τῶν ποδῶν αὐτοῦ προσκυνῆσαι αὐτῷ, *and I fell down at his feet to worship him.* (Cf. Rev. 22:8.)

ἐχόντων τὴν μαρτυρίαν Ἰησοῦ, *who have the testimony of Jesus.* Who are these? The apostle himself answers: "The one who believes in the Son of God has His testimony within himself" (1 John 5:10).

Ἡ γὰρ μαρτυρία τοῦ Ἰησοῦ ἐστι τὸ πνεῦμα τῆς προφητείας, *for the testimony of Jesus is the spirit of prophecy.*

(1) Some conclude that this sentence is a periphrastic way of referring to the prophets, that they have the testimony of Jesus; that is, the command to testify that Jesus is the only Savior.

(2) Others explain it in this way: that in these words it is declared who they are who have the testimony of Jesus, namely, those who have received from God the gift of prophecy, that is, the ability to explain the mysteries of the kingdom of heaven.

(3) Still others explain it in this way: that all prophecies refer to Jesus as the ultimate goal. This explanation is to be preferred to the others.

v. 11 Καὶ εἶδον τὸν οὐρανὸν ἀνεῳγμένον, *and I saw heaven opened.* The opening of heaven is the symbol of a new vision.

καὶ ἰδού, ἵππος λευκός, καὶ ὁ καθήμενος ἐπ᾽ αὐτόν, *and behold, a white horse, and the one sitting on it.* The rider is Christ. The white horse denotes Christ's purity and holiness, as well as the eternal blessedness and glory into which He entered through His suffering (Luke 24:26) because conquerors used to make a triumphal entrance, riding on white horses.

καλούμενος Πιστὸς καὶ Ἀληθινός, *called Faithful and True* (Rev. 1:5, 3:14). In that triumphal entrance, heralds would proclaim the glorious titles of the conqueror.

καὶ ἐν δικαιοσύνῃ κρίνει καὶ πολεμεῖ, *and in righteousness He judges and makes war.* He judges His enemies and fights against them.

v. 12 Οἱ δὲ ὀφθαλμοὶ αὐτοῦ ὡς φλὸξ πυρός, *and His eyes were like a flame of fire.* This signifies: (1) Christ's omniscience; (2) His wrath against the ungodly; (3) the vengeance He wishes to exact on the Antichrist and his followers.

καὶ ἐπὶ τὴν κεφαλὴν αὐτοῦ διαδήματα πολλά, *and upon His head were many diadems.* These are a symbol: (1) of ultimate power, for He is the King of kings and Lord of lords (v. 16; 1 Tim. 6:15); (2) of a threefold kingdom, namely, of power, of grace, and of glory.

ἔχων ὄνομα γεγραμμένον ὃ οὐδεὶς οἶδεν εἰ μὴ αὐτός, *having a name written which no one but He knows,* (1) because His divinity is incomprehensible and inscrutable; (2) apart from divine revelation no one knows anything about His name, that is, His person, office, and benefits (Mat. 11:27).

v. 13 καὶ περιβεβλημένος ἱμάτιον βεβαμμένον αἵματι, *and clothed in a robe dipped in blood.* This signifies: (1) that His body, which is like His garment, was made red with His blood, which was shed for our sins (Gen. 49:11, Luke 22:44); (2) that by His suffering, death and resurrection, He has powerfully conquered all His enemies and has tread upon them as one treads upon red grapes in a winepress, so that He was sprinkled with their blood (Isa. 63:23), as would happen both in bloody battles and in the winepress.

καὶ καλεῖται τὸ ὄνομα αὐτοῦ, Ὁ Λόγος τοῦ Θεοῦ, *and His name is called "The Word of God,"* namely, the personal (*hypostaticum*) Word.

v. 14 Καὶ τὰ στρατεύματα τὰ ἐν τῷ οὐρανῷ ἠκολούθει αὐτῷ ἐφ' ἵπποις λευκοῖς, *and the armies that are in heaven were following Him on white horses*. This is referring to the army of all the faithful and elect.

The white color of the horses and garments signifies that Christ, by His blood, has acquired for believers the pure white robe of righteousness and salvation.

v. 15 Καὶ ἐκ τοῦ στόματος αὐτοῦ ἐκπορεύεται ῥομφαία ὀξεῖα, *and out of His mouth comes a sharp sword*. This sword stands for (1) the efficacy of the word, for by the word men are conquered, so that they submit obediently to Christ; (2) stern judgment against His enemies.

Καὶ αὐτὸς ποιμανεῖ αὐτοὺς ἐν ῥάβδῳ σιδηρᾷ, *and He will rule them with a rod of iron*. This iron rod will crush them in His wrath, unless they are willing to submit to His scepter and stop opposing Him and His kingdom.

Καὶ αὐτὸς πατεῖ τὴν ληνὸν τοῦ οἴνου τοῦ θυμοῦ καὶ τῆς ὀργῆς τοῦ Θεοῦ, *and He treads the winepress of the wrath and fury of God*. When He suffered, He was crushed like grapes under the winepress of divine wrath, so that His blood flowed copiously. But after His resurrection and ascension, He tramples all His enemies under His feet and subjects them to the winepress of divine wrath, under which they will be tortured for all eternity (Isa. 63:3, Rev. 14:19-20).

v. 16 Καὶ ἔχει ἐπὶ τὸ ἱμάτιον, *and He has upon His robe, etc*. The name mentioned earlier in v. 13 represents His divinity, but this name denotes His saving office as King.

v. 17 ἑστῶτα ἐν τῷ ἡλίῳ, *standing in the sun*, that is, in plain sight of men and of all creatures, standing publicly before them all.

συνάγεσθε εἰς τὸ δεῖπνον τοῦ μεγάλου τοῦ Θεοῦ, *gather together for the supper of the great God*, that you may consume the great abundance of food prepared for you by God. This signifies the notable defeat of the enemies of the Church: that Christ will defeat and kill the Antichrist and his followers, together with their entire army, in a notable battle, so that all the birds can feast on their dead bodies (Jer. 7:34, 12:9; Eze. 39:17). This will be fulfilled figuratively when, on the Day of the Last Judgment, the angels gather the infernal birds with their trumpets for the judgments of God that are to be brought against the damned.

v. 19 Καὶ εἶδον τὸ Θηρίον, *and I saw the beast*, the Antichristian papal kingdom. Καὶ τοὺς βασιλεῖς τῆς γῆς, *and the kings of the earth*, who cling to him.

v. 20 ὁ Ψευδοπροφήτης, *the false prophet*, the head of the Antichristian kingdom. Εἰς τὴν λίμνην τοῦ πυρὸς, *into the lake of fire*, into the fire of hell. They will fight in vain against this judgment.

v. 21 Καὶ οἱ λοιποὶ, *and the rest*, who had gathered together as one with the beasts for battle against Him who was sitting on the white horse; that is, against Christ and His Church.

Chapter 20

This chapter is composed of the beginning of the seventh and final vision, and also includes a partial repetition of the things that were stated in the preceding chapters. There are three parts:
  I. The binding of the dragon;
  II. His release;
  III. The things that follow his release.

v. 1 Καὶ εἶδον ἄγγελον καταβαίνοντα, *and I saw an angel descending*. This angel is the Son of God.

ἔχοντα τὴν κλεῖδα τῆς ἀβύσσου, *having the key of the abyss*, of hell and death (Rev. 1:18, 9:1), with which the abyss, that is, hell, could be opened and shut. Καὶ ἅλυσιν μεγάλην, *and a great chain*, which stands for His divine power, which He maintains against the devil, death and hell.

v. 2 Καὶ ἐκράτησε τὸν δράκοντα, *and He laid hold of the dragon*, etc. He restrained the devil's power, which he had wielded up to this point with God's permission.

v. 3 ἵνα μὴ πλανήσῃ τὰ ἔθνη ἔτι, *so that he should no longer lead the nations astray*, misusing them as his instrument for persecuting Christians.

Various interpretations have been posited concerning this binding of Satan, which Alcazar lists in his commentary on this passage. From an erroneous exposition of this passage the error of the Chiliasts arose. They concluded that Christ would reign in this world for a thousand years after His resurrection from the dead, and that His people would live in complete joy and peace. Some, such as Eusebius (Book III, *Hist. Ecl.*, ch. 22, 25) attribute this error to Cerinthus as the primary author. Others attribute it to Papias, Bishop of Hierapolis, who was followed by Irenaeus, Apollinarius, Victorius Pictaviensis, Tertullian, Lactantius, Book VII, ch. 24. Their authority, in turn, influenced Jerome, so that he wrote on Jeremiah chapter 9: "Even though he does not approve of this conclusion, nevertheless he does not condemn it, since so many outstanding men embraced and followed it." And yet, commenting on Daniel chapter 7 and on Ezekiel chapter 36, he rejects this conclusion. Augustine, Book XX, *De Civitate Dei*, ch. 7: "The first resurrection is poorly understood by some in our ranks, and is even turned into some ridiculous fables." See the whole section where he admits that he himself once thought the same thing. In this same place he says: "That opinion is tolerable, if certain spiritual delights are thought to be awaiting the saints on that Sabbath through the Lord's presence, and I also once held that opinion." Compare Luis Vives on the same passage.

Pope Damasus condemned this opinion about the kingdom of Christ being administered on this earth in a human and bodily way for a thousand years after the resurrection, even branding the Apollinarians, together with their leader Apollinarius the Laodicean, as heretics because they held tenaciously to this opinion (Cf. Baronius, Vol. 2, *Annal. Ann. 118*, sect. 2), although the same opinion was tolerated in Papias, Justin, Irenaeus and Tertullian (cf. Baronius, Vol. 2, *Annal. Ann. 118*, sect. 5).

(1) Some conclude that these thousand years should begin immediately after the time of Christ, and so they count a thousand years during which Satan should be bound, after which time the Antichrist would appear. Thus John Wycliffe explains it, together with Foxe, *In Martyrol.*, p. 426. According to this computation, we are taken up to the time of Hildebrandt Gregory VII, who barred the ministers of the Church from marrying. At that time the Saracenes destroyed many churches in the East.

(2) But it is better to say that these thousand years began after the three hundred years of persecution that took place after the birth of Christ, because it seemed that Satan was loose during that whole time, since he raged against the Church like a lion. Gualterus Brutus, with Foxe, p. 480. According to this computation, the thousand years ended around the year A.D. 1300. During that century, superstitions began to grow and bands of monks began to increase. Those who embrace the first conclusion explain the binding of the devil in this way, that the devil was hindered by the power of the preaching of the Gospel, so that he could not seduce men so freely and drive them to idolatry. Those who embrace the second opinion explain the binding of the devil in the following way: that the devil could not stir up persecu-

tions and wars against Christians with as much violence as he had done at first and as he would do again.

Jacobus de Teramo, *Consolatio Peccatorum*, second-to-last page, edit. 1484: "The captivity of the devil began in A.D. 312, when the Empire arose in Constantinople." And afterwards: "At the time of Emperor Albert of Austria the devil completed the thousandth year of his captivity, in the year A.D. 1308. For once Constantine joined himself to Christ, he became a very fierce protector of the Church. He bravely removed the huge storm of persecution at the hand of tyrants and powerfully held them in check. But in the year 1308, the devil was loosed again when the Muhammadans and Saracenes violently invaded Christian territory. At that time the Turkish Empire under the Ottomans received its largest increase."

Therefore, the devil was bound by Christ at the time of Constantine the Great, who was converted to the Christian religion around the year A.D. 308. Under his rule, those terrible persecutions that were stirred up so forcefully against the Christian Church by the pagan emperors came to an end.

But when peace was restored to the Church through Constantine, then it was as if the devil was bound with a great chain, so that he was less able to force pagan idolatry upon men and to propagate it through the same kind of persecutions. Yes, it is true that various heresies were introduced into the Church at the devil's instigation both at the time of Constantine and afterwards. But the persecutions of the pagan emperors, with which this passage is dealing, began to subside at that time. If, then, Satan was bound at the time of Constantine, then the thousand years ended in A.D. 1308, when Satan was again loosed in order to stir up the Ottoman Turks against Christians. From that time on, much more severely than before, the Saracenes began to attack Christians; they seized the majority of the eastern territories of the Roman Empire, including even Constantinople, the capital of the Eastern Empire.

Philip Nicolai, Book II, *De Regno Christi*, ch. 5: "The angel is the Bishop of Rome. The binding of Satan is the restriction of the Muhammadan heresies at the time of Pontiff Hormisdas and Emperor Justin, so that the end of the thousand years began in the century before."

v. 4 Καὶ εἶδον θρόνους, καὶ ἐκάθισαν ἐπ' αὐτούς, *and I saw thrones* (namely, of judgment), *and they sat upon them,* namely, those who would judge and who would award eternal blessedness to the souls of the martyrs for the testimony they gave.

κρίμα ἐδόθη αὐτοῖς, *and judgment was given to them.* They were given authority to execute judgment.

καὶ τὰς ψυχὰς τῶν πεπελεκισμένων, *and* (sc. I saw) *the souls of those who had been beheaded, etc.,* the souls of the holy martyrs who had been killed by the pagan emperors for their confession of Christ.

This is a reference to those who were struck down by the ax, a common form of punishment used by the pagan Roman emperors. By way of synecdoche, this applies to all the ways in which the godly were punished.

καὶ οἵτινες οὐ προσεκύνησαν τῷ Θηρίῳ, *and* (sc. the souls of those) *who did not worship the beast,* the holy confessors who did not allow themselves to be convinced to cling to the Antichrist.

Καὶ ἔζησαν καὶ ἐβασίλευσαν μετὰ τοῦ Χριστοῦ τὰ χίλια ἔτη, *and they lived and reigned with Christ for the thousand years.* They lived and reigned with Christ in eternal happiness and glory.

(1) Some take these thousand years indefinitely, for eternity, since the happiness of the blessed is eternal (Exo. 20:6; 1 Sam. 18:7; 1 Kings 19:18; Dan. 7:10). They say that the millennium in vv. 4–6 signifies eternity, while in vv. 2 and 7 it refers to a limited time, which should not seem surprising in a prophetic book.

(2) But it should be noted that it says τὰ χίλια ἔτη, *the thousand years,* namely, the same ones mentioned in v. 3. Therefore, it is better to say that the reference is to those thousand years during which Satan was bound, not that these souls ceased to live and reign with Christ afterwards, when the thousand years were completed and Satan was again released, but those thousand years were specifically mentioned for the following reasons, both because it might have been in doubt what the state was of those martyrs and confessors who had died a godly death during those thousand years—how the souls of those who had been loosed from their bodies were faring during all that time, since the peace that was brought upon the Church by Constantine seemed

to have benefited them little; and because something important happened to the Church when those thousand years were fulfilled; namely, Satan was again released and the Church was again subjected to terrible persecutions.

(1) Therefore, since the terrible persecutions stirred up against Christians by the pagan emperors during the first three centuries after Christ's birth preceded the binding of Satan that took place under the rule of Constantine, John introduces in his vision the souls of those beheaded martyrs, that is, those who were put to death for their testimony of Jesus, and he reveals their happiness and the glorious comfort they have now received. (2) When Satan was bound, that is, when those external persecutions that the Church suffered under the Gentiles came to an end, various heresies arose in the Church under each Antichrist—both the Eastern and the Western. For just as Pelagianism gave birth to the papal errors, so also Arianism led to the Muhammadan madness. Therefore, John links the souls of the martyrs with the souls of those who did not worship the beast, that is, those who guarded their souls against the papistic and Muhammadan heresies. (3) Then Satan would be released, and the madness of both Antichrists, the Eastern and the Western, would rage horribly against the Church. Therefore, on a secondary level, these souls can also be understood as the souls of those who are killed in the Turkish and papistic persecutions for their confession of the truth.

He proclaims the following concerning the souls of these godly martyrs and confessors: (1) that thrones of judgment were given to them as a sign of their authority to execute judgment (v. 4). This judgment is distinct from the Final Judgment (v. 11). Therefore, it is a reference to the judgment that the souls separated from their bodies will execute during the thousand years against their persecutors by whom they were killed. For just as the blood of the godly cries out to heaven from the earth and demands to be avenged against those who shed it (Gen. 4:10, Heb. 12:24), so also their souls in heaven cry out from under the altar, and they demand that their blood and that of their brethren be avenged (Rev. 6:9).

He likewise proclaims (2) that they live, namely, in heavenly peace, tranquility and glory. The tyrants thought that those whom they put to death were extinguished, body and soul. But the Holy Spirit testifies that the souls of the godly immediately escape death and live in heavenly glory (Wisdom 3:2).

And he proclaims (3) that they reign with Christ, namely, all their enemies—the devil, the flesh, the world and all those who opposed them—have been conquered (Luke 23:42–43). But since the life and glory of the godly also has a beginning in this life (John 3:36, Col. 3:3, Heb. 6:5), a secondary explanation can be added concerning the happiness and the state in which the souls of the godly live even in this life, namely, the souls that have not yet been released from their bodies.

1. They are given authority to execute judgment against their persecutors, because by their prayers they obtain this from God, that even in this life examples of divine wrath and vengeance are brought upon their enemies (Rev. 18:20). (Cf. the history of the death of the pagan emperors who fomented such persecutions.)

2. The souls of the godly live, namely, with that spiritual life that is from God (Eph. 4:18). They live for God (Eph. 4:18). They live by faith in the Son of God (Gal. 2:19). Indeed, Christ lives in them (Gal. 2:20). Those who do not share in His spiritual life are dead before God (Mat. 7:22, 1 Tim. 5:8). Thus John adds that the rest of the dead did not come to life again, for they are alienated from the life that is from God (Eph. 4:18).

3. They reign with Christ, for they also conquered the world by faith before their death (1 John 4:4, 5:4). They rule over sin (Rom. 6:12), and so they are called kings (Rev. 1:6) and a royal priesthood (1 Pet. 2:9), and the Church is called "the kingdom of heaven."

Furthermore, since this happiness, dignity, and glory of the blessed souls will not cease when they are reunited with their bodies as they are raised from the dust, but will rather increase and become complete, namely, because their bodies will then share in the glory, therefore the things that John says in this passage can be extended in a secondary sense to the state of these souls. For on that day of regeneration, the apostles and the rest of the martyrs will judge their persecutors (Mat. 19:28). They will be counselors in the judgment of Christ, and with their vote their will condemn the ungodly (1 Cor. 6:2; Rev. 2:26, 3:21). Then all the godly will inherit the kingdom (Mat. 25:34) and will be admitted into the full possession of eternal life.

Therefore, by no means should one conclude that at the end of those thousand years the glory and blessedness of those souls will come to an end. For the conjunction "until" in this passage includes the preceding time, yet not in such a way as to exclude the subsequent time. (Cf. Gen. 28:15; 1 Sam. 15:35; 2 Sam. 6:23; Psa. 110:1; Isa. 22:14, 42:4; Mat. 28:20.)

v. 5 Οἱ λοιποὶ τῶν νεκρῶν οὐκ ἀνέζησαν, *the rest of the dead did not live again*, etc. The reference is to those who are spiritually dead in sins (Mat. 8:22; Eph. 5:14; 1 Tim. 5:8; Rev. 3:1); who tenaciously adhered to the pagan or Antichristian errors; who worshiped the beast; who were not put to death for their testimony of Jesus, but are dead in sins; who were not raised to spiritual life; who remained in unbelief, and thus, in death (John 3:36).

During that whole time when the saints were living and reigning in the way just described, the ungodly were neither living nor reigning, but they remained entangled in the death of sins, persevering in impenitence and unbelief, and thus were exiled from spiritual life and the kingdom of heaven until those thousand years were completed. And again, it cannot be inferred from the conjunction "until" that the ungodly would be brought to life again and would reign with Christ after exactly one thousand years, for they crossed over from the death of sins to the second death, which is eternal death. Rather, the conjunction "until" denotes continuation and duration, so that the sense is, for as long as the ungodly would not live and reign, so long will the saints live and reign with Christ. Wherefore, since the saints live and reign with Christ forever, even so the ungodly would be exiled forever from that life and kingdom. Augustine, Book XX, *De Civitate Dei*, ch. 9: "When it is said that the rest of the dead did not live until the thousand years were over, it should be understood in this way: they did not live at that time when they should have lived, namely, by crossing over from death to life, and therefore, when the day for the resurrection of their bodies comes, they will not go forth from their tombs to life, but to judgment, that is, to damnation, which is called the second death." They will rise with their bodies at the end of the age, but not to spiritual life.

Αὕτη ἡ ἀνάστασις ἡ πρώτη, *this is the first resurrection*. It is (1) spiritual, namely, a resurrection from sins in which the godly arise from sins through repentance and faith in Christ. They become partakers of spiritual life, and they cross over from death to life and into a kingdom. This spiritual resurrection is distinct from the resurrection of the body, which will follow on the Last Day. (2) It is a blessed resurrection in which the souls of the elect are transferred into heavenly glory and a heavenly kingdom. Augustine, Book XX, *De Civitate Dei*, ch. 10: "Just as souls can fall spiritually, that is, they can sin, so also are they able to rise spiritually, John 5:25, Rom. 6:4."

v. 6 Μακάριος καὶ ἅγιος ὁ ἔχων μέρος ἐν τῇ ἀναστάσει τῇ πρώτῃ. Ἐπὶ τούτων ὁ θάνατος ὁ δεύτερος οὐκ ἔχει ἐξουσίαν, *blessed and holy is the one who has a part in the first resurrection. The second death has no power over them*. For the one who believes in Christ and rises again from sins spiritually through Him (Luke 2:34, Col. 3:1, Eph. 5:4), so that he walks with Christ in newness of life (Rom. 6:4) "he will live, even though he dies" (John 11:25).

The second death is eternal death, never-ending torments in hell (Rev. 2:11, 20:14).

ἀλλ' ἔσονται ἱερεῖς τοῦ Θεοῦ καὶ τοῦ Χριστοῦ, καὶ βασιλεύσουσι μετ' αὐτοῦ χίλια ἔτη, *but they will be priests of God and of Christ, and they will reign with Him for a thousand years*, offering spiritual sacrifices to God in this and in the future life, and sitting on the throne of Christ (Rev. 3:21). At the end of those thousand years, Satan will certainly again be released, but he will not be able to wrest them away from this happiness and from the throne of heavenly glory.

Therefore, the fruits of the spiritual resurrection are: (1) the reward of blessedness; (2) the testimony of holiness; (3) the longed-for release from death; (4) a spiritual priesthood; (5) an eternal kingdom.

v. 7 Καὶ ὅταν τελεσθῇ τὰ χίλια ἔτη, λυθήσεται ὁ Σατανᾶς, *and when the thousand years are completed, Satan will be released*, etc. Lyranus makes the following comment on this passage: "Here a renewed persecution of Christians is being described. Some interpret it as the persecution of Saladin. But to me it seems better to interpret it with reference to the Tatars, who, in the year A.D. 1202, departed from their country and put many people to death, both Christians and pagans." But he adds: "It seems that this prophecy has still not been fulfilled, and since I am neither a prophet nor the son of a prophet, I do not wish to say anything about the future, except that which can be drawn from the Holy Scriptures or the sayings of the saints. Therefore, I will leave the exposition of this letter to those who are wiser than I."

At the end of those thousand years, when Satan was released (v. 2), God will again permit him to employ the Gentiles as his instruments for stirring up persecutions against Christians.

v. 8 καὶ ἐξελεύσεται πλανῆσαι τὰ ἔθνη τὰ ἐν ταῖς τέσσαρσι γωνίαις τῆς γῆς, *and he went out to deceive the nations that are in the four corners of the earth*, in all corners of the earth, in the four parts of the inhabited world.

τὸν Γὼγ καὶ τὸν Μαγώγ, *Gog and Magog*. Some understand Gog and Magog generically as "the persecutors of the Church, for the persecution by Gog and Magog that befell the Jewish Church at the time of the Maccabees was a type of the persecution of the Christian Church that will take place shortly before the second coming of Christ. The Syrian enemies and persecutors of the Israelite Church are called Gog and Magog, Eze. 38:2, 39:1."

But this is especially a reference to the Turks, descended from the Tatars, who will attack the Church with violent persecutions.

ὧν ὁ ἀριθμὸς ὡς ἡ ἄμμος τῆς θαλάσσης, *whose number is as the sand of the sea*, because the Turk leads a great army with him into battle.

v. 9 Καὶ ἀνέβησαν, *and they went up*, namely, those people whom Satan gathered for battle (v. 8). Ἐπὶ τὸ πλάτος τῆς γῆς, *upon the breadth of the earth*. They will fill all things far and wide.

καὶ ἐκύκλωσαν τὴν παρεμβολὴν τῶν ἁγίων, *and they surrounded the camp of the saints*, that is, the Christians, καὶ τὴν πόλιν τὴν ἠγαπημένην, *and the beloved city*, namely, the City of God, the Christian Church.

Καὶ κατέβη πῦρ ἀπὸ τοῦ Θεοῦ, *and fire from God descended*. God will put an end to their tyrannical endeavors by means of the Last Judgment, when fire will consume heaven and earth.

v. 10 Καὶ ὁ Διάβολος, *and the devil, etc.* The torments of the evil spirits will be increased in the Last Judgment.

καὶ τὸ θηρίον καὶ ὁ ψευδοπροφήτης, *and the beast and the false prophet* (Rev. 19:29).

v. 11 Καὶ εἶδον θρόνον λευκὸν μέγαν, *and I saw a great white throne.* This represents the judicial tribunal of Christ. It is white, because Christ will judge the whole world in righteousness (Acts 17:31).

καὶ τὸν καθήμενον ἐπ' αὐτοῦ, *and the One sitting on it.* This is Christ, the Judge of the living and the dead.

οὗ ἀπὸ προσώπου ἔφυγεν ἡ γῆ καὶ ὁ οὐρανός, *earth and heaven fled from before His face.* On the Day of Judgment, the heavens will pass away with a great noise, etc. (2 Pet. 3:10).

v. 12 Καὶ εἶδον τοὺς νεκρούς, *and I saw the dead,* etc, namely, after they were raised from the dust of the earth by Christ the Judge. Ἑστῶτας ἐνώπιον τοῦ θεοῦ, *standing before God,* before Christ, who is true God and Man, to whom the Father has given all judgment (John 5:22).

καὶ βιβλία ἠνεῴχθησαν, *and books were opened.* (1) The book of divine omniscience (Psa. 139:15), in which are written all the things that all men, through the whole time of their lives, have ever thought, said, done, etc. Nothing escapes this omniscience of God. All those things will be manifested in the judgment. (2) The book of human conscience, in which the thoughts, words and works of every man are written with the pen of truth. For it is clear from the end of this verse and from the next verse that these are the kinds of books in which the works of every single man are written. (3) The book of Holy Scripture, according to which the judgment will be established: believers will be absolved and justified on the basis of the Gospel; unbelievers will be condemned on the basis of the Law (John 12:48, Rom. 2:16). Augustine, *Homil. 17 in Apoc.,* near the middle: "The opened books are the Testaments of God, for the Church will be judged according to both Testaments." These books will be opened in judgment, because on the Day of Judgment, the thoughts, words and actions of every man, even the most deeply hidden ones, will be brought to light before angels and men and will be judged on the basis of the Word (1 Cor. 4:5).

Καὶ Βιβλίον ἄλλο ἠνεῴχθη, *and another book was opened.* God will reveal in the judgment before men and angels those who are numbered among the elect.

ἐκ τῶν γεγραμμένων ἐν τοῖς βιβλίοις, *on the basis of the things written in the books.* Luther: "*aus der Schrifft in den Büchern.*"

v. 13 Καὶ ἔδωκεν ἡ θάλασσα τοὺς ἐν αὐτῇ νεκρούς, *and the sea furnished the dead who were in it*. Augustine, Book XX, *De Civitate Dei*, ch. 15: "Some appropriately take the sea in this passage as a representation of this present age. 'The sea furnished the dead,' because they came in whatever state they were found." Likewise, in the preceding chapter he writes: "This event, 'the sea furnished the dead,' undoubtedly took place before the dead were judged, and yet the judgment is said to have taken place first. Therefore, by way of recapitulation, he is adding something that he had omitted. But he retains this order, and, for the purpose of explaining the order, he also repeats in the proper place what he had said about the dead being judged. For although he says that 'the sea furnished the dead who were in it, and death and hell gave back those who were in them,' he soon adds what he had said a little earlier, 'and each one was judged according to his deeds.' This is the very thing he had said above, 'and the dead were judged according to their deeds.'"

But it is better to say that "the sea furnished the dead who were in it" means that those who had drowned in the sea were called back to life by Christ on the Day of Judgment.

καὶ ὁ θάνατος καὶ ὁ ᾅδης ἔδωκαν τοὺς ἐν αὐτοῖς νεκρούς, *and death and Hades furnished the dead who were in them*. Augustine on this passage: "Death and hell gave them back, because they were called back to the life from which they had passed away. 'Death,' because of the good, who were only able to endure death, not hell. 'Hell,' because of the wicked, who also pay the penalties of hell."

The sense is that the dead who are outside of the sea, including the living who had gone down to hell, were likewise called back to life by Christ the Judge and led before the judicial tribunal.

Piscator concludes that "three classes of the dead are being described. One is of those who were buried in the sea. The second is of those who were not buried in the sea or in the ground, but were devoured by wild animals or incinerated. The third is of those who lay in their graves." For Hades can be translated as "the grave." There are also others who follow Piscator, but it is better to take Hades as "hell."

Καὶ ἐκρίθησαν ἕκαστος κατὰ τὰ ἔργα αὐτῶν, *and they were judged, each one according to their deeds*, as the testimonies either of faith or of unbelief.

v. 14 Καὶ ὁ θάνατος καὶ ὁ ᾅδης ἐβλήθησαν, *and death and Hades were cast*, that is, some, and indeed, most of those whom death and hell had given back. Piscator: "Hell is said to have been cast into a lake of fire. But it is not exactly correct to say that hell was cast into hell."

We reply: (1) The sense is that the ungodly, who were among those who were raised up from the earth and brought back to life from hell, were cast into the flames of hell. (2) Augustine, Book XX, *De Civitate Dei*, ch. 15: "The devil—and, at the same time, the whole horde of demons—is meant by these names, for he is the author of death and of the infernal punishments." (3) Some explain it this way: "Death is utterly wiped out and hell is destroyed, so that the devil no longer has any power over God's elect, for he has been cast into the lake of fire, together with all the persecutors of the Church (1 Cor. 15:54–55)."

v. 15 Καὶ εἴ τις οὐχ εὑρέθη, *and if anyone was not found*, that is, not found among the number of the elect.

Chapter 21

There are two parts to this chapter:
I. A brief description of eternal life, with an earnest entreaty that the godly should most certainly be brought into it, while the ungodly should be excluded from it;
II. A new description of that heavenly joy and habitation.

v. 1 Καὶ εἶδον οὐρανὸν καινὸν καὶ γῆν καινήν, *and I saw a new heaven and a new earth*, both of which will be created by God on the Day of Final Judgment. Isaiah's prophecy (Isa. 65:17, 66:22) to which John refers back in this passage, properly treats of Christ's spiritual kingdom, which He gathers to Himself in this life from all nations through the preaching of the Gospel, which He will administer in a new way once the old ceremonies of the Law have been abolished, renewing this kingdom by the Holy Spirit. But since the completion of this glorious renewal will only take place in the age to come, therefore John is also referring to it here.

v. 2 Καὶ ἐγὼ Ἰωαννης εἶδον τὴν πόλιν τὴν ἁγίαν, *and I, John, saw the holy city*, etc. Rupert on this passage: "Now at last, at the end of this vision or revelation, John is finally shown the sum of the entire work that Jesus Christ has built at such great expense, with so many gracious gifts of His Spirit; namely, the holy city of Jerusalem, which is the Church of God—not such as it is during this pilgrimage on earth; nor such as it will stand on Christ's right hand during the Last Judgment, as described shortly before, where it will stand, not without a degree of fear, until the Lord's wrath passes and He casts those on His left into eternal flames; but such as it will exist after the judgment in eternal glory, pure and whole, with all foreigners having been expelled, fully enjoying the vision of God."

καταβαίνουσαν ἀπὸ τοῦ Θεοῦ ἐκ τοῦ οὐρανοῦ, *coming down from God out of heaven*. This took place in the vision so that the holy city might be rendered visible to John, since the heavenly Jerusalem will remain in heaven.

Augustine, Book XX, *De Civitate Dei*, ch. 17: "The city is said to come down from heaven, because the grace with which God made it is heavenly, etc. And indeed, it comes down from heaven from its very beginning, since throughout the time of this age its citizens continually grow by the grace of God, which comes from above through the washing of regeneration in the Holy Spirit sent from heaven. But by the Last Judgment of God, which will be administered through His Son Jesus Christ, its glory will appear so great and so new, that no traces of anything old will remain, since our bodies also will pass over from their old corruption and mortality to a new incorruption and immortality."

Primasius on this passage: "He is describing the Church of the future, when it will not be like it is now, as the Church endures the mixture of good and bad dwelling together. For only the good will reign with Christ; they will faithfully remain with Him and within this heavenly Jerusalem, which is the mother of us all."

In contrast, Bernhard, Book III, *De Consid. ad Eugen.*, applies this to the "Church Militant," which, he says, "is called the New Jerusalem coming down from heaven, because it is established and modeled after the pattern of that heavenly city."

Both opinions can be combined, since the Church Militant and the Church Triumphant are one Church. It is apparent from the words immediately following that this New Jerusalem is a symbol of the Church Militant. It is clear from v. 11 that it is a symbol of the Church Triumphant. Therefore, both the citizens of the heavenly Jerusalem and their heavenly habitation are being described. Properly and chiefly this passage is dealing with the heavenly and eternal blessedness of the godly that is to be anticipated in heaven and in eternal life after this life ends, as is apparent (1) from the Old Testament prophecies to which John alludes in this passage (Isa. 25:28, 65:17, 66:22; Eze. 37:27). For the words themselves, in the description they offer and in the reference to 2 Pet. 3:13, show that these prophecies deal with the glory and blessedness of eternal life. (2) From the words of the preceding chapter (Rev. 20:11–12), where a description of the Final Judgment is set forth. (3) From the author's aim. For in the preceding chapters of this book, John prophesied concerning various persecutions, calamities, and adversities that threatened the Church. Therefore he wants to add to those things, as is fitting, the glorious destruction of them all that is to be expected in heaven, so that the minds of the godly, by considering such an outcome, may be patiently and powerfully fortified against all tribulation. (4) From the very words of the description. "I saw a new heaven, etc." Therefore, he is speaking about the blessedness and glory that will come after the destruction of the first heaven, the first earth, and the sea. Verse 3, "Behold, the tabernacle of God, etc." This dwelling of God will be consummated in eternal life, where God will no longer dwell among the elect separably, as in this life, but inseparably. Verse 4, "And God will wipe away every tear… death will be no more." These things will take place in the future life (1 Cor. 15:26; Psa. 30:6; Psa. 126:6; cf. Rev. 7:14 ff.; Augustine, Book XX, *De Civitate Dei*, ch. 17). (5) From the contrast. In verse 8, the lake burning with fire and brimstone, which is the second death, is set in contrast to this city. Murderers, fornicators, etc., are removed from this city. (6) From the fuller description of this city that is added in v. 10 ff. of this chapter and in chapter 22.

Nevertheless, the Church Militant on earth and the Church Triumphant in heaven are one Church under one Head, which is Christ (Heb. 12:12), since the believers also are said to have eternal life in this life (John 3:36)—a life that is hidden with Christ in God (Col. 3:3; Isa. 25:8; Rev. 7:17).

Therefore, since believers at times experience in their hearts a foretaste of that blessedness and glory, certain parts of this description can be applied to the saints in the Church Militant as it still exists here on earth, with respect to its commencement and to a certain degree. Thus Paul applies the saying in Isa. 65:17, "I saw a new heaven, etc.," to regeneration, which takes place in this life (2 Cor. 5:17; cf. Gal. 4:26).

The city is said to come down out of heaven, because on the Day of Judgment the souls of the elect will descend from heaven, that they may again be united with their resurrected and glorified bodies, and thus, body and soul, be taken up into heavenly glory and blessedness.

ἠτοιμασμένην, *prepared*, with perfect righteousness, wisdom, holiness.

ὡς νύμφην κεκοσμημένην τῷ ἀνδρὶ αὐτῆς, *as a bride adorned for her husband.* "For the marriage of the Lamb has come" (Rev. 19:7). Therefore she is adorned with perfect righteousness and holiness in her soul, and with heavenly glory in her resurrected body, and she is led into the palace of heavenly blessedness and glory. She is compared to a bride, because Christ has betrothed her to Himself and has loved her with a fervent love and is loved, in turn, by her (Hos. 2:19).

v. 3 Ἰδού, ἡ σκηνὴ τοῦ Θεοῦ μετὰ τῶν ἀνθρώπων, *behold, the tabernacle of God is with men*, with the elect and blessed men. Καὶ σκηνώσει μετ᾽ αὐτῶν, *and He will dwell with them*, forever, in heavenly blessedness and glory.

καὶ αὐτὸς ὁ Θεὸς μετ᾽ αὐτῶν ἔσται, Θεὸς αὐτῶν, *and God Himself will be with them, their God*. He will be "all in all" (1 Cor. 15:28).

v. 4 Καὶ ἐξαλείψει ὁ Θεὸς πᾶν δάκρυον, *and God will wipe away every tear, etc.*, so that in this way, "those who sowed in tears may reap in joy" (Psa. 126:6).

καὶ ὁ θάνατος οὐκ ἔσται ἔτι, *and death will be no more*. That final enemy of Christ and of the faithful will be destroyed (1 Cor. 15:26, 54) and will be swallowed up in victory (Isa. 65:19, 1 Cor. 15:54).

ὅτι τὰ πρῶτα ἀπῆλθεν, *for the first things have passed away*, and all things have been made new (2 Cor. 5:17).

v. 5 Ἰδού, καινὰ πάντα ποιῶ, *behold, I am making all things new* (Isa. 43:19, 2 Cor. 5:17).

ὅτι οὗτοι οἱ λόγοι ἀληθινοὶ καὶ πιστοί εἰσι, *for these words are true and faithful* (Rev. 19:9).

v. 6 Γέγονε, *it is done*. "The form of this world has passed away" (1 Cor. 7:31). The judgment is established, and to whomever a place has been assigned by the judicial sentence, in that place he shall remain for all eternity.

Ἐγώ εἰμι τὸ Ἄ καὶ τὸ Ὦ, *I am the Alpha and the Omega* (Isa. 41:4, 44:6, 48:12; Rev. 1:8, 11, 17).

Ἐγὼ τῷ διψῶντι δώσω ἐκ τῆς πηγῆς τοῦ ὕδατος, *to the one who thirsts, I will give of the fountain of the water* (Isa. 55:1; John 4:10, 14; John 7:37; Rev. 22:17).

v. 7 Ὁ νικῶν κληρονομήσει πάντα, *the one who overcomes will inherit all things*, namely, the things that have been promised to the sons of God and the elect in eternal life.

Καὶ αὐτὸς ἔσται μοι ὁ υἱός, *and he will be My son,* and therefore also an heir (Rom. 8:17).

v. 8 δειλοῖς δὲ, *but to the cowardly,* that is, those who, for fear of death, deny the heavenly truth, who fear men more than God, who despair of the grace of God.

καὶ ἐβδελυγμένοις, *and to the abominable,* those who indulge in terrible and abominable acts, but especially those who stir up monstrous persecutions against the Church of God.

v. 9 εἷς ἐκ τῶν ἑπτὰ ἀγγέλων, *one of the seven angels,* the ones mentioned above.

τὴν νύμφην τοῦ Ἀρνίου τὴν γυναῖκα, *the Bride, the Wife of the Lamb,* the Church Triumphant of the elect in heaven.

v. 10 ἐπ᾽ ὄρος μέγα καὶ ὑψηλόν, *onto a great and high mountain,* so that I could view the whole city of God from its summit.

v. 11 ἔχουσαν τὴν δόξαν τοῦ Θεοῦ, *having the glory of God,* that is, the heavenly glory given to her by God.

Ὁ φωστὴρ, *the light,* the light of glory shining from her.

v. 12 τεῖχος μέγα καὶ ὑψηλόν, *a great and high wall,* which signifies peace and security; no danger from any enemies threatens her.

πυλῶνας δώδεκα, *twelve gates.* Some think these stand for the twelve patriarchs from whom the people of God came into existence and thus receive entrance into the heavenly Jerusalem. But it is better to interpret them as the twelve apostles, who showed the way into this city in the word of the Gospel.

ἐπὶ τοῖς πυλῶσιν ἀγγέλους δώδεκα, *twelve angels at the gates.* They are the guardians of this city (Psa. 34:8).

ἅ ἐστι τῶν δώδεκα φυλῶν, *which are of the twelve tribes.* The twelve tribes of the children of Israel stand for the whole multitude of the elect (Gal. 6:16; cf. Rev. 7:4).

v. 13 ἀπὸ ἀνατολῆς πυλῶνες τρεῖς, *three gates on the east.* The gates are facing the four corners of the earth, because God will gather His elect from the four corners of the earth (Mat. 24:31). Through the preaching of the Gospel, the apostles invited the nations from all parts of the world to the kingdom of Christ, and they showed the gates of the heavenly Jerusalem to all men, as if pointing with their index finger.

v. 14 Καὶ τὸ τεῖχος τῆς πόλεως ἔχον θεμελίους δώδεκα, *and the wall of the city had twelve foundations.* Augustine, *In Psal.* 86: "How is it that the prophets or apostles are foundations, and how is Christ Jesus the foundation other than which no foundation can be laid? How shall we think of this, except in the sense that He is plainly called the Holy of Holies, and thus, figuratively, the Foundation of Foundations." Juan de Torquemada, Book II, *Summae,* ch. 19: "A thing is called a foundation in two different ways. In one sense, it is that to which the bottom part of the building adheres, which, nevertheless, is not included in the building, like solid ground or rock or a cliff. In another sense, a foundation is the bottom part of the building upon which the rest of the building is founded. Christ is the foundation in the first sense as that which holds up the whole building. But the foundation in the second sense applies nicely to others, namely, the apostles."

There is a single foundation of the Church, which is Christ (1 Cor. 3:11, Eph. 2:25). The apostles are said to be foundations of the Church because of the doctrine which they preached about Christ. There were twelve apostles, wherefore twelve foundations are listed. At the same time, there remains a single foundation of the Church, since they are called foundations, not because of their person, but because of their doctrine, and all of them built upon that one foundation (Mat. 16:18, 1 Cor. 3:10).

v. 15 κάλαμον χρυσοῦν, *a golden rod,* a measuring rod.

ἵνα μετρήσῃ τὴν πόλιν, *to measure the city.* The measurement represents the size and stability of this city.

καὶ τοὺς πυλῶνας αὐτῆς καὶ τὸ τεῖχος αὐτῆς, *and its gates and its wall,* the height and breadth of the gates and of the walls.

v. 16 Καὶ ἡ πόλις τετράγωνος κεῖται, *and the city is laid out as a square.* In eternal life, all things will be precisely equal. Nothing there will be twisted or curved. The square shape also denotes the beauty, magnitude, and stability of this city.

ἐπὶ σταδίους δώδεκα χιλιάδων, *twelve thousand stadia*, and thus on every side there were three thousand stadia, which amounts to more than three hundred German miles.

Τὸ μῆκος καὶ τὸ πλάτος καὶ τὸ ὕψος αὐτῆς ἴσα ἐστί, *its length and breadth and height are equal*. This signifies that the city will remain unshaken and will never fall into ruin.

v. 17 μέτρον ἀνθρώπου, *the measurement of a man*, that is, as many cubits are understood as belong to a man, from the elbow to the tip of the middle finger.

ὅ ἐστιν ἀγγέλου, *which is of an angel*, which the angel, who was appearing to John in the form of a man, was using.

v. 18 ἡ ἐνδόμησις τοῦ τείχους αὐτῆς ἴασπις, *the structure of the wall was of jasper*. Perfect righteousness is depicted with this gem that is more precious than gold.

καὶ ἡ πόλις, *and the city*, that is, the pavement of the city is of pure gold, which symbolizes the purity of the Church Triumphant in heaven. Just as everything shines brightly in glass, so also nothing will escape the notice of the elect in heaven.

v. 19 καὶ οἱ θεμέλιοι τοῦ τείχους τῆς πόλεως, *and the foundations of the wall of the city*. Luther: "*Der Mauren und der Stadt.*"

ὁ θεμέλιος ὁ πρῶτος ἴασπις, *the first foundation of jasper*. These gems signify the apostolic doctrine, which is more precious than all gems. For by it, men are invited to this city. Indeed, the city of God is built by it. A Chaldaic paraphrase of Song of Solomon 5:13, on the words, *His hands are full of hyacinths*. "And for the twelve tribes of His servant Jacob there were arranged all around the breastplate holy golden moldings, engraved on twelve pearls with the three parts of the world, Abraham, Isaac and Jacob. Ruben was engraved on a sardius stone, Simeon on a topaz stone, Levi on a sapphire, Judah on a carbuncle, Issachar on an emerald, Zebulon on a jasper, Dan on a beryl, Naphtali on an agate, Gad on an amethyst, Asher on a chrystolet, Joseph on an onyx, Benjamin on a ligurius. These were similar to the twelve celestial signs, shining like lamps and polished in their settings, like the teeth of an elephant, and radiant like jewels."

v. 21 Καὶ οἱ δώδεκα πυλῶνες δώδεκα μαργαρῖται, *and the twelve gates were twelve pearls*. Pearls represent the ecclesiastical ministry on the earth (Mat. 13:45). For just as men enter a city through its gates, so God leads us into the heavenly Jerusalem through the ministry.

ἡ πλατεῖα τῆς πόλεως χρυσίον καθαρόν, *the street of the city was pure gold*, for in this heavenly Jerusalem there will be nothing impure, nothing corruptible. In this life, we have nothing more precious than gold, pearls, and jewels. Therefore the Scripture describes the beauty and glory of the heavenly Jerusalem in a symbolic and figurative way by means of these precious things.

v. 22 Καὶ ναὸν, *and a temple*, namely, an external temple made of stone, οὐκ εἶδον ἐν αὐτῇ, *I did not see in it*, such as there once was in the earthly Jerusalem.

ὁ γὰρ Κύριος ὁ Παντοκράτωρ ναὸς αὐτῆς ἐστι, καὶ τὸ Ἀρνίον, *for the Lord Almighty is its temple, and the Lamb*. In eternal life there will no longer be a place for the visible and external signs by which God manifested Himself to His people in the Old Testament, namely, through the temple and the ark of the covenant. For then God will allow Himself to be seen face to face (1 Cor. 13:12).

v. 23 Καὶ ἡ πόλις οὐ χρείαν ἔχει τοῦ ἡλίου, *and the city has no need of the sun*. Christ is the temple and the lamp of the heavenly Jerusalem, for He will live with the elect in person. He will speak with them with His own voice. He will illuminate the city inside and out with His heavenly splendor. He will be the light and joy of the elect, and He will communicate to them the very heavenly glory that He earned for them and promised them in the Gospel.

v. 24 Καὶ τὰ ἔθνη τῶν σωζομένων ἐν τῷ φωτὶ αὐτῆς περιπατήσουσι, *and the nations of the saved will walk in its light*. The saved from the nations will walk in its light, that is, they will be made partakers of heavenly blessedness, happiness, and glory.

καὶ οἱ βασιλεῖς τῆς γῆς φέρουσι τὴν δόξαν, *and the kings of the earth bring their glory*. There will be an abundance of all good things in this city, as if all the kings of the earth had brought all their treasures into it. And the kings and rulers who promoted the kingdom of Christ in this life will shine with glory ahead of the rest.

v. 25 Καὶ οἱ πυλῶνες αὐτῆς οὐ μὴ κλεισθῶσιν, *and its gates will never be shut* (Isa. 60:11). There will be perfect security and freedom there. This is why it says that its gates will not be closed by day, because there will be no night there.

νὺξ γὰρ οὐκ ἔσται ἐκεῖ, *there will be no night there*. In this life, night comes after day. But in eternal life there will be perpetual day and light, so there will be no need for the gates to be closed at night, as the gates of the cities of this earth are closed at night. Nor will there be any need there for sleep or for the refreshment of nocturnal rest, as there is in this life (1 The. 5:7), for all the infirmities of this life will be gone.

v. 26 Καὶ οἴσουσι τὴν δόξαν καὶ τὴν τιμὴν τῶν ἐθνῶν εἰς αὐτήν, *and they will bring the glory and the honor of all the nations into it*. Many people from the nations will be brought to the glory of this city.

v. 27 Καὶ οὐ μὴ εἰσέλθῃ εἰς αὐτὴν πᾶν κοινόν, *and no common thing will ever enter it* (Acts 10:14), καὶ ποιοῦν βδέλυγμα καὶ ψεῦδος, *or anyone who commits abomination or tells lies*, unlike in the Church Militant, where many hypocrites and unholy people are intermingled with the godly (Isa. 35:8, Rev. 22:15).

εἰ μὴ γεγραμμένοι, *but only those written, etc.*, only the elect children of God.

Chapter 22

There are two parts:
  I. The things that pertain to the description of the heavenly Jerusalem mentioned earlier, namely, the river of the water of life and the tree of life;
  II. The confirmation of those things that John has seen thus far, but especially of heavenly joy.

v. 1 Καὶ ἔδειξέ μοι καθαρὸν ποταμὸν ὕδατος ζωῆς, *and he showed me a pure river of the water of life.* (1) Some think this river signifies the delight and joy that will flow in the elect from the beatific vision of God. It is called "the river of the water of life" because it will never run dry. It proceeds from the throne of God and of the Lamb because it flows from the vision of God, wherefore it is added immediately that "the throne of God and of the Lamb will be in it, and they will see His face."

(2) Others take it to be the river of consolation and the abundance of all good things (Eze. 4:1). (3) It is most simply understood as a symbol of the Holy Spirit. This is clear (i) from its designation as a river (John 7:38); (ii) from the properties attributed to it, which are either essential, such as, first of all, its essential and virtual clarity, and secondly, its power to give life; or personal, such as the fact that it proceeds from the throne of God and of the Lamb, that is, from the Father and the Son.

These explanations can be combined. The Holy Spirit proceeds from the Father and the Son in a manner that is inscrutable and incomprehensible, and thus great comfort, perfect joy, and an abundance of all the heavenly good things (Psa. 36:10–11) that the Holy Spirit imparts to the blessed in eternal life are carried by the river of the water of life. It is clear as crystal because the heavenly consolation and gladness is in every way pure, untainted by pain or sadness, and is communicated to all the elect abundantly.

Ὕδωρ ζωῆς, *the water of life*, which streams continually from an ever-flowing fountain. This is a reference to the Garden of Paradise, which was watered by four rivers emanating from a single fountain (Gen. 2:7).

In the first and the last chapters of the Bible, there is a testimony concerning the mystery of the Trinity: the entire Trinity is active in the first and the last works; namely, in creation and in glorification.

v. 2 ξύλον ζωῆς, *the tree of life*, another reference to the Garden of Paradise, in the midst of which stood the tree of life, which was a symbol of eternal life. (1) Therefore, some understand this tree of life as the blessedness of eternal life. (2) Others take it as the blessed themselves, for the tree of life is said to have stood on both sides of the river, and therefore the singular is used for the plural, so that the sense is, many trees were planted on both sides of the river. Therefore, since the river signifies the joy of blessedness, the trees planted on both sides of the river represent the blessed, who are watered with the stream of that joy. Since their joy will never end or be interrupted, they are said to bear fruit every month. In all the powers of the soul and senses of the body there will be special joys, which will produce powers of the same kind. Their leaves are said to be for the healing of the nations, because the attendant joy of the blessed, indicated by the leaves, is sufficient for relieving all the sickness of body and mind. (3) But since the Holy Spirit is signified by the river of the water of life, therefore the tree of life is most naturally taken as a symbol of Christ, who gives believers eternal life and was prefigured by the tree of life in Paradise (Gen. 2:9). For as the fruit of that tree would have preserved human life and health until man was transferred into heavenly life, so Christ, who is the true tree of life, gives heavenly and eternal life to the elect, since they have been transplanted into Him through true faith and have been made His spiritual branches. This tree of life stands on both sides of the river, (i) because the Holy Spirit, by His divine power, has united the human and divine nature in Christ; (ii) because Christ furnishes the elect with consolation and the joy of eternal happiness perpetually and without limit, so that joy, consolation, and life will always be joined together in them.

Christ is referred to as a Lamb in v. 1 on account of the expiation of sins and the acquisition of benefits. He is called the Tree of Life in v. 2 on account of the distribution of the acquired benefits.

ποιοῦν καρποὺς δώδεκα, *bearing twelve fruits.* (1) As the tree of life bears its fruit throughout the whole year, so Christ distributes His benefits throughout the course of this entire life as well as the future life. (2) He utilizes the ministry of the apostles for the purpose of this distribution (Rev. 21:14). (3) The elect will never grow tired of these heavenly fruits which the tree of life communicates to them, but will always experience new joy, new comfort and new pleasure. (4) The fruit of this tree will last forever.

Καὶ τὰ φύλλα τοῦ ξύλου εἰς θεραπείαν τῶν ἐθνῶν, *and the leaves of this tree for the healing of the nations.* When the nations feed on the leaves of this tree in this life by true faith, that is, when they embrace the Gospel with true faith, they receive from it healing for their soul. This tree of life will preserve such healing of soul and body for all eternity, so that, in this way, life and health will be perpetually maintained.

v. 3 Καὶ πᾶν κατανάθεμα οὐκ ἔσται ἔτι, *and there will no longer be any curse.* The curse stands for a man who is devoted to destruction. There will not be anyone like this in the Church Triumphant. Some interpret this in a general sense concerning anything that God hates.

καὶ ὁ θρόνος τοῦ Θεοῦ καὶ τοῦ Ἀρνίου ἐν αὐτῇ ἔσται, *and the throne of God and of the Lamb will be in it.* God and Christ will reign forever in the Church Triumphant, and the Holy Spirit, who proceeds from the Father and the Son and is one with them in essence, will not be separated from them.

καὶ οἱ δοῦλοι αὐτοῦ δουλεύσουσιν αὐτῷ, *and His servants,* the elect, *will serve Him,* not with tedium or with toilsome labor, but from a deep desire of the heart and with sincere joy, as the angels serve God (Psa. 103:20; Dan. 7:10).

v. 4 Καὶ ὄψονται τὸ πρόσωπον αὐτοῦ, *and they will see His face,* they will know Him perfectly, and from that beatific vision of God there will arise in them unspeakable joy (1 Cor. 13:12).

καὶ τὸ ὄνομα αὐτοῦ ἐπὶ τῶν μετώπων αὐτῶν, *and His name on their foreheads.* It will be evident to all men and angels that they are children of God (1 John 3:2), which was still hidden in this life and could not be read on anyone's forehead.

v. 5 Καὶ νὺξ οὐκ ἔσται ἐκεῖ, *and there will be no night there, etc.* Since the glory of the Lord will illuminate this city, and the Lamb will be its lamp, there will be no alternating between light and darkness (James 1:17). Instead, there will be perpetual light, the perpetual brightness of the sun. And for this same reason there will be no need for lamps or for sunlight; the darkness of ignorance, error, and injustice will be completely banished.

βασιλεύσουσιν εἰς τοὺς αἰῶνας τῶν αἰώνων, *they will reign forever and ever*, as the glorious conquerors of death and hell.

v. 6 Καὶ εἶπέ μοι, *and he* (that is, the angel) *said to me.*

ὁ Θεὸς τῶν ἁγίων προφητῶν, *the God of the holy prophets*, who long ago sent the holy prophets to men (Luke 1:70) and foretold the future things through them.

ἃ δεῖ γενέσθαι ἐν τάχει, *which must soon take place* (Rev. 1:1).

v. 7 Καὶ ἰδου, ἔρχομαι ταχύ, *and behold, I am coming soon.* These are the words of Christ.

Μακάριος ὁ τηρῶν τοὺς λόγους τῆς προφητείας, *blessed is the one who keeps the words of this prophecy.* With these words, Christ confirms the testimony of the angel and of all the things written by John in the Book of Revelation.

v. 8 Καὶ ἐγὼ Ἰωάννης ὁ βλέπων ταῦτα, *and I, John, who sees these things.* With these words, John himself confirms his testimony—the things he has written in this Book of Revelation—since he saw everything with his own eyes and heard everything with his own ears.

ἔπεσον προσκυνῆσαι, *I fell to worship.* I am the very one whom the angel so diligently cautioned, because I wanted to worship him.

(1) Costerus, Part 2, *Concion.*, p. 70: "The angel did not permit himself to be worshiped by John the Baptist, because he detected in John the height of apostolic and angelic purity." We reply: (i) He is confusing John the Baptist with John the Evangelist. (ii) This is obviously a fallacy of cause.

(2) The Anglo-Remenses suggest, *In Annot. Apoc.*: "The angel did not want to be worshiped because John had been deceived, mistaking the angel for Christ and attributing divine honor to him." Bellarmine answers them,

Book I, *De Sanct. Beat.*, ch. 14, arguing "that John gave only due honor to the angel, and that the angel did well in not permitting this worship out of reverence for the humanity of Christ."

(3) Smaltius, *In Refut. eorum quae examinationi 100. errorum objecit Schmiglecius*, p. 48: "What is said of John in Rev. 22 can be taken as the same action that was reported in Rev. 19. For at one and the same time, indeed, at the very same hour it may have also occurred in such a way that John wanted to do twice that which the majesty of the angel seemed to require. Thus he was warned by the angel twice not to do it, which sufficiently indicates that such a thing could have been done at an earlier time, and perhaps was done, but now, since all the angels and believing men have been admitted into one family and serve one Lord, it should no longer be done. For there is a difference between the worship of angels and the worship of other things, which constituted idolatry: no other individuals should be worshiped, since they have no divine authority, nor is there any command to worship them. But the angels should not be worshiped, because, although they have a certain divine authority, nevertheless it is all subject to the authority of Christ, and somehow it came to pass after Christ was exalted that they are no longer permitted to be worshiped, for they, together with the faithful, are subject to Christ Himself, who is the Savior of the faithful." And on page 53: "God once permitted the angels to be worshiped. Indeed, the very fact that the angel forbad John to worship him, seems tacitly to imply that it could once be done, unless something new should intervene, namely, that the angel became a fellow servant of John, which was not previously the case at the time of the other forms of divine worship under the Old Testament." We reply: It is a false hypothesis that the angels in the Old Testament were worshiped, and that Christ effected some change among the angels.

v. 10 Μὴ σφραγίσῃς τοὺς λόγους τῆς προφητείας τοῦ βιβλίου τούτου, *do not seal up the words of the prophecy of this book*. Do not hide or conceal them, but proclaim them to all. For there are some things that God wishes to seal, that is, to keep hidden for awhile (Dan. 8:26, 12:4; Rev. 10:4).

Ὅτι ὁ καιρὸς ἐγγύς ἐστιν, *for the time is near*, namely, the time is coming when those things that are written in this book will be fulfilled.

v. 11 Ὁ ἀδικῶν ἀδικησάτω ἔτι, *let the unjust remain unjust still*. The angel responds to the objection that John might have made to this command.

214

What if the revelation of these mysteries gives occasion for some to become even worse, and to harass the Church even more, and to wallow even more in the mire of sins? The angel replies, Let the unjust, etc. You should not be silent about the revelation of these mysteries on account of the ungodly and the obstinate. Rather, commend those things to God's judgment. Those people will not improve, but will become even worse. For since those obstinate men refuse to be corrected, God, in His just judgment, will hand them over to their depraved desires (2 Tim. 3:13), so that they are blinded and hardened more and more by the devil.

ὁ δίκαιος δικαιοθήτω ἔτι, *let the righteous remain righteous still*, let him persevere in uprightness, and let him increase daily in holiness. At the same time, there is also a promise that God will increase His grace and blessing in the faithful so that they persevere in godliness and daily grow in it more and more.

v. 12 Καὶ ἰδού, ἔρχομαι ταχύ, *and behold, I am coming soon*. These again are the words of Christ.

καὶ ὁ μισθός μου μετ' ἐμοῦ, *and My reward is with Me*, etc., that I may give rewards of grace to those who faithfully served Me and who confirmed their faith with the testimony of good works. But I will bring against the ungodly and impenitent all the punishments they have earned.

v. 13 Ἐγώ εἰμι τὸ Ἄ καὶ τὸ Ὦ, *I am the Alpha and the Omega* (Rev. 1:8, 11).

v. 14 Μακάριοι οἱ ποιοῦντες τὰς ἐντολὰς αὐτοῦ, *blessed are those who do His commands*. These are again the words of the angel. Yet some attribute them to John. Blessed are those who believe in Christ and love their neighbor, for this is the summary of all the divine precepts (1 John 3:23).

ἵνα ἔσται ἡ ἐξουσία αὐτῶν ἐπὶ τὸ ξύλον τῆς ζωῆς, *so that they will have the right to the tree of life*, so that they may have the right and power to enjoy the fruits of the tree of life in the heavenly Paradise.

καὶ τοῖς πυλῶσιν εἰσέλθωσιν εἰς τὴν πόλιν, *and may enter by the gates into the city*, into the heavenly Jerusalem, that is, that they may become partakers of eternal life.

v. 15 Ἔξω δὲ οἱ κύνες, *but outside are the dogs*. Outside of the heavenly Jerusalem are the dogs: (1) impure men who let themselves be used as women (Deu. 23:17); (2) false teachers (Phi. 3:2); (3) impudent blasphemers (Mat. 7:6); (4) in general, all those who lead a lewd and impure life (2 Pet. 2:22).

πᾶς ὁ φιλῶν καὶ ποιῶν ψεῦδος, *everyone who loves and does a lie*, those who love that which is contrary to pure teaching and holy living.

v. 16 It was the angel speaking in verses 14 and 15. In this verse Christ is speaking again, just as He had spoken with John in verses 12 and 13.

Ἐγὼ Ἰησοῦς ἔπεμψα τὸν ἄγγελόν μου μαρτυρῆσαι ὑμῖν, *I, Jesus, sent My angel to testify to you*, to you bishops in Asia Minor, ταῦτα ἐπὶ ταῖς ἐκκλησίαις, *these things to the churches*, that you should set them forth to the churches which have been committed and entrusted to your care. Luther: "*an die Gemeinen.*"

This passage powerfully proves the divinity of Christ against the Photinians, for the sending of the angels is the proper work of the true God alone. Indeed, Enjedinus, who brazenly twists even the clearest of Scripture passages, is unable to spread his darkness over this fact.

Ἐγώ εἰμι ἡ Ῥίζα καὶ τὸ Γένος Δαβίδ, *I am the Root and the Offspring of David*. Luther renders this in a combined sense: "*Ich bin die Wurzel des Geschlechtes David*," who arose from David as from a root. According to My human nature, I sprang up from the family of David, as a plant from a root (Isa. 11:1). But, at the same time, I am the root of David according to My divine nature, much older than David, indeed, begotten of My heavenly Father from all eternity. And I supported, preserved, and nourished the offspring of David, as a root supports, preserves, and nourishes a tree (Rom. 11:18).

ὁ Ἀστὴρ ὁ λαμπρὸς καὶ ὁ ὀρθρινός, *the bright and the Morning Star*. Just as the morning star brings the day and the sunrise with it, so I kindle the light of divine knowledge in the hearts of men (2 Cor. 4:6, 2 Pet. 1:19). I bring them the light of divine grace, favor, and help. The Syriac version has, "As that bright, that morning star." He is called this in a much more excellent way than the angels (Job 38:7).

v. 17 Καὶ τὸ Πνεῦμα καὶ ἡ νύμφη λέγουσιν, ἐλθέ, *and the Spirit and the Bride say, "Come!"* The Holy Spirit speaks through the Bride, or the

Bride speaks by inspiration of the Holy Spirit. This signifies the spiritual and burning desire with which the Church awaits the coming of Christ, who is the spiritual Bridegroom of souls (Rom. 8:23; 2 Cor. 5:2, 4; 2 Tim. 4:8); who will lead her into the joys of the heavenly wedding banquet.

Καὶ ὁ ἀκούων εἰπάτω, ἐλθέ, *and let the one who hears say, "Come!"* Likewise from a deep desire for His coming.

Καὶ ὁ διψῶν, *and the one who thirsts*, who thirsts for consolation and happiness, ἐλθέτω, *let him come*, let him come to Me, the Fount of Grace, and let him drink from it.

Καὶ ὁ θέλων, λαμβανέτω τὸ ὕδωρ ζωῆς δωρεάν, *and the one who wishes, let him freely take the water of life*.

v. 18 Συμμαρτυροῦμαι, *I bear witness*. Tertullian, *Adv. Hermogenem*, ch. 17, takes this generally concerning the whole New Testament canon. "The office of Hermogenes teaches that it was written. If it was not written, then let him fear that woe that is directed toward those who add or subtract."

v. 19 Ἀφερέσει ὁ Θεὸς τὸ μέρος αὐτοῦ, *God will take away his part*, God will damn him so that he may have no part in the kingdom of heaven.

v. 20 ὁ μαρτυρῶν ταῦτα, *He who bears witness to these things*, is Christ the faithful Witness.

Ἀμήν, *Amen*. With these spiritual words, the Bride of Christ, which is the true Church—every believing soul—answers Christ.

v. 21 Ἡ χάρις τοῦ Κυρίου, *the grace of the Lord*. Just as John began this book with a blessing from Christ, even so he brings it to a close.

217

www.ingramcontent.com/pod-product-compliance
Lightning Source LLC
Chambersburg PA
CBHW050551160426
43199CB00015B/2621